HIRED, FIRED OR SICK & TIRED?

A PRACTICAL GUIDE TO YOUR JOB RIGHTS

LYNDA A C MACDONALD

NICHOLAS BREALEY
PUBLISHING
LONDON

First published in Great Britain by
Nicholas Brealey Publishing Limited in 1995
21 Bloomsbury Way
London WC1A 2TH

Reprinted 1995 (with corrections)

ISBN 1–85788–105–2 (Hardback)
ISBN 1–85788–106–0 (Paperback)

British Library Cataloguing in Publication Data
A catalogue record for this book is available from the British Library.

Printed and bound in Finland by Werner Söderström Oy

Contents

Great care has been taken in the writing of this book to ensure accuracy and legal correctness. However, the author cannot, under any circumstances, accept responsibility for any omissions or errors.

Throughout this book words signifying the masculine gender (e.g. he, him) are intended to include the feminine gender (e.g. she, her).

Introduction

Do you know whether or not you have a proper contract of employment? If not, does this mean that you have no employment rights? What are your options if your employer cuts your pay, or changes your hours of work, without your agreement?

Can your employer refuse to pay you if you are off sick? On strike? Suspended from work on suspicion of misconduct? And what if you find out you are being paid a rate of pay much lower than other employees doing the same job?

What is your minimum entitlement to annual holidays? What rights do the new maternity leave provisions give you? What is the minimum notice your employer must give you if you are dismissed? Made redundant? And how much redundancy pay would you get? What are your chances of succeeding in a claim for unfair dismissal and how do you go about it?

If you are certain you know the answers to all these questions, then you do not need to read this book. If, however, you hesitated in some of your answers, then undoubtedly you will benefit from gaining additional knowledge about your employment rights. All the above questions, and many, many more, are answered in this book.

Knowing your employment rights gives you choices. Ignorance and innocence will not help you achieve your rights in employment. If your rights are breached and you recognise that they are being breached, then you can choose whether to take action, or whether to do nothing. In practice, many employees do nothing in the face of blatant illegality because they quite simply do not know that their employer is breaking the law. Many employers are equally ignorant of basic employment law and may genuinely not know that they are acting illegally towards you.

The objective of this book is to inform. The key aim is to give you knowledge of your employment rights so that you may, if you choose, tackle any issue where your rights are being abused. In so doing you will not only benefit yourself, but you will also be raising standards in employment for others in the future.

In addition to providing information about your employment rights, this book also gives guidance on what you can do if you wish to make a claim against your employer for breaching your rights. The book will be of interest not only to employees, but also to non-employed people, to those who are actively seeking work, and to people who have recently been dismissed or made redundant. Employers may also benefit substantially from reading it!

Throughout the book the emphasis will be on what your employer can and cannot legally do, and the remedies available to you if you are denied your rights, suffer breach of your conditions of employment, or are treated unfairly or discriminated against. Case studies and examples are provided throughout to emphasise the various points discussed.

You may choose to read through the whole book from beginning to end, and many readers will find that all of it will be of direct interest and relevance. An alternative option is to select the chapters which are of particular interest to you and concentrate on those. The book is fully cross-referenced throughout, allowing you to refer easily to different sections of the book to locate the information which is of greatest personal interest to you.

Good luck!

PART I: BEGINNING WORK

1
Identifying Your Employment Status

Employed or not?

Anyone who works for someone else in exchange for money has a contractual relationship with that person or company. There is, however, a distinction between a person who is employed (under a contract of employment) and someone who is self-employed, or working for a company through an agency or contracting company. This situation constitutes a contract for services rather than a contract of employment, and does not normally entitle the person to any employment rights.

This book concerns itself primarily with those who are employed under a contract of employment. Information is given in this chapter to help you to judge whether or not you are employed. Chapter 2 examines your

1

entitlement to receive a contract of employment, and the various elements of such a contract.

In most cases it is obvious whether the relationship between you and your 'employer' is one of employment or self-employment. Some cases, however, may be borderline.

To establish whether or not you are an employee, you should consider the key factors listed below. The answers to some or all of these questions will determine whether or not you are employed. The more questions which can be answered 'yes', the more likelihood there is that you are an employee of the company.

- Are you engaged to perform work as an employee (as opposed to being a person in business on your own account)?
- Are you carrying out work which is an integral part of the company's business?
- Are you working under the direction and control of the company?
- Are you obliged to do the work you are given (as opposed to having freedom to accept or reject work)?
- Is the company obliged to give you work to do?
- Are you obliged to do the work personally (instead of substituting someone else to do your work from time to time)?
- Does the company hire any other people needed to help you in your work (rather than you supplying your own helpers)?
- Does the company supply your tools / equipment?
- Do you work exclusively for one company (rather than working for several companies)?
- Have you worked for the company on a continuous basis for a relatively long period of time?
- Are you paid a regular fixed wage or salary?
- Does the company deduct tax and national insurance payments? (Note that this factor is generally not regarded as strong evidence of employment, although by contrast, registration for VAT would normally be a strong pointer towards self-employment).
- Do you receive company benefits, e.g. pension scheme, holiday pay?

CASE STUDY

Mr Long worked for his employer, Plant Movements, for many years as a foreman. Early in 1990 the company offered him a choice of two sets of conditions of employment, one of which was similar to his present contract and the other headed 'self-employed'. The self-employed version provided for a higher rate of pay, but would remove entitlement to holiday pay and company sick pay. In most other respects the two sets of conditions were the same.

(CASE STUDY CONTINUED)

From then on both parties adopted the self-employed version of the contract and Mr Long continued to work for the company, receiving the higher rate of pay. He received his P45 and all outstanding holiday pay. He also obtained a sub-contractor's tax certificate from the Inland Revenue.

The following year, Mr Long was dismissed from the company and he subsequently submitted a claim to an industrial tribunal for unfair dismissal.

Q Was Mr Long still an employee of the company when he was dismissed? (If he was not, then the industrial tribunal would not have jurisdiction to hear his claim).

A The industrial tribunal found that after the adoption of the self-employed version of the contract, everything had carried on as before, except that Mr Long understood that he would not be paid for holidays or sickness absences. Mr Long was at all times under the direction and control of the company and provision of work was guaranteed. Their decision was that Mr Long was in fact and in law an employed person.

Based on the case *Plant Movements Ltd* v *Long*.

Even if the company labels your working relationship as one of self-employment, an industrial tribunal may still conclude that you are an employee, depending on an analysis of the various factors involved. The analysis would give different weightings to the various factors, depending on the circumstances of the particular case.

A dispute over status could occur if, for example, you are dismissed and wish to make a claim to an industrial tribunal. The tribunal would first of all need to establish whether or not you had been an employee. To decide this, they would look at the actual facts of the case, and not at the label which the two parties put on the working relationship.

Tribunals have often ruled that the intention of the parties concerned is not the only factor which affects contractual status. Generally, tribunals will take a broad and flexible approach to the question of whether or not someone is employed, as every case is different.

CASE STUDY

Michael McCarthy and his son James were both carpenters and had worked exclusively for one company for over five years. They were both designated by the company as self-employed, and neither had a written contract. Mr McCarthy senior was paid a gross sum to cover both his own and his son's pay and neither received any holiday pay or sick pay.

However, both father and son were directed and supervised in their work by the company, they worked regular hours as required by the company and, although they supplied their own tools, these were only the basic tools used

(CASE STUDY CONTINUED)

by carpenters and not heavy plant or equipment.

When their services were no longer required, they were dismissed without notice or pay in lieu of notice, and with no redundancy payments.

Q Were the two men employees of the company (in which case they would have been entitled to notice and redundancy pay)?

A The tribunal concluded that both men were employees of the company, and not independent contractors as the company argued. This conclusion was reached by weighing up the various factors involved and in particular with reference to the fact that both men worked under the control and direction of the company.

Based on the case *Basil Wyatt & Sons Ltd* v *McCarthy and another.*

Special categories of worker

Agency workers

Many contract staff and 'temps' are in fact agency workers – i.e. they are contracted out by one company to work for another.

As an agency worker, you may be employed by the agency, and the factors listed at the beginning of this chapter should help you to determine your status. It has been established by industrial tribunals that agency workers sometimes are not employees of the agency, but assume the status of self-employed in law, even although the individual may never have regarded himself in that light.

Under the law, agencies are required to regard themselves as the employer for PAYE and National Insurance purposes – but that is all. In all other respects, individuals may technically be self-employed, and as a result lack many rights that they might otherwise have had.

This is not surprising – the relationship between an Agency and a contract worker or 'temp' lacks many of the features which normally form an employment contract. For example:

- The agency has no control over the individual's duties or conditions of work.
- Notice can be given by a third party (i.e. the client).
- There is normally no pension or holiday entitlement.
- There is no obligation for the agency to provide work for the worker, or for the individual to accept work from the agency.
- There is no element of 'care' for the employee by the agency.
- There may be no element of continuity.

Equally, agency workers would have difficulty showing that they were employees of the client company — although this could well occur in the case of a long-term, full-time contract, provided a substantial number of the factors listed at the beginning of this chapter could be answered in the affirmative.

CASE STUDY

Mr Ironmonger was employed as a building assistant by Unilever Engineering for 34 years until he retired in 1983 at age 60. The company wished to retain his services, and arranged for him to return through an employment agency. He was to work as clerk of works, engaged on the construction of a new factory. In 1985, when this contract was due to terminate, Mr Ironmonger received a new letter of appointment from the agency transferring him to Birds Eye Walls, a subsidiary of Unilever. In January 1987, Birds Eye Walls told the agency they no longer needed Mr Ironmonger's services and his employment was terminated. Mr Ironmonger subsequently made a claim for unfair dismissal against the employment agency.

Q Was Mr Ironmonger an employee of the employment agency?

A The Employment Appeal Tribunal, to whom this case was referred, found that Mr Ironmonger was not an employee of the Agency. His working arrangements were inconsistent with normal employment contracts in several ways: Mr Ironmonger could have been on the books of any employment agency, there was no written contract, the agency had no direct control over Mr Ironmonger's duties, notice of termination could be given by a third party (i.e. Birds Eye Walls), there was no pension or holiday pay, and there was no obligation for the agency to provide work for Mr Ironmonger. Consequently Mr Ironmonger could not claim unfair dismissal.

Based on the case *Ironmonger* v *Deering Appointments*.

CASE STUDY

In 1987 Mr Nixon registered with an employment agency when looking for work as a fitter/machinist. He signed a contract with the agency which stated that he was engaged as a temporary worker under a contract for services. Thereafter he accepted a work placement which kept him employed for just over three years until he was told that his services were no longer required. Because the employment agency had no other work to offer Mr Nixon at that time, he claimed a redundancy payment. The agency, however, disputed his claim, arguing that he was not their employee, but had worked for them on a self-employed basis.

(CASE STUDY CONTINUED)

Q Was Mr Nixon an employee of the employment agency?

A No, the tribunal took the view that Mr Nixon was not an employee of the agency. Their reasoning in reaching this conclusion was based mainly on the fact that Mr Nixon's contract contained no obligation on the agency to provide work, and no obligation on Mr Nixon to accept work.

Based on the case *Pertemps Group plc* v *Nixon*.

Contract staff/consultants

Individuals working for a company as contract staff or consultants are not normally employees of that company unless their relationship with the company satisfies a substantial number of the factors listed at the beginning of this chapter. Often, contractors and consultants work for an agency, or are self-employed. Typically contractors perform short-term work, rather than being 'employed' over a long period. Usually they do not receive wages from the company, but rather submit regular invoices for payment to the agency on completion of agreed work.

Office holders

Office holders include such people as company directors, trustees, trade union officials, club secretaries, magistrates and the clergy. Generally office holders are not employees, although it is possible for someone to hold an office and be an employee of the organisation as well. This is often the case with company directors.

Technically the distinction between an office holder and an employee is that the duties of an office holder are normally defined by the office held, and the post exists independently of the person who fills it. There would not usually be a contract of employment.

The police and prison officers are office holders in law, although they may also be employees, depending on the usual tests. Whatever their employment status, they are excluded from much of the protection enjoyed by the majority of employees and are prevented from being members of independent trade unions. They are, however, entitled to protection under the Sex Discrimination Act and the Race Relations Act.

Partners

Generally partners are not employees. The business relationship between partners is one of people doing business together, which is quite different from an employer / employee relationship.

There is, however, a type of partner called a 'salaried partner' who appears to the outside world as a 'normal' partner but who is in fact just a glorified employee. A salaried partner would enjoy the same employment rights as an employee.

Homeworkers

Individuals who work for a company at home may be employed or self-employed. Their status will depend on the factors listed at the beginning of this chapter. In particular, where there is a minimum obligation on both sides to provide / accept work, where the employer provides the equipment to do the job and where a worker has been working from home on a full-time basis for several years, then there is a good chance that the person would be classed as employed in law.

Trainees

Trainees involved in government-sponsored training schemes are not employees, as they have no contract of employment with the training body concerned. Other types of trainees may be employees, depending on the type of contract they have with the company.

Rights of part-time employees, casual workers and temporary staff

It is important to define the meaning, for the purpose of this book, of part-time employees, casual workers and temporary staff.

In December 1994 the Government announced that all existing distinctions based on the number of hours worked per week were to be removed from employment protection legislation.

The effect of this decision is that all part-time employees, regardless of hours worked, now share the same employment rights as full-timers (with existing qualifying periods of service applying to both categories of worker). The Government's hand was forced by a House of Lords decision in March 1994 which effectively gave the same unfair dismissal and redundancy pay rights to part-time employees as those enjoyed by full-timers (after two years service).

Casual workers are those who work for a company on an 'as required' basis, and are paid only for the hours they work, often not being entitled to any company benefits except wages.

CASE STUDY

Mr O'Kelly worked as a wine waiter on a casual basis in a large hotel in the Trusthouse Forte Group. He was regarded as a regular casual and given preference over other 'casual' staff when it came to compiling work rotas. He had no other employment.

(CASE STUDY CONTINUED)

Q Was Mr O'Kelly an employee of Trusthouse Forte?

A Mr O'Kelly was not employed under a contract of employment. The key factor in determining the answer was that there was no mutuality of obligation between Mr O'Kelly and Trusthouse Forte. Mr O'Kelly had the right to choose whether or not to accept work when it was offered, and was free to work elsewhere. Equally Trusthouse Forte was not under any obligation to provide any work to Mr O'Kelly.

Based on the case *O'Kelly and Others* v *Trusthouse Forte plc.*

Casuals then are usually regarded as self-employed in law and do not enjoy any employment rights. In certain circumstances they may, however, be temporary employees, for example in the event that a casual employee worked regularly and continuously for a substantial number of hours a week over a long period of time. In such circumstances certain employment rights could be gained (although this would be an unusual situation). Most casuals work irregular hours on a 'wages only' type agreement, and therefore have few rights.

Temporary staff may be employed on a short-term contract, or may be engaged through an employment agency. Occasionally, they may be self-employed, although few companies are keen to engage self-employed persons as temps. for a variety of reasons.

The rights of temporary staff, if employed, depend on length of service, in the same way as the rights of permanent staff. If, on the other hand, you work through an employment agency, it is unlikely that you have any employment rights (see the list at the beginning of this chapter).

Questions and Answers

Q The employment agency I work with deducts tax and national insurance from my pay. Surely this means they are my employer?

A No, it doesn't. Employment agencies are required in law to regard themselves as the employer for PAYE and National Insurance purposes — but not in other respects. Generally agency workers are not regarded as the employees of employment agencies.

Q If I work through an employment agency, am I entitled to sick pay and holidays?

A No, except for statutory sick pay. There is, in any event, no law obliging employers to pay wages to employees who are off sick or on holiday, although many employers choose to do so.

Q I am self-employed, but have worked exclusively for one firm for over two years. What 'employment rights' do I have?
A The answer to this depends on whether you are, in law, an employee of the firm for whom you work. There are many factors which are taken into account when determining whether an individual is an employee, or self-employed. The fact that you have worked exclusively for one company for over two years points towards employment, but other factors (listed at the beginning of this chapter) would also be taken into account. If, in law, you are an employee, then you would have the same employment rights as any other employee.

Q I work for a company part-time and am based at home. The company provides all the equipment and material I need to produce the goods. They insist I am self-employed, but I have never regarded myself in this light. How can I clarify the issue?
A Sometimes 'homeworkers' (as they are known) are classed as employees of the company, sometimes not. Various factors are taken into account in determining their employment status, in particular whether there is a minimum obligation on both sides to provide/accept work, whether the employer provides the equipment to do the job and how long the worker has been working from home on a full-time basis.

If you are in law self-employed, you should ensure that your tax and national insurance liabilities are being properly taken care of. Ask your 'employer' about this if you are in any doubt.

Q I work as a receptionist for a company for 10 hours a week. There are rumours that the company is planning to cut staff numbers and my job may be redundant. I have been told that part-timers are not entitled to redundancy pay. Is this true?
A No, it is not true. Since 1994, part-timers have the same redundancy pay and unfair dismissal rights as full-time workers. You would be entitled to redundancy pay if your job is made redundant, provided you have at least two years service.

Q I have just started work on a temporary contract to cover another employee's maternity leave. Does the fact the job is temporary affect my rights?

A Yes, but only in the sense that many rights are service-related. In particular, you normally require two years service for unfair dismissal and redundancy rights. As it is unlikely you will attain two years service (unless your contract is extended), then you will not gain these rights. Other rights, however, apply to all employees regardless of length of service. Some examples of these are the right not to be discriminated against on the grounds of sex or race, the right to receive statutory sick pay, certain maternity rights, trade union rights, and protection against unlawful deductions from your pay.

2
Your
Contract of
Employment

A contract of employment can exist whether or not anything has been put into writing.

Provided you have been formally offered a job, and have clearly accepted it on the terms offered, then from that moment on a contract of employment exists in law. This could happen, for example, if an unconditional verbal offer follows an interview and you immediately accept it. If your prospective employer subsequently withdraws the offer, then you could pursue a breach of contract claim. Of course, proving it would be a different matter! Any serious and worthwhile employer would ensure that a verbal offer of employment was quickly confirmed in writing, with full details of the main terms of employment stated clearly, but this does not alter the fact that an employment contract can be entered into verbally.

There is indeed no legal requirement for a contract of employment to be in writing (except for apprentices). What is a legal requirement is for certain specified terms to be given to you in writing. This is known as the 'written

11

statement of key terms and conditions of employment', or just the 'written statement'. For details of these terms, see the section later in this chapter 'The terms and conditions of your employment which must be in writing'.

If you are not issued with written terms and conditions within two months of beginning work, you should ask your employer to provide them. In the event that you are still refused any written information, you would have the right to complain to an industrial tribunal.

CASE STUDY

Jayne had worked as a contracts assistant for Western Engineering for 4 months on a part-time basis. She worked three days a week from 09.00 – 13.00 hours. Her offer letter stated her salary, defined her hours of work and gave a brief description of the job she was expected to do. She had been told during her interview about the company's terms regarding holidays, and informed that she would not be entitled to company sick pay.

Jayne was concerned, however, that she had not been provided with a proper contract of employment and worried that her employment rights could thus be adversely affected.

Q Did Jayne have a contract of employment with Western Engineering?

A Yes. The fact that Western Engineering did not provide Jayne with a written statement of her key terms of employment would not affect Jayne's employment rights. In law a contract existed because Jayne was doing the job and being paid a salary.

However, Jayne was legally entitled to receive a written statement because her employment had continued for more than one month. She should have asked her employer to provide proper written terms of employment and if she still did not receive them, then she could, if she wished, make a complaint to an industrial tribunal.

The written statement is often referred to as the contract of employment, but in reality it is only a summary of the main provisions of the contract.

Apart from certain legal requirements (see below), employers are free to offer whatever terms and conditions they wish to prospective employees, and individuals are free to accept or reject these, or negotiate a better deal if they can.

There are a number of statutory provisions which benefit you as soon as you have entered into a contract of employment. Some of these are dependent on length of service and, where this is so, indication is given in the summary below.

- *The right to a written statement of the main terms and conditions of your employment.* You are entitled to receive this within two calendar months of starting work, your employment continues for at least one month.
- *The right to an itemised pay statement* (see Chapter 4). This right exists where the company employs 20 or more staff.
- *The right to equal pay* (for men and women) for work that is judged to be equal, for work rated as equivalent (under a job evaluation scheme), or for work of equal value. This is explained more fully in Chapter 4.
- *The right to statutory sick pay* if you cannot attend work on the grounds of personal sickness, provided you are eligible (see Chapter 4).
- *The right to payment in cash* where existing employees have established a contractual right.
- *The right to time off work* for the following:
    Public duties;
    Trade union duties, activities and training;
    To look for work when under notice of redundancy
    (subject to two years service).
    These rights are explained more fully in Chapter 5.
- *The right not to be discriminated against on the grounds of sex or race* (see Chapter 6).
- *The right to maternity benefits* (see Chapter 7). Note that the right to receive statutory maternity pay is dependent on a minimum of six months service.
- *The right to belong, or not to belong, to a trade union of your choice,* and to take part in trade union activities (see Chapter 11).
- *The right to notice of termination of your employment* (for minimum notice periods, which are service related, see Chapter 12).
- *The right to a written statement detailing reasons for dismissal.* This right, which is dependent on a minimum of two years' service, only arises if you request such written reasons. This means that your employer has no obligation to provide written reasons unless you ask for them (see Chapter 12).
- *The right not to be unfairly dismissed,* which, under most circumstances, begins only when you have gained two years' service (see Chapter 13).
- *The right to redundancy pay,* subject to a minimum of two years' service (see Chapter 14).
- *The right to continuity of employment and protected employment rights when the business is transferred to a new employer.* This could occur in the event of a take-over or merger.
- *The right to guaranteed pay if you are laid off* (i.e. if your employer has no

work for you to do) (see Chapter 14).
● *The right to a safe system of work.* The subject of Health and Safety is large
and complex, and, regrettably, outside the remit of this book.

It is interesting to note that in Britain (at present) there is no statutory
right to holidays (paid or unpaid). This means that a company could offer
you a contract of employment stating that you would receive no time off
for holidays whatsoever. It is highly likely that no reasoned individual
would work for such an employer, but the company would not be breaking
any law!

Furthermore you have no automatic right to be paid your wages / salary
during periods of sickness absence. (The question of statutory sick pay is a
separate issue: both are dealt with in Chapter 4, *Sick Pay – Statutory and
Contractual*).

Contracts of employment – general information

The contract of employment forms the basis of the relationship between the
employer and the employee and is therefore a very important document
from the point of view of both parties.

Illegality

Contracts of employment can only be enforced if they are legal. This means
that if you work under a contract of employment which contains provision
for some illegal act to be committed, then you will not be able to use the
contract to enforce your rights. The most common form of illegal contract
in this context is one which contains a term which results in part of an
employee's pay not being declared for income tax purposes.

The sources of contractual terms

Contractual terms are generally divided into four groups or sources:

● *Statutory terms:* these apply automatically to all contracts of employment
and take precedence over the other groups.
● *Express terms:* terms which are spelled out (usually in writing, but may
also be agreed verbally).
● *Implied terms:* terms which are not spelled out which may be implied into
the contract through common law or custom and practice.
● *Incorporated terms:* these are terms which become part of the contract of
employment through separate documents, e.g. collective agreements,
pension scheme rules.

Each of the four groups is considered more fully below.

Statutory terms

Statutory provisions such as the Health and Safety at Work Act, the Equal Pay Act and the Wages Act are imposed into all employment contracts. In addition, the statutory rights listed on pages 13–14 automatically form part of every contract of employment, whether or not reference is made to them. Such terms take precedence over all others.

CASE STUDY

Clive was offered a position as Civil Engineer with Mason Construction Ltd. His terms of employment were clearly spelled out in a document headed 'contract of employment' which he had signed. In a section entitled 'absence from work due to sickness', the contract stated: 'if, during the first six months of your employment, you are absent from work due to sickness, you will not be entitled to any payment whatsoever from the company'.

Q Could Mason Construction legally refuse to pay Clive any money if he was off work due to sickness, as stated in the contract?

A No, this clause would be illegal, and therefore unenforceable. There is a law which requires all employers to make specific payments of statutory sick pay to employees who are off work due to sickness, regardless of length of service. Clive would therefore be entitled to receive statutory sick pay, despite the fact he had signed a contract which stated the opposite. (For full information on sick pay, please refer to Chapter 4).

Any term in a contract which appears to deny you your statutory rights will be null and void, except in certain very limited circumstances. If in doubt, you should ask your employer to clarify the situation.

Express terms

Express terms are those which are specifically agreed between you and your employer. Usually such terms are in writing, but it is equally valid for an express term to be agreed verbally – although more difficult to prove!

Your employment offer letter is a likely source of several express terms of your contract, such as pay and hours. It is unlikely, however, that all your contractual terms will be contained in that document. Many of the express terms of your contract may be included in a written statement of terms and conditions, in an employee handbook, or in a union agreement.

Implied terms

Implied terms are those which are often left unsaid, but which would be regarded by the courts as forming part of the contract. More detailed information is given about this area later in this chapter.

Incorporated terms

Certain terms stated in documents such as trade union agreements, works rules, disciplinary procedures and pension scheme rules may be incorporated into contracts of employment. Incorporation is usually done by means of a clause such as 'Your entitlement to sick pay is as set out in the company's current union agreement'. However, the law now limits the number of employment-related items which can be incorporated in this way to sick pay, pensions, disciplinary rules, appeals and notice periods.

Fixed-term contracts

A fixed-term contract is one with a specified start date and a specified finish date. It is the existence of a specific termination date that makes the contract fixed-term. The actual duration of the contract can be any length of time agreed between the employer and employee. If you are in any doubt over whether your contract is fixed-term or permanent, you should seek clarification from your employer as soon as possible. The existence of a fixed-term may give you the advantage of guaranteed employment for the whole duration of the contract, although there is the obvious disadvantage of lack of permanence.

A fixed-term contract will automatically expire on the nominated termination date. It might be said that notice of termination is, in effect, given when the contract is entered into since both parties know its expiry date at that point. Nevertheless, expiry of a fixed-term contract is a dismissal in law.

Indeed, it is common for fixed-term contracts to contain no notice clauses, although there is no reason why notice periods cannot be included. If there is a notice clause in a fixed-term contract, your employer could legally terminate the contract early, provided you were given the period of notice stipulated in the contract. If notice periods are not included, this would normally mean that both parties were bound to maintain the contract (i.e. not terminate it) until the expiry of the agreed fixed period.

If, therefore, you are offered a fixed-term contract, be quite sure that you intend to remain with the employer for the whole duration of the contract. Acting in your favour, however, is the fact that a fixed-term contract without a notice clause would give you guaranteed employment for the specified period. So, if the employer were to terminate such a contract early (other than for reasons of gross misconduct on your part), then this would constitute a breach of contract. This would entitle you to make a claim for damages equivalent to your agreed rate of pay for the total outstanding portion of the contract. A change of mind could be expensive!

One key difference between a normal contract of employment and a fixed-term contract is the right of the employer to 'contract away' your unfair dismissal and redundancy rights. Indeed this is the only situation where these rights can be removed from you.

The unfair dismissal rights may be contracted away by means of a written clause in the contract prohibiting you from making a claim for unfair dismissal on the grounds of non-renewal of the contract. This can be done where the following conditions are met:

- The contract is for one year or more;
- The dismissal occurs upon the expiry of the fixed-term contract (i.e. the contract is not renewed);
- You are issued the disclaimer in writing, and agree to it, before the contract expires.

CASE STUDY

Peter was employed by Gibbons Shipping Company as a consultant engineer on a fixed-term contract for three years. His employment began on 1 July 1991. He had signed a contract which contained an exclusion clause along the following lines: 'This contract is for a fixed-term of three years, commencing on 1 July 1991. You agree, when the contract comes to an end, not to pursue a claim against the company for unfair dismissal'.

On 31 January 1994, Peter's manager explained that the company no longer needed his services and informed him that his contract would be terminated at the end of February, giving him one month's notice.

Q Could Peter make a claim for unfair dismissal?

A Yes, because the contract was being terminated prior to the expiry of the fixed-term. To comply with the law, Gibbons would have to permit Peter to work through to the end of the contract, i.e. the end of June 1994, or pay him for the outstanding portion of the contract, i.e. five months pay in lieu of notice.

If a fixed-term contract which was originally for a year or more is extended (without any change to its terms) then the original waiver clause will be extended with it. However if the contract is renewed (i.e. a new contract, perhaps with some different terms, replaces the original one), and the employer wishes to continue the exclusion clause, then the new agreement must itself be for at least one more year. If these provisions are not met, then the exclusion clause will not be valid.

Similarly your right to redundancy pay may be contracted away – in this case where the contract is for two years or more.

If a fixed-term contract is for less than a year, there can be no such exclusion clauses. Any exclusion clause included in a fixed-term contract for a period which is too short, or such a clause inserted into any other employment contract, will be void and unenforceable in law. You can simply disregard its existence.

Also, if your employer terminates the contract early, and provided you have sufficient qualifying service (normally two years), you would still be legally entitled to bring a claim for unfair dismissal and / or redundancy pay. An exclusion clause only applies to termination of the contract upon the expiry of the agreed term.

It is also useful to note that if you are employed on a series of consecutive fixed-term contracts, this will amount to continuous employment in law and will give you many other statutory rights.

Another type of contract which you may encounter is a 'contract for performance'. The key feature of such a contract is that it will expire on the occurrence of a particular event or completion of a specific task (for example a construction company employing workers to work on a specific building project). When the particular task that you are employed to do is complete, such a contract is said to be 'discharged by performance'.

This situation, unlike the expiry of a fixed-term contract, does not constitute a dismissal in law so you would not usually find exclusion clauses contained within it.

Terms and conditions of employment which must be in writing

All employees who continue in employment for at least one month must be given, within two months of starting work, a written statement setting out their main terms and conditions of employment.

A written statement is not in itself a contract of employment, but rather a statement setting out the key terms which the employer believes form part of the contract. The written statement must include:

- *Who the parties to the contract are (i.e. your name and the company's name).*
- *When your employment began.*
- *Whether or not any previous employment counts as continuous service (for example with an associated company).*
- *The scale or rate of pay.*

- *The intervals at which remuneration is paid (e.g. weekly, monthly).*
- *Normal working hours, and any rules as to hours of work. (Note there is, at present, no legislation in Britain placing a maximum number of hours on the working week, except for drivers of goods vehicles and public service vehicles).*
- *Any entitlement to holidays, including public holidays, and entitlement to holiday pay.*
- *The job title. (At present there is no legal obligation to give an employee a job description, although a brief job description will do as an alternative for a job title).*
- Any rules / terms relating to sickness, notification of sickness and pay during sickness absence.
- Pension arrangements, and a statement as to whether the employee's employment is contracted-out of the State pension scheme.
- If the contract is for a fixed-term, the termination date.
- The length of notice which the employee is entitled to receive and obliged to give (N.B. minimum notice periods are defined in law – see Chapter 12, *Giving Notice*).
- The name or job title of the person to whom employees can apply if they wish to raise a grievance, and the steps involved in the appeals procedure.
- Disciplinary rules (except for employers with less than 20 employees).

Trade Union Reform and Employment Rights Act 1993
The Trade Union Reform and Employment Rights Act, which was enacted in 1993, made certain additions to the Written Statement mandatory, as follows:

- *The place of work and the employer's address.*
- Any mobility requirements.
- *The likely duration of a period of temporary employment.*
- Notification of any collective agreements which directly affect the terms and conditions of the employment.
- Certain details relating to overseas assignments of one month or more.

There is no defined format or style for your terms and conditions of employment, although the law states that certain terms should be contained within one document known as a 'principal statement'. These are the items shown in **bold italic** in the above list.

CASE STUDY

Mr Mears worked for a small security company for 14 months, during which he was absent from work due to sickness for a period totalling about seven months. His written terms of employment made no reference to company sick pay (i.e. continuation of wages during periods of sickness absence), and he applied to an industrial tribunal for a declaration as to what terms ought to have been included in his contract.

Q Was Mr Mears legally entitled to company sick pay under his contract of employment, given the absence of any written term covering the subject?

A In this case the Court of Appeal decided that there was evidence to show that it was the normal practice of the company not to pay wages during sickness absence, and that this fact was well-known to employees. Furthermore Mr Mears had not at any time asked for sick pay. The decision was therefore that Mr Mears's contractual terms excluded the right to be paid wages during periods of sickness absence.

Based on the case *Mears v Safecar Security Ltd.*

There is no legal requirement for you to sign the written statement, although your employer will probably ask you to do so. A signature provides the employer with evidence that the written statement has been issued and received. There is no real advantage to you in refusing to sign, unless you clearly disagree with one or more of the terms, in which case the best course of action is to discuss and resolve the difference with your employer as soon as possible.

Any changes to the terms and conditions in your employment must, by law, be notified to you in writing within one month of the change taking place. There is no obligation on your employer to issue a complete new contract, just a written note of the items which have been changed.

If your employer fails to provide you with a written statement, or gives you inaccurate or incomplete information, then you can apply to an industrial tribunal. The tribunal will make a declaration as to what should have been included in a properly prepared written statement. This would then clarify the issue for you. The tribunal will not, however, assist you if you feel that your terms and conditions are unfair, or if the terms have been worded to be deliberately vague. They will merely make a statement as to what was agreed between you and your employer. There will be no monetary compensation.

To make a claim to an industrial tribunal in this context, you should first wait until the deadline for providing a written statement has expired, i.e.

two months after the start of your employment. Thereafter your claim may be brought to tribunal at any time during your employment.

Your implied rights

It would be unusual for a contract of employment to specify absolutely every term applicable to the employee. Implied terms are those which you and your employer are assumed to have agreed, even although there has been no express agreement. Terms may be implied into contracts:

- Through common law (see below);
- By the conduct of the parties (i.e. both you and your employer act as if the term was agreed);
- Because they are necessary due to 'business efficacy' (this simply means that without the term the contract would not be workable);
- Because they are so obvious that it is not necessary to include them in the written terms and conditions;
- Through custom and practice (see below).

CASE STUDY

Mrs Herbertson worked for Ladbroke Racing Ltd. and had received a written statement which defined her normal working week as 5 days or 35 hours. However for the last 32 months she had worked a rota involving six days a week for three weeks followed by a complete week off. Subsequently Ladbroke tried to return Mrs Herbertson to the original terms of her contract.

Q Was the company within its rights to require Mrs. Herbertson to work in accordance with the original written statement, i.e. a 5-day, 35-hour week?

A No, the company was in breach of contract. Because of the conduct of the parties during the preceding 32 months, the 6-day pattern represented the true term of Mrs Herbertson's contract and this took precedence over the written statement.

Based on the case *Ladbroke Racing Ltd v Herbertson*.

Common law

Common law duties are imposed on both employer and employee in an employment relationship. The main common law obligations affecting your employer are as follows:

- *To pay salary or wages*. Normally this is covered by a written term in the contract. The actual amount of wages to be paid is entirely a matter for agreement between you and your employer. Since the abolition of Wages Councils there are no longer any minimum rates of pay in Britain.

For details of legal and illegal deductions from your wages, see Chapter 4, *Deductions from Wages – Legal and Illegal*.

- *In certain limited circumstances, to provide work.* Employers are not generally required by law to provide you with work to do, as long as you continue to receive your pay.

  Circumstances in which there might be a duty to provide work include cases where pay depends on the amount of work provided (piece-working or commission-only based employment), or where lack of work could affect the competence or reputation of the individual (e.g. theatre performers).

  So, legally at least, you cannot complain if your employer keeps you idle!

- *To maintain the employment relationship* (the duty of cooperation). This includes the obligation on your employer not to destroy the mutual trust and confidence upon which cooperation is built, to treat you with reasonable courtesy and consideration, and to provide reasonable support to enable you to do your job. Such support could include support in dealing with serious workplace problems, or possibly the provision of necessary training.

- *To take reasonable care.* This provision is generally restricted to the requirement for the employer to provide a safe system of work and a safe working environment. In practice, this common law duty has been largely overtaken by the Health and Safety at Work Act 1974 and other subsequent health and safety legislation.

- *To compensate or reimburse employees* for expenses and liabilities incurred in the course of their employment.

Custom and practice

Terms may be implied into an employment contract through custom and practice. This can occur where the terms are regularly adopted over a period of time in the company, or in the particular trade or industry, or in a particular locality. It would be assumed that both employer and employee knew of the term and agreed to it as part of the contract without any need to put it in writing.

Such terms will only be implied into contracts if they meet all of the following criteria. They must be:

- *Reasonable* – i.e. fair and not arbitrary or capricious;
- *Certain* – i.e. clear-cut;
- *Notorious* – i.e. generally established and well known.

If your employer breaches any of the implied terms of your contract, then you have a choice of courses of action. These choices are explained in Chapter 3, *Breach of Implied Terms*.

CASE STUDY

Marion worked for a Paper Mill and had been employed for the last eight years. Each year the company had paid out a Christmas bonus equivalent to two weeks' wages. One year, Marion's manager informed her that she would not be entitled to a bonus that year. The manager maintained that the bonus was discretionary and therefore it was within the company's rights to withhold it.

Q Was Marion contractually entitled to her Christmas bonus?

A It is likely that in a case such as this an industrial tribunal would find that because the bonus had been paid to all employees for several years, it had become a contractual entitlement through custom and practice.

Your duties to your employer

As stated above, common law duties are imposed on both employer and employee in an employment relationship. The main common law obligations on you as an employee are:

- To be ready and willing to work.
- To be honest in your dealings with people.
- To cooperate with your employer. This includes obeying lawful and reasonable orders (provided the orders are in accordance with your contract, and do not endanger your safety).
- To be loyal and faithful. This includes the duty not to compete with your employer, not to disclose confidential information, not to accept secret profits and not to steal from your employer.
- Not to impede your employer's business, which includes the duty not to withdraw your labour (go on strike), or your goodwill.
- To maintain the employment relationship through good conduct.
- To take reasonable care and skill in performing your duties.
- To take reasonable care of the employer's property.

If you fail to comply with any of the above duties, then it is likely that you will be in breach of your contract of employment. In this context this means that your employer may have justified reason to give you a disciplinary warning or dismiss you.

Probationary periods

Many employers operate a practice of placing new employees on probation for an initial period of, typically, six months. This is generally good practice on behalf of employers who wish to assess the competence and suitability of new employees over the first few months of their employment.

The concept of a probationary period has no meaning in law, however, and in no way affects your continuity of employment, length of service or employment rights. This is the case whatever the length of your probationary period – your employment rights remain unaffected.

Restraint clauses and restrictive covenants – what they mean

It is possible that you may be asked to sign a document known as a restraint clause, or a restrictive covenant. Alternately such a clause may be written into your contract of employment. Such a document will seek to restrict what you may do during your employment, and more importantly perhaps, after you have left employment with that particular company.

Generally, it may be fair for your employer to expect you to sign such a document, provided the content and scope of the terms of the restraint clause are clear and reasonable. It is understandable that employers wish to protect themselves from, for example, ex-employees who set up business in competition against them and then steal all their customers! If you refuse to sign a restraint clause or restrictive covenant which is reasonable in its content and scope, your employer may regard your refusal as breach of your duty of fidelity (see next Chapter, *Breach of Implied Terms*). If you are in any doubt, therefore, you should discuss your objections with your employer and try to resolve them, rather than simply refuse to sign the document.

CASE STUDY

Mr Green worked for a company called Robb. During the course of his employment he secretly copied the list of Robb's customers' names and addresses. He subsequently left Robb and set up his own business. He intended using the list he had copied to induce Robb's customers to transfer their business to him.

Q Was Mr Green in breach of the terms of his contract in taking the list of customers for his own benefit?

A Yes. The court decided that there was a clear breach of the implied term that Mr Green should serve Robb with good faith. His actions therefore amounted to a breach of contract.

Based on the case *Robb* v *Green*.

Restraint clauses

A restraint clause may seek to prevent you from doing some or all of the following during your employment:

- Working for one of your employer's competitors during your spare time ('moonlighting');
- Doing work for another employer, or on your own account, during work time;
- Making secret profits from the employment, for example by using your employer's customer lists or contacts for personal profit;
- Divulging your employer's trade secrets, or any confidential information.

Moonlighting

Working at a second job, or carrying out work on your own account in your spare time is not illegal, since it is generally considered that individuals should be free to sell their labour to anyone they choose.

CASE STUDY

Mr Froggatt, an odd-job man, was dismissed when his employer found out that he had been doing some work for a competitor in his spare time.

Q Could this dismissal be justified on the grounds of breach of the duty of fidelity?

A No, the dismissal was unfair. The industrial tribunal hearing the case found that the nature of the work Mr. Froggatt did for the competitor company was not likely to pose any serious threat to his employer.

Based on the case *Nova Plastics Ltd* v *Froggatt*.

However, if what you do in your spare time is in serious conflict with your employer's business interests, then it would be quite reasonable for your employer to object, or to seek to prevent you (contractually) from doing it.

The sorts of situations in which your employer may be able to legitimately prevent you from moonlighting are:

- If you work for another employer during your working hours;
- If you work for a company which is a direct competitor of your main employer in a way which could damage the business interests of your employer;
- If your secondary employment is of a kind that could cause you to need higher amounts of sick leave;
- If, due to your second employment, you are likely to come to work tired.

In the types of cases described above, you could well be in breach of your contract of employment, and your employer would certainly be justified in seeking to prevent you from undertaking such activities.

Restrictive covenants

A restrictive covenant is a post-termination restraint clause which may seek to prevent you from doing some or all of the following after you have left your employment:

- Working for a competitor company;
- Setting up your own business in competition with your ex-employer, such as would damage his business interests;
- Inducing your ex-employer's customers to do business with you in your new employment (non-solicitation clause), or having any dealings whatsoever with such customers (non-dealing clause);
- Divulging your employer's trade secrets, or any confidential information.

It is worth noting, however, that employers cannot use restrictive covenants merely to prevent competition, as such clauses may be regarded in law as being contrary to public interest. The restriction must be no wider than is necessary to protect the employer's business interests.

So although a restrictive covenant set up purely to guard against competition is unenforceable in law, a restriction may be justified where the employer is genuinely seeking to protect confidential information, the relationships it has with its customers or suppliers, or the goodwill of the business generally.

CASE STUDY

Frances was a hairdresser employed by Ashley's Hair Salon, a privately-owned hairdresser in Harrow. She had signed a restrictive covenant which stated that she would not, within three years of the termination of her employment with Ashley's, start up her own hairdressing business within 25 miles of London.

Six months after resigning from her employment at Ashley's, Frances started up a hairdressing business in Croydon.

Q Would Ashley's be able to legally enforce the restrictive covenant against Frances by obtaining an injunction to stop her from opening her own business?

A Almost certainly not. It is likely that a court would find that the terms of the restraint were too wide. Firstly the period of the restraint (three

(CASE STUDY CONTINUED)

years) is unnecessarily long and secondly the area of the restraint would be much larger than the area of Ashley's business. Thus the restraint is far wider than is needed to protect the legitimate interests of the employer.

For a restrictive covenant to be enforceable in law, it must fulfil the following conditions:

- It must seek only reasonable protection;
- It must be no more than is necessary to protect a legitimate business interest.

In particular, three factors would be considered in the event of a dispute:

- *The type of restriction.* If, for example, a sales representative is employed to sell double glazing, it may be possible for the employer to restrict his future activities within the Glass and Glazing Industry, but not to prevent him from working as a sales representative for another type of company.
- *The geographical area.* If an employer operates only in one area of Britain, for example Yorkshire, a clause preventing the employee from setting up business anywhere in Britain would be too wide to be legally enforceable.
- *The duration of the restriction.* A restriction must not last longer than is necessary to protect the employer. A period of six months to one year is normal.

If a restraint clause or restrictive covenant is wider than necessary to protect the employer's legitimate business interests, it will be unenforceable in law.

CASE STUDY

Mr Shapiro was the chairman of Hanover Insurance Brokers Ltd. His contract contained a number of clauses restricting his activities for 12 months after termination of employment, including restrictions on canvassing, soliciting or endeavouring to take away any of the company's customers. There was also a clause prohibiting Mr Shapiro from enticing any of the company's employees to work for him.

When Mr Shapiro left Hanover along with three of his colleagues and set up an insurance broking business through another company, Hanover sought to enforce the restrictive covenant through the courts.

Q Was Mr Shapiro legally entitled to solicit Hanover's clients, or attempt to poach Hanover's employees?

(CASE STUDY CONTINUED)

A The High Court in this case agreed to grant an injunction to prevent Mr Shapiro and his colleagues from soliciting Hanover's customers. This was clearly within the remit of the terms of the restrictive covenant. This decision was upheld by the Court of Appeal.

With regard to poaching staff, however, the Court decided that employers should not be able to enforce restrictive covenants preventing ex-employees from poaching members of their workforce. A restrictive covenant seeking to prevent such poaching was against the principle of fair competition, and as such was unenforceable.

Based on the case *Hanover Insurance Brokers Ltd & another v Shapiro & others.*

If you consider that a restraint clause or restrictive covenant which your employer has asked you to sign is too wide, inappropriate for you, or otherwise unreasonable, then you would be wise to discuss your objections directly with your employer, rather than just refusing to sign it. There have been instances of employees being dismissed for refusing to sign a restraint clause. It is always better to try to sort out such differences in a rational way before the matter can escalate into a major problem.

Questions and Answers

Q My employer has not provided me with any written documentation regarding my terms and conditions of employment, despite the fact that I have been employed for almost a year. Does this mean I don't have a contract of employment?

A No, the fact that you are working for the company and being paid means that you have a contract of employment, and the same employment rights as any other employee.

Your employer should, however, have provided you with a document setting out the main terms of your employment in writing. Such a written statement must, in law, be given to all employees, within two months of starting work. You are therefore entitled to ask for such a written statement. Nevertheless, the fact that you have not received one does not put you at any legal disadvantage.

Q My company's rules and conditions on overtime working are not clear. I have been told I might be asked to work weekends sometimes. Do I have to comply?

A Strictly speaking, your employer can only oblige you to work over-time if it is stated in writing (in your terms and conditions of employment) that you are required to do so if asked, or if your hours of work are described as 'flexible'. You should check your terms and conditions / contract of employment, or alternatively ask your employer for clarification. If your employer recognises a trade union, then you could also ask the union representative for advice.

Q How many weeks' holiday entitlement must my employer give me in law?

A None. There is currently no law in Britain stipulating any minimum holiday entitlement, paid or unpaid. Holiday arrangements are therefore up to each employer to decide. The only obligation your employer does owe you in this respect is to put into writing any entitlement to holidays, (including public holidays) which is being offered to you as part of your contract.

Q I have asked my manager for a job description, but, after 6 months, I still haven't received one. Surely the company is obliged to give me a job description?

A No, there is no law compelling companies to produce job descriptions for employees. The only aspect of your job content which must be stated in writing is your job title. This, of course, is not necessarily very meaningful! Keep asking, because obviously it is helpful for you to have your job duties clarified, but you cannot legally insist on it.

Q My contract states that, if I am off sick, then I will receive company sick pay 'at management discretion'. This seems very vague. Is it legal?

A Yes. The company's only obligation with respect to sick pay (i.e. continuation of wages or salary during periods of sickness absence) is to state in writing what terms apply to you with regard to sickness, notification of sickness and pay during sickness absence. There is no need for the company to be specific as to the amounts of sick pay you would get, only to state the general rules applicable in the event of sickness.

Statutory sick pay must be paid to you, however, provided you qualify for payment. This is a separate issue covered in a later chapter.

You could ask your employer to clarify what usually happens in practice when employees are off sick, and what factors influence management in exercising their discretion.

Q I have been engaged on a fixed-term contract for two years. The contract contains a clause that, when the contract terms expires, I agree not to make any claim for unfair dismissal. I signed the contract at the time, but am now wondering whether such a clause is legal?

A Yes, it is quite legal. Such a waiver clause may be included in a fixed-term contract which is for one year or more, and will be valid provided you have agreed to it before the contract expires.

Q My employer has, for many years, operated a flexible retirement policy whereby employees can choose to retire at age 60 or work on until age 65 if they wish. I will be 60 in a few months time, and my manager has told me I will have to retire, and he has given me no reason. I am in good health and would like to continue working. Can I be forced to retire at 60?

A Sometimes terms of employment can become part of an employment contract through custom and practice. This can occur where the terms have become regular practice in the company over a long period of time, and are generally established and well known. It sounds as if your flexible retirement policy fits this bill, and consequently you would have the right to choose to work on to age 65 in the same way as other employees have done over many years.

If you are forced to retire at age 60 against your will, you may have a valid claim for unfair dismissal.

Q I joined a new company recently and was told that there would be a six month probationary period, after which my job performance would be assessed. Now I have been informed that the probationary period is to be extended for another three months. How will this affect my employment rights?

A It will not affect your employment rights in any way. Many employment rights are dependent on length of service, but your service began on the day you started work, and the existence and length of any probationary period does not affect this.

Q If I want to take on a second job in my spare time, can my employer stop me?

A Possibly – it depends on what your contract of employment says on the subject, and on the nature of your second job.

Working at a second job in your spare time is not illegal, but if your spare time activities are in serious conflict with your employer's business interests, then it would be quite reasonable (and legal) for your employer to seek to stop you. This would normally be achieved by writing a 'restraint clause' into your contract of employment.

Employers often wish to prevent their employees from taking up any secondary employment with companies in the same industry, especially competitor companies, or from working in a second job where the work might result in your coming to your main job tired.

Check your employment contract, or ask your manager what your company's rules are on this subject.

Q I work as a salesman. My employer has asked me to sign a document called a 'restrictive covenant', which (if I sign it) will prevent me from working for any other company as a salesman for six months after I leave. Could my employer enforce this agreement if and when I actually leave my present job?

A In principle, yes, although the legality of such a clause depends on it being reasonable in scope. Six months is a reasonable time period for a restrictive covenant to be applied, but it may be that your company is being over-ambitious in expecting to prevent you from working as a salesman for any other organisation whatsoever.

To be enforceable, such a restriction must be no wider than is necessary to protect the employer's business interests. In your case it is likely such a clause would only be enforceable if it restricted you from working for competitor companies (rather than any company) within a defined geographical limit.

You should discuss the wording of the proposed restrictive covenant with your employer in order to reach agreement on what is a reasonable restriction − i.e. one which protects your employer's business interests without imposing unreasonable restrictions on you if and when you leave.

PART II:
DURING EMPLOYMENT

3
Breach of
Contract

Breach of contract occurs when the employer acts in a manner inconsistent with the terms (express or implied) in the contract. This would include a situation where the employer changes one or more of the key terms of the contract without the employee's agreement. This will usually be illegal unless a clause in the contract states specifically that a particular change can be made. An example of this might be where the employer has reserved the right (stated in writing) to change shift patterns from time to time.

So, once a contract is entered into, both you and your employer are bound by its terms, and neither of you can alter them without the agreement of the other.

However, throughout the course of your employment, it is likely that certain changes to the terms of your contract will become necessary or desirable. For example, your salary may be reviewed and increased, and it would certainly be highly unusual for an employee to object to that sort of change! Other terms may be altered to introduce new working methods for example, which may not be so welcome.

Nevertheless the fact remains that unless there is a 'flexibility clause' written into the contract, then your employer will be in breach of contract if he tries to alter any of the terms and conditions of your employment without your agreement. What you may do about this is explained later in this chapter.

35

There is, however, another issue to consider. If your employer reduces your pay, then it would seem logical that this would amount to a breach of contract, unless you have agreed to a pay cut. But suppose the pay cut is equivalent to a penny per month – perhaps brought about by a hiccup in the computer's method of calculating salaries. Would this constitute breach of contract?

The answer, of course, is no. Not every breach of contract will be serious enough to be considered fundamental to the contract. The breach must be serious enough to go to the very root of the contract of employment, if you are to have a chance of resisting it.

Normally when a breach of contract occurs, it is as a result of something which the employer has actually done without your agreement. But what if your employer states his intention to change the terms of your contract at some date in the future? Provided the proposed change is a fundamental one, and your employer's statement is a real statement of intent, and not just a vague proposal, then an 'anticipatory breach' is said to occur.

In this situation you are entitled to treat the anticipatory breach in the same light as an actual breach which has already happened.

CASE STUDY

Robert worked for a housing organisation as administrative supervisor. In October the company began conducting a salary and jobs review throughout the organisation. Robert was informed by his manager that his job title would be altered to administrative officer as from 1 January the following year. He was told that salaries and job responsibilities were still under review, that there might be further changes, and he would be informed about these as soon as possible.

Q Has Robert's employer breached his contract of employment?

A In a case such as this, no fundamental breach of contract has occurred. Although Robert has been given a different job title, that does not amount to a clear indication from his employer that his salary, status or job responsibilities will change. As long as the review is still going on, there can be no anticipatory breach of contract.

One of the dangers here is that you might be tempted to act too hastily. You need to be sure that the so-called anticipatory breach is in fact a clear and unequivocal statement of intent to take a specific action to alter the terms of your contract at a future date.

It can sometimes be difficult to distinguish between a clear statement of intent and a proposal which is open for discussion. If your employer is just proposing to alter salary structures, change working practices or introduce a new shift system, then this would in no way breach your contract of employment. It is advisable, therefore, to be cautious in your reactions to such situations.

CASE STUDY

Ms Mercer-Brown worked as a personal secretary, but was asked to take on switchboard duties which were outside the scope of her contract. When she refused, discussions took place with her union, the AUEW. After a while the union's General Secretary wrote to her saying it was time something was finalised, and he expected her to cooperate with her employer. Ms Mercer-Brown promptly resigned.

Q Did the situation described give rise to an anticipatory breach of contract?

A The tribunal concluded that Ms Mercer-Brown had acted prematurely in resigning because the General Secretary's letter was simply a request to cooperate. The letter did not mean that the employer definitely intended to insist that she undertake switchboard duties.

Based on the case *Mercer-Brown* v *AUEW*.

Breach of express terms

A breach of contract may involve a unilateral change to one of your express terms. Some examples of breach of express terms are given in the following paragraphs:

Pay

Clearly pay is central to the contract of employment. For this reason, if your employer in any way alters the amount you are paid, or the timing of your pay, then this could well amount to a breach of contract.

On the other hand, there is normally no legal obligation on employers to increase pay, for example on an annual basis. Such an obligation would only occur if your contract of employment clearly stated that you were to be given a specific pay rise after a defined period of time, or if there was an implied term to the same effect, perhaps on account of custom and practice within the company.

CASE STUDY

Angela began work for Munro Petroleum as an assistant accountant in January 1994. Her offer letter stated that her salary would initially be £18,000 per annum for the first six months of her employment, and then,

(CASE STUDY CONTINUED)
subject to satisfactory performance, would be increased to £20,000. The pay
rise did not materialise despite Angela's requests for a review. As far as she
was aware her performance in the job had been satisfactory.

Q Is Munro Petroleum in breach of contract in not awarding Angela the
pay rise?
A Yes, because the pay rise was a firm promise, and was stated as a
contractual entitlement at the time Angela was recruited.

Fringe benefits
Terms which entitle you to certain fringe benefits are normally regarded in
law as part of your remuneration package. Consequently any alteration to
these benefits without your consent could also amount to a breach of
contract. Cases of such breach of contract which have occurred include
reduction of the contribution an employer made towards his employee's
telephone bill; removal of an employee's entitlement to a company car; and
withdrawal of a petrol allowance.

Job content
Unwanted changes to the tasks that you are asked to perform may amount
to a breach of contract. This could include transfer to another job, imposition of new tasks which are completely outside the scope of the original job
description, or transfer to less skilled work. To constitute breach of contract
such changes would have to be imposed on you without your consent,
instituted on a permanent rather than temporary basis, and contrary to your
original contract of employment.

CASE STUDY
Millbrook Furnishing Industries employed a number of skilled sewing
machinists. When business became slack, the machinists were transferred to
less skilled work until business in their original department picked up again.
The transfer, however, was of an unlimited and uncertain duration and it was
not clear whether the employees would suffer a reduction in wages as a result
of the transfer.

Q Did Millbrook Furnishing Industries breach the contracts of the sewing machinists?
A Yes, given the circumstances of the particular case. However, in a case
where a transfer is genuinely on a purely temporary basis, and provided
there is no reduction to wages, then it is likely that an employer would not be
acting in breach of contract.

Based on the case *Millbrook Furnishing Industries Ltd* v *McIntosh & others*.

Before jumping to any sudden conclusions on this subject, it would be advisable to check the wording of your contract of employment or job description. It may be that there is a 'flexibility clause' which entitles your employer to alter the work which you do from time to time. More information about flexibility clauses is provided later in this chapter.

CASE STUDY

Ms Glitz was appointed as a 'copy typist/general clerical duties clerk' in a small company called Watford Electric Company Ltd. After she had worked there for three years, her employer obtained a duplicating machine and asked her to operate it. She had not been told when she was recruited that this might be one of her job duties. Ms Glitz subsequently had problems with the machine as the vapour from it gave her headaches. Ultimately she was dismissed because there was no other work for her to do.

Q Was Watford Electric Company in breach of Ms Glitz's contract in requiring her to operating the duplicating machine?

A The Employment Appeal Tribunal decided in this case that the operation of a duplicating machine fell within the scope of general clerical duties, and so Ms Glitz lost her case.

Based on the case *Glitz* v *Watford Electric Co Ltd*.

Status

If your employer reduces the amount of responsibility which you have in your job leading to a loss of status, this may amount to a breach of contract. This would only occur, however, if you could show that an important part of your work had been removed, involving a significant loss of status.

Working hours

It would almost certainly be a breach of contract for an employer to increase an employee's hours without agreement. Further, it may be a breach to alter working patterns or shift systems.

Again this would amount to breach of contract only where the changes were made without your agreement, where they were substantial and not minor, and where there was no flexibility clause in the contract entitling the employer to alter your hours of work or change working schedules.

CASE STUDY

Mr Webb worked as a platemaker in the pre-press department of the web offset section of BPCC Purnell Ltd, a printing company. The platemakers

(CASE STUDY CONTINUED)
worked a triple shift pattern involving night shift work every three weeks, for which a shift premium was paid. Mr Webb's average gross weekly wage was £305.

Mr Webb's contract of employment contained a clause which stated that there would be total flexibility between all pre-press departments. In May 1989 BPCC announced that they would have to close the web department, but all employees would be redeployed. Thereafter Mr. Webb was transferred to another pre-press department and was told that until further notice he would work days only. This change would have resulted in a reduction to Mr Webb's gross earnings of about £80 per week.

Q Is Mr Webb entitled to regard his employer's actions as a breach of contract, given the flexibility clause in his contract?

A The tribunal in this case took the view that BPCC was entitled to transfer Mr Webb to a different department, and, within reason, to a different shift pattern. They also decided, however, that the flexibility clause did not entitle the employer to reduce Mr Webb's pay by such a substantial amount. This latter action amounted to a fundamental breach of contract.

Based on the case *BPCC Purnell Ltd* v *Webb*.

It is worth noting that a case like this could also be taken up under the Wages Act. For further details and another case study on the subject, please refer to Chapter 4, *Deductions from Wages, Legal and Illegal*.

Holidays
An attempt to shorten your holiday entitlement could amount to a breach of contract if the change was one of a fundamental nature.

Place of work
Unless your contract contains a mobility clause (i.e. a clause entitling your employer to transfer you to another location), it is likely that any attempt to force you to work in a different place would amount to a breach of contract.

Even where a mobility clause exists, the employer still has an implied obligation to give you reasonable notice of the transfer, in particular if the transfer requires you to move house.

Where your employer moves premises from one address to another, this technically gives rise to a redundancy situation. For full details on this, please refer to Chapter 14.

Disciplinary procedure
If you are subject to disciplinary action and your employer fails to follow the terms of the disciplinary procedure correctly, then this may amount to a

breach of your contract. For example if the disciplinary procedure allows the employer to demote an employee as 'punishment' for serious misconduct – but only in a situation where a previous written warning has been given – it would be a breach of contract for the employer to demote the employee where there had been no previous written warning.

CASE STUDY

Ms Dietmann worked as a social worker for Brent London Borough Council. Following an enquiry, the Council decided that Ms Dietmann was guilty of gross misconduct resulting from her alleged negligence in carrying out her duties. Thus she was dismissed summarily (without notice).

Under the Council's disciplinary procedure which was incorporated into her contract, Ms Dietmann would normally have been entitled to eight weeks' contractual notice on dismissal (except if the dismissal was for gross misconduct). She should also have been allowed a hearing to explain her side of things, which she was not given.

Q Did Ms Dietmann have a case for breach of contract against Brent Borough Council?

A The Court of Appeal decided in this case that Ms Dietmann's conduct did not amount to gross misconduct as defined in the Council's disciplinary rules, and that she was therefore entitled to eight weeks' notice on dismissal. Furthermore the employer was in breach of contract in denying her a disciplinary hearing. She received damages totalling 16 weeks' net pay.

Based on the case *Dietmann* v *Brent London Borough Council.*

Breach of implied terms

Proving breach of contract resulting from a breach of an implied term is difficult. The situation may well not be black and white. Some instances are as follows:

Mutual trust and confidence
It has been well established in law that employers must not, without reasonable cause, behave in a manner likely to destroy or seriously damage the relationship of trust and confidence between employer and employee.

Breach of this implied term can therefore cover a wide range of possible circumstances. Actual cases include an employer who unreasonably insisted that an employee should undergo a psychiatric examination; and a situation where a letter containing serious and false allegations against a particular employee was left visible on a computer screen for all to see.

CASE STUDY

Ms Protopapa was a hotel telephone supervisor with over 13 years' service. One day, having suffered from severe toothache, she arranged a dental appointment without consulting her manager. Later the manager severely reprimanded Ms Protopapa for her conduct in a manner which embarrassed and upset her. Following the reprimand Ms Protopapa resigned from the company.

Q Did the manager's conduct towards Ms Protopapa constitute breach of mutual trust and confidence?

A The tribunal in this case found that the rebuke issued to Ms. Protopapa had been officious and insensitive and she had not deserved that sort of treatment. She had been humiliated, intimidated and degraded to such an extent that there was a breach of trust going to the root of the contract. The employer appealed against the tribunal's decision, but the appeal tribunal supported the original tribunal's decision.

Based on the case *Hilton International Hotels (UK) Ltd* v *Protopapa*.

Even where the breach of trust is a result of the behaviour of another employee, and not the company as a whole, the employer may still be liable for breach of contract. This depends on whether the employee whose behaviour gave rise to the breach of contract is acting 'in the course of his employment'. Thus the company whose employee left the letter visible on the computer screen was liable for that behaviour since the employee concerned (a supervisor) was acting in the course of his employment.

Support
Breach of the duty to provide reasonable support to employees may also amount to breach of contract. Actual instances include an employer who failed to take proper steps to support a ward sister in dealing with an insubordinate member of nursing staff; and another employer who failed to make enough effort to protect an employee who was harassed and abused after working normally during a strike.

Safety
Under the implied duty to take care, employers could well be in breach of contract (not to mention the Health and Safety at Work Act) if they fail to provide a safe system of work. A breach of contract could occur, for example, if your employer failed to investigate properly, or failed to take seriously, a genuine complaint about a safety issue which an employee had raised.

At this stage a word of caution may be required! It is quite conceivable that employees could be tempted to over-react, or react over-hastily, to their employer's behaviour. In order to constitute a breach of contract, your employer's conduct must go right to the heart of the working relationship, i.e. be so serious as to be completely inappropriate and intolerable. Disagreements, personality clashes and work-place conflicts would not necessarily give rise to a breach of contract situation!

Variations to your contract of employment

It is important to distinguish between a breach of contract on the one hand and a variation to the contract on the other. If your employer imposes new terms on you without your agreement, then this is a breach of contract. If, however, you agree to accept new terms, then the contract will have been 'varied'.

Flexibility clauses

The most common situation in which your employer has the right to change the terms of your contract of employment, is one in which the contract contains a flexibility clause.

A flexibility clause is a statement in your contract which is phrased in such a way as to give the employer the right to alter certain terms and conditions like hours of work, work location, or job duties. The existence of a flexibility clause means that, in effect, you have agreed in advance to allow the employer to alter certain terms of your employment.

CASE STUDY

Mr McCallum worked for ICI Ltd, and under the terms of his contract the company was entitled, at its discretion, to transfer him from one operation to another carrying a higher or lower rate of pay. Mr McCallum was instructed to move from his job of estimator to lower paid work as a tradesman, but he objected to this and left.

Q Was the company within its rights to require Mr McCallum to transfer to lower paid work?

A The terms of Mr McCallum's contract clearly gave the company the right to transfer employees to lower paid work, therefore Mr McCallum had no legal grounds on which to contest the decision.

Based on the case *ICI Ltd* v *McCallum*.

Problems in this area often occur when an employer asks an employee to carry out duties which are not in the person's job description. There may, however, be a clause in the job description along the lines of 'you are required to undertake, at the direction of the company, any duties which reasonably fall within the scope of your capabilities'. In this case you would be well advised to comply, provided the new job duties are reasonable and you have the skills to perform them.

The method of performing a job could also fall within the job description. Despite this, it has been shown in practice that, if your company decides to alter your method of work (for example asking you to do work on computer instead of manually), then this would not necessarily amount to a breach of contract.

When you consider it, this approach is based on common sense – it is clear that employers need to move with the times and introduce new technology from time to time. Computerisation is a common example – so where you have previously done work manually and your employer introduces a new computer system which you are required to operate, this is likely to be perfectly reasonable in a legal sense. Its reasonableness will, however, depend on your being given proper support (i.e. training) to learn how to use the new computer system.

Other types of flexibility clauses might refer to working hours or shift patterns. A term might read: 'The company operates different shift systems and reserves the right to amend or alter these systems'.

Your employer may also wish to reserve the right to alter your place of work, or transfer you to another location. A mobility clause would normally define your employer's right to do this, with a clear definition of the scope of the clause. In other words, you are only obliged to move to another place of work within the geographical limitations defined in the mobility clause.

It is clear then that a flexibility clause within your contract of employment will entitle your employer to vary certain terms and conditions of your employment without being in breach of contract.

One final point – if your contract of employment has a union agreement incorporated into it, then in effect you have agreed to delegate the right to alter certain terms of your employment (i.e. those covered by the agreement) to the union in question.

Thus if the union makes a new agreement with your employer, your terms will be varied according to the new agreement. In this situation it makes no difference whether or not you are a member of the union – you are still bound by such changes. This may be rather surprising to some readers who are not union members.

How the employer can vary your contract

Clearly your employer may need to alter employees' terms of employment from time to time to cope with changes in business needs and activities, but it is important that fair procedures are observed.

Suppose that your employer wishes to make a change to one of the terms of its employment contracts, and supposing there is no flexibility clause in the contract which permits this. If employees refuse to agree to the change, can the employer just go ahead anyway?

This very scenario happens frequently throughout the country, when companies institute pay-cuts or changes to working practices, causing considerable unrest within their workforce, and possibly across the industry as a whole. So how do they get away with it?

The law recognises that sometimes it is crucial for a company to be able to make changes to the terms and conditions of employment of a group of employees, or of the whole workforce. An example of this could be where a company would have to go into liquidation unless it could substantially cut its overhead costs — thereby necessitating pay cuts. The underlying principle is whether there are 'sound business reasons' for the employer to make the change.

In order to avoid the risk of breach of contract claims, what the employer may do is terminate employees' contracts of employment rather than vary them. If, at the same time, the employer offers re-employment on the revised terms, employees who are prepared to go along with the changes can accept the offer of re-employment, carry on working on the new terms, and retain their continuity of employment.

This approach may, of course, lead to claims of unfair dismissal. But, provided certain steps (listed below) have been followed through, and the employer has behaved reasonably, it is unlikely that an industrial tribunal would consider such dismissals unfair. This is especially so if the majority of employees affected have accepted re-employment on the changed terms.

The correct procedure for an employer to follow in order to institute major changes to the terms of employees' contracts is as follows:

- Consider whether there are sound business reasons (and not just reasons of administrative convenience) for making the changes.
- Make an individual offer to vary the contract of employment to every employee affected, and fully explain the proposals. This should clearly be an offer, not a firm or non-negotiable statement of intent.
- If employees refuse to accept the new terms, hold discussions and listen to the reasons for the rejection of the proposals. (If employees agree to the proposals at this stage, then the remaining steps below would not be required).
- Take reasonable steps to overcome any objections raised by employees in connection with the proposals. An example of this might be to offer to pay for taxis to take employees home, if a new shift pattern involves finishing work after the last bus.

- Follow up such consultations in writing, recording the position so far, noting any particular objections and specifying any other options which might be explored.
- Warn employees who continue to resist the proposed changes that the consequence could be termination of their existing contract of employment (i.e. dismissal).
- Ultimately, if employees still fail to agree to the change, terminate their contracts of employment (with proper notice) and at the same time offer them re-employment on the new terms. Employees are of course free to accept or reject the offer of re-employment. If they reject it they are effectively dismissed.

Remedies open to you if your employer changes the terms of your contract without your agreement

If your employer alters the terms of your employment contract without following the procedure outlined above, and provided you have not agreed to the changes, then you have a choice of courses of action:

- *To do nothing, and continue to work under the revised terms.* In this case you will be deemed to have accepted the new terms after a 'reasonable' period of time. Unfortunately 'reasonable' in this context is not defined in law. The moral of the story is that if you wish to take action against your employer for breach of contract, do it promptly. At the very least you should tell your employer that you do not accept the change, preferably in writing.

   Note that even if you have not signed any document agreeing to the changes, the fact that you continue to work under the new terms will mean that, in law, you have accepted them, unless you notify your employer to the contrary.

CASE STUDY

Tessa worked as an advertising supervisor in the offices of a local newspaper. Due to financial difficulties, the company instituted pay cuts amongst its supervisory staff. This was done without consultation and without the agreement of the staff affected. Tessa was unhappy about the pay cut, but continued to work for the company whilst she looked around for another job. Three months later, having found another job, she resigned.

Q What are Tessa's chances now of taking legal action against her ex-employer on account of the imposed pay-cut?

A In this case because Tessa has continued to perform her job without protesting against the change, it is likely that a claim for breach of

(CASE STUDY CONTINUED)
contract would fail. The fact that she has continued to work for three months after the change would imply acceptance of the revised rate of pay.

● *Refuse to work under the new terms* if, for example, they involve a change in duties or hours, and wait to see if your employer dismisses you. It is advisable to be aware that if you choose this course of action then refusal on your part to comply may well lead to your dismissal.

If you are dismissed in these circumstances, you may have a claim for unfair dismissal, depending on how the employer has handled the situation. If, however, your employer has followed a fair procedure as outlined above, then it is unlikely that a claim for unfair dismissal would succeed. For full details of unfair dismissal, please refer to Chapter 13.

● *To continue working under protest, but sue your employer for damages for breach of contract* (if you have lost out financially). Working under protest simply means making your objections to the change known to management. If the breach involves a pay-cut, it is likely that the court would award you damages equivalent to the difference between your old rate of pay and the new one, backdated to the date of the imposition of the pay-cut.

CASE STUDY

Mrs Burdett-Coutts worked as a school dinner lady for Hertfordshire County Council. The council announced a series of amendments to the employment contracts of dinner ladies which had the effect of reducing pay. Mrs Burdett-Coutts and some of her colleagues continued to work, but did so under protest. At the same time they brought a High Court action for damages for breach of contract, claiming arrears of wages, and seeking a declaration that the Council was not entitled to vary their contracts in this way.

Q Did Mrs Burdett-Coutts succeed in her claim?

A Yes, the Court decided that the council was trying to vary the contracts unilaterally and that this was illegal.

Based on the case *Burdett-Coutts & others v Hertfordshire County Council.*

If the breach involves a change in hours or duties, then your only possible remedy from the court would be a declaration that the variation was unlawful. This has less chance of succeeding than a claim involving actual financial loss.

To sue for breach of contract, there is no service requirement. This means that your length of service with the company is immaterial – your claim will be eligible to be heard.

This type of claim would have to be made in the ordinary courts and not in an industrial tribunal.Note that if your employer terminates your contract in accordance with its notice terms, and offers you re-employment as discussed earlier, you will not legally be able to pursue this option.

● *To resign (without notice) and claim (unfair) constructive dismissal.* For this to succeed, you would have to be able to prove that your resignation was caused entirely by your employer's unreasonable actions.

In order to pursue a claim for constructive dismissal, you require a minimum of two years' service. An industrial tribunal will consider whether your employer's behaviour was such that no reasonable employee could be expected to put up with it. For full details of constructive dismissal, refer to Chapter 13.

CASE STUDY

Mrs Elsworthy and her husband both worked for UB (Ross Youngs) Ltd. There was a clause in their contracts entitling the company to transfer them to different shifts. Mrs Elsworthy, after having worked for the company for eight years, was transferred to the job of production supervisor, which involved shift work. In practice she worked on the same shift as her husband although there was no specific arrangement or contractual term guaranteeing this.

The year after her transfer, UB Ltd. devised a new shift pattern as a result of which Mr and Mrs Elsworthy would be working on different shifts and therefore rarely able to spend time together at home. Mrs Elsworthy expressed her concern about this and a number of meetings were subsequently held between her, her union representative and management. The reasons for the new shift pattern were explained to Mrs Elsworthy, and although alternative employment was considered for her, this was found not to be practicable. Mrs Elsworthy subsequently resigned, claiming that her employer had breached her contract of employment and that she had been constructively dismissed.

Q Did Mrs Elsworthy succeed in her claim?

A Yes. The tribunal commented that the company, although entitled to transfer Mrs Elsworthy to a different shift, had amended the shift pattern in a way such as to make it impossible for her to continue in the employment relationship. This situation had the effect of destroying the mutual trust and confidence (one of the key implied terms) between the parties.

Based on the case *UB (Ross Youngs) Ltd* v *Elsworthy*.

Questions and Answers

Q My employer has cut my pay by 25 per cent. What can I do about it?

A You have a choice of courses of action:

- *To continue working, but make your objection to the pay-cut known to management, and sue your employer for breach of contract through the ordinary courts.* Such a claim for breach of contract has a good chance of succeeding and the outcome could be that the court would award you compensation equivalent to the difference between your old rate of pay and the new one, backdated to the date of the imposition of the pay-cut.
- *To resign (no need to give notice) and claim (unfair) constructive dismissal.* In order to pursue a claim for constructive dismissal, you require a minimum of two years service. (More information about constructive dismissal is given in Chapter 13).

It is important to be aware that, if you do nothing, and continue to work under the revised terms, you will be deemed to have accepted the pay-cut after quite a short period of time, and will consequently have no means of taking legal action later on. So, if you wish to take any action at all, then do so promptly.

Q My boss has told everyone in my department that we will not receive any pay increase this year. Surely we are entitled to a cost-of-living increase at the very least?

A No, unfortunately not. There is no law obliging employers to increase pay once you are in employment.

Q I work in a small shop. My employer wants to extend the hours the shop is open, and has told me I have to work from 11.00 – 7.00 each day instead of 9.00 – 5.00, as from next month. Does he have the right to do this?

A Not without your agreement. However, it is not unreasonable in principle for your employer to want to extend the shop's opening hours, therefore the best outcome would be if you could discuss your hours and reach some agreement which is acceptable to both of you.

Q I work shifts on the basis of one week from 06.00 – 14.00 hours and from 14.00 – 22.00 hours the second week. Now my employer is planning to introduce a 24-hour, 3-shift system, including weekends. I don't want to work night shift, but what will happen if I refuse?

A Firstly, you should check your contract of employment to see whether your hours of work are precisely defined as you have stated. If so, your employer cannot force you to work different hours without your agreement. You would be entitled to refuse to work night shift, and your employer could not (legally) penalise you for refusing.

If, on the other hand, your hours of work or shifts are described in your contract as flexible, or if there is a clause saying that your hours of work or shifts can be changed according to your employer's needs, then any refusal to work a different shift pattern would amount to a breach of contract on your part. This means that your employer could possibly dismiss you for refusing to work night shift.

Please read the section on 'Breach of express terms' thoroughly to find out more, as this is a complex subject.

Q My employer has told me he wants to change my job description. This will involve my taking on new duties and additional responsibility. What is the legal position in a case like this?

A Major changes to the tasks that you are asked to perform imposed on you without your consent may amount to a breach of contract on the part of your employer. This would normally be the case only if you were asked to carry out tasks which were completely outside the scope of the original job description, or outside your capabilities.

Check, however, whether there is a 'flexibility clause' in your contract which entitles your employer to alter the work which you do from time to time. In this case, you would be obliged to comply with the changes, provided they are reasonable.

Look at it another way – perhaps this a challenging opportunity for you to develop your skills by taking on new duties and responsibilities! It could be a change for the better.

Q A new supervisor has been recruited into the department where I work, and I have been advised that he is to take over some of the key tasks which have been part of my job since I started work here three years ago. This will, in practice, remove the most interesting aspects of my job from me, and reduce my responsibility and status. Can I do anything about it?

A If your employer actually reduces the amount of responsibility which you have in your job, leading to a loss of status, this may amount to a breach of contract. You could then well succeed in a claim for constructive dismissal if you can show that an important part of your work has in fact been removed, involving a significant loss of status. To claim constructive dismissal, you must have at least two years service, and resign promptly once the changes are introduced (additional information about constructive dismissal is provided in Chapter 13). You would be well advised to wait and see whether the changes actually happen, however, rather than take action too soon.

Q My company is introducing computerisation into the department where I work. This will change my job completely as I will have to work with a keyboard rather than producing my work manually. I have been offered training on the new computer system, but I am uneasy about such a major change. Does my employer have the right to change my job like this?

A Yes, changes to the method of doing a job are generally within the scope of the law. It is understandable that employers wish to take advantage of new technology and expect their employees to learn new systems.

You do have the right in a situation such as this to be given adequate training and support in learning the new system. Why not discuss your fears and doubts with your boss, and see what training and coaching will be available to you?

Q My contract of employment contains a statement that my employer reserves the right to alter my working hours according to the needs of the business. Is it legal to have such a clause in a contract of employment?

A Yes, this is known as a 'flexibility clause' and is perfectly legal. If your employer does ask you to change your working hours in the future, you would be obliged to comply. The only exception to this would be if the new hours of work were totally unreasonable, or if there was some very strong objective reason why you would be unable to comply with them. Simply finding the new hours inconvenient would not, for example, constitute such a reason.

Q My employer has asked me to move to another office about eight miles from my present place of work. The job will be the same, but it is farther away from where I live, so I would prefer to remain where I am. Can I be forced to move?

A Unless your contract contains a mobility clause (i.e. a clause saying that your employer is entitled to transfer you to another location), it is likely that any attempt to force you to move would amount to a breach of contract. This means that you are entitled to refuse to move.

Q Recently my boss accused me of making a serious mistake which in fact related to work which had nothing to do with me. I felt humiliated and upset. Since then I have the feeling that he is trying to 'get at me' as he criticises everything I do. Is there any legal action I can take?

A Yes, but it is fairly drastic, and you would have to have a very strong case to succeed. It has been established in law that employers must not, without reasonable cause, behave in a manner likely to destroy or seriously damage the relationship of trust and confidence between employer and employee.

If you have at least two years service, you could resign and claim constructive dismissal on the basis that the treatment meted out to you by your boss was in breach of this 'duty of trust and confidence'. However, you would have to act quickly to have a chance of succeeding with such a claim. Details are given within this chapter and in Chapter 13, *What is Constructive Dismissal?*

4

Your Pay

Contractual and non-contractual pay

The amount of pay you receive for doing a particular job is a matter for agreement between yourself and your employer. There are no longer any minimum rates of pay in force in Britain since the abolition of Wages Councils in August 1993.

Your written terms of employment should specify the amount of your pay, your pay period (weekly, monthly, etc.) and your method of pay (bank credit transfer, cheque, etc.).

Your pay may be made up of a number of different elements, for example:

- Basic pay
- Bonus payment
- Overtime
- Commission
- Standby or call-out payment
- Regional allowance / weighting
- Shift allowance, etc.

The term 'remuneration' is often used to mean your total pay (including any of the above which you receive). 'Remuneration' may also be intended to include fringe benefits, e.g. company car, medical insurance, pension scheme, free lunches.

One important point which you should be clear about is whether or not a particular element of your pay is a contractual right. In other words, is your employer obliged to pay you the element of pay in question?

If your contract contains a clause along the lines of 'The company may, from time to time, pay you a bonus at the end of the financial year', this is

53

unlikely to indicate a contractual obligation on the part of your employer to pay you a bonus. So you may get the bonus, or you may not, depending on the discretion of your employer.

On the other hand if the clause is worded along the lines of 'The company will pay you a bonus at the end of each financial year', then this is almost certainly a guarantee that a bonus will be paid to you. In this second situation, if the bonus is not paid, you would have a claim for breach of contract.

In addition, if a bonus (or other element of pay) is paid on a regular basis over a long period of time, it may become an expected part of the remuneration package, and thus create a contractual entitlement. This would mean that the bonus had actually become a contractual entitlement through custom and practice, even if it was not originally intended to be so, and was not specifically included in the contract of employment.

If you are in any doubt about whether an element of your pay is contractual or non-contractual, then you should check your contract of employment and/or ask for clarification.

Overtime

Whether or not overtime is payable, and whether or not you are obliged to work overtime if asked to do so, are matters which your written terms and conditions should make clear. Again, if you are not sure, then it would be advisable to ask, so that you know precisely what your obligations and entitlements are. There are many instances of disputes over whether or not an employee is obliged to work overtime, and it is better for you to have a clear understanding as to your terms in this respect.

CASE STUDY

Mr Kirkpatrick was a service engineer employed by Lister-Petter Ltd. He was required to work overtime under his contract of employment, but initially was exempted from a stand-by rota because he had no experience of the work required, which was refrigeration maintenance. After attending training courses on the subject, however, he was asked to join a 24-hour stand-by rota. When he persistently refused to do so because of family commitments, he was dismissed.

Q Was the employer within his rights to insist that Mr Kirkpatrick work the stand-by rota?

A Yes, the tribunal in this case decided that because Mr Kirkpatrick was contractually required to work overtime, that meant he was obliged to work on the stand-by rota if asked. The company acted reasonably in dismissing him for refusing to do so, especially since the stand-by rota was necessary to the company's business interests.

Based on the case *Kirkpatrick v Lister-Petter Ltd.*

It is common for companies to pay for overtime hours (hours worked over and above your normal working week) at an enhanced rate of pay, typically time and a half, or double time. This, however, is not a legal requirement, and it is perfectly acceptable legally for an employer to pay for overtime at single time (i.e. based on your normal rate of pay).

Some employees are not paid for overtime hours – for example managers and professional staff who may be paid a fixed monthly salary and be expected to work whatever hours are necessary to get the job done. This is perfectly legitimate provided it is spelled out to the employee in writing. It is entirely a matter between you and your employer.

Your right to an itemised pay statement

Employees have a statutory right to receive an itemised pay statement where the company employs 20 or more staff. The statement must be given to you at the time of payment and include:

● The gross amount of your wages or salary;
● The amounts of all fixed deductions, and the purposes for which they are made, e.g. trade union subscription;
● The amounts of all variable deductions and the purposes for which they are made, e.g. income tax, national insurance;
● The net amount of wages or salary payable to you (i.e. the amount you actually receive);
● If different elements of your net pay are paid in different ways, e.g. one element is paid in cash, another by cheque, the amount and method of each part-payment.

CASE STUDY

Mr Pritchett worked for Game World (Developments) Ltd. and for over three years received wage packets which showed his tax / national insurance deductions. Suddenly he ceased to receive wage packets at all, although he was still paid the same amounts of wages in cash. He suffered no financial loss.

Q Did Mr Pritchett have any legal claim against his employer for failing to provide itemised pay statements, given that he suffered no financial loss?

A Yes. An industrial tribunal awarded Mr Pritchett an amount of money equivalent to the full amount of the unnotified deductions over the relevant period of time – this amounted to £398.

Based on the case *Pritchett* v *Game World (Developments) Ltd.*

So if your employer fails to provide you with an itemised pay statement, or fails to include the proper information, then you can apply to an industrial tribunal for a decision as to what items should be included. The tribunal may or may not award monetary compensation, depending on the circumstances. Note, however, that an industrial tribunal will not deal with questions of accuracy in the statements – such problems would need to be resolved internally with your company's payroll department.

Deductions from wages – legal and illegal

All employees are protected under the Wages Act 1986. What your employer can and cannot deduct from your pay is strictly governed by this piece of legislation which introduced clear restrictions with regard to deductions from wages.

For a deduction to be legal, it must satisfy one of the following conditions:

● It is required or authorised by legislation, for example income tax and national insurance payments. *Or*
● It is covered by a clause in your contract of employment and you have received a copy of the appropriate clause before any deduction is made. *Or*
● You have agreed to it in writing in advance of any deduction being made.

There are, however, exceptions to the above rules. They do not apply in the following circumstances:

● Where there has been an over-payment of wages or expenses;
● In the case of disciplinary proceedings provided for in legislation, e.g. police disciplinary proceedings;
● Where there is a court or tribunal order requiring payment by you to your employer;
● Where you have participated in a strike or other industrial action.

CASE STUDY

Sarah, a 16 year-old school-girl, obtained a part-time job as a waitress in a local restaurant. She worked two evenings a week for 3–4 hours each evening. There was no written contract of employment.

One evening a customer accidentally knocked against Sarah causing her to spill some food on to another customer's jacket. Although the accident was not Sarah's fault, the restaurant manager informed her later that money

(CASE STUDY CONTINUED)

would be deducted from her tips in order to compensate the customer. It was the practice of the restaurant to pool all tips and pay them over to staff each week. Over the next few weeks a total of £40 was deducted from Sarah's tips.

Q Did the restaurant manager, under the circumstances, have the legal right to deduct any money from Sarah's tips?

A No. Despite the fact that Sarah was a 16 year old 'casual' worker who worked only 6–8 hours a week, and the fact that the money was deducted from her tips and not her basic wage, the deduction was illegal. Sarah could take legal action against her employer to force him to repay the money he had deducted.

Your employer is not allowed to deduct money from your wages for lateness, misconduct or damage to company property, etc. unless either there is an express term in the contract entitling him to do so, or you have agreed to it in writing in advance. Retrospective consent to a deduction from wages will not entitle your employer to make such a deduction.

This effectively prevents employers from putting pressure on employees to agree to give consent to deductions in respect of conduct which has already taken place.

CASE STUDY

Charlie had worked for 18 months as a maintenance engineer for a small family-run building firm. Charlie's boss, Mr Duncan, permitted Charlie to drive his car both on company business and occasionally privately. On two previous occasions during the last 12 months, Charlie had been involved in minor accidents involving damage to Mr Duncan's car. Mr. Duncan had warned Charlie that if it happened again, he would require him to pay for the damage.

One evening in November, Charlie skidded on ice and hit a lamp-post causing considerable damage to the car. Later he discussed the matter with Mr Duncan and agreed to pay half the cost of the vehicle's repairs. Mr Duncan said he would obtain an estimate for the repairs and notify Charlie accordingly.

Two weeks later, Charlie resigned from the company, giving one week's notice. When he received his final pay packet, he noticed that about £600 had been deducted from his pay, leaving him with a net pay of £43. On checking, he verified that the repair to the vehicle had been estimated at £1,200.

Q Did Mr Duncan have the legal right to deduct £600 from Charlie's final pay packet?

(CASE STUDY CONTINUED)

A No, a verbal agreement to pay for damage to the vehicle did not entitle Mr Duncan to deduct money from Charlie's wages.

There are other situations which may arise during which you may not be entitled to be paid your normal wage or salary. These include periods of absence due to sickness or holidays. Whether or not you are entitled to be paid during such periods of absence will depend entirely on what your contract of employment says. There is no legal requirement for an employer to give employees paid holidays (or any holidays at all), nor to pay salary during periods of sickness absence. (Note that for periods of sickness absence, statutory sick pay may be payable – this is an entirely separate issue from continuation of wage/salary during periods of sickness. Full details are given later in this Chapter under the heading 'Statutory sick pay').

If you choose to take part in a strike, then your employer is not obliged to pay you.

If you think that your employer has made an illegal deduction from your wage or salary, you can make a claim to an industrial tribunal to seek reimbursement of the sum involved. You must do so within three months of the deduction taking place.

Furthermore, if a tribunal order is made to reimburse you an amount which was illegally deducted from your pay, then your employer cannot subsequently sue you for the money. This means that the money is yours to keep whatever happens subsequently.

You should not hesitate to raise any query over deductions from pay with your employer. It is better to resolve queries or differences directly rather than take formal proceedings to tribunal. If, however, your employer refuses to agree to reimburse you a sum of money which you believe has been illegally deducted, then you have every right to take the case to an industrial tribunal where the matter can be resolved fairly.

CASE STUDY

Mr Yemm and three others were entitled under their contracts of employment to basic pay and shift allowances. Their employer, British Steel, was entitled under the contracts of employment to change employees' shift patterns. A dispute arose, however, when British Steel altered the shift pattern with the result that Mr Yemm and his colleagues received less pay for shift work than before. Mr Yemm and his colleagues made a complaint to an industrial tribunal, claiming that they should have been paid the same shift allowances as they had received before the change.

(CASE STUDY CONTINUED)

Q Could the tribunal consider a claim under the Wages Act under the circumstances described above?

A This issue went to appeal in 1993. The Employment Appeal Tribunal decided that the reduction in pay caused by the change in shift pattern could amount to a deduction from wages within the scope of the Wages Act. The case was subsequently remitted to a different tribunal to determine the outcome.

Based on the case *Yemm & Others* v *British Steel plc*.

Over-payment of wages

What happens if your employer has over-paid you and wishes to recover the relevant amount of money from you? The answer is that recovery may be legal. It could, however, be illegal if:

● The employer has misled you into believing you were entitled to the sum in question;
● You were genuinely unaware that your employer was going to reclaim the money, and you had already spent it;
● The over-payment was not primarily your fault.

Attachment of earnings

Where a person has been ordered by a court to pay a debt, fine or family maintenance, but has defaulted on payment, the court may require the employer to make deductions from the person's pay. This is known as an attachment order.

The normal deduction rate will be the amount the court considers reasonable to deduct from the employee's pay, taking into account the person's individual circumstances and financial needs.

There are similar rules applying to non-payment of council tax, where the local authority may issue an attachment order to your employer to enforce payment by deduction from wages. Non-council-tax payers beware!

Special provisions for retail employees

It is common in retail employment for employers to have a clause in employees' contracts of employment giving them the right to make deductions from wages on account of cash shortages or stock deficiencies.

There is additional legal protection for people who work in retail employment as regards such deductions. The deductions must firstly comply with the rules regarding authorisation which have already been stated in this section, and in addition must comply with another important rule.

The additional protection is a rule that the deduction must not exceed 10 per cent of your gross wage payable on any pay-day. So if a cash shortage amounted to more than 10 per cent of your pay, then your employer would have to deduct the total amount in instalments over two or more pay days. This rule does not apply, however, to final payment of wages, i.e. your last pay if you leave your job.

Your employer is also under certain obligations to notify you in writing of the full amount of any shortfall, and issue a written demand for payment from you.

Equal pay for men and women

Since the introduction of the Equal Pay Act, employers are obliged to treat men and women equally in terms of pay and fringe benefits, if they are employed on 'like work', work rated as equivalent under a job evaluation scheme, or work judged to be of equal value. These three factors are described more fully below:

Like work
'Like work' is work which is the same or of a broadly similar nature. There are no hard and fast rules for proving that jobs are similar and a flexible approach is taken. Trivial differences would not be taken into account. Also, job titles will not be a factor – it is what each employee actually does which will determine whether or not their work is 'like work'. Your job description (if you have one) should be a useful source of information if you wish to compare what you do with the job duties of an employee in another job or department.

Work rated as equivalent
This applies where the job of a man and the job of a woman have been rated as equal under a properly conducted job evaluation scheme. It is important to remember that a properly conducted job evaluation study will have evaluated the job, and not the person doing it. Thus the resulting job grades may be used as the basis for the company's pay structure, and this will normally be assumed to be free of any sex bias.

If a job evaluation system is in operation in your company, equal pay can only be challenged where it can be shown that the job evaluation scheme itself discriminates against women (or against men).

Work of equal value
Where there is no job evaluation scheme, but one job makes equal demands on the job holder as another, then the 'equal value' clause may apply.

Factors which are taken into account in establishing whether two jobs are of equal value are effort, skill, decision making and other significant factors.

Material differences

Your employer may, of course, still pay you a different amount from another employee if there are material differences (i.e. personal differences) between the two cases which have nothing to do with the sex of the individuals. For example, you may be paid less if you have less experience, fewer qualifications, have worked for the company for a shorter period of time, or have performed less well than another employee. This is perfectly legitimate.

CASE STUDY

Ms Enderby was employed with Frenchay Health Authority as a speech therapist, a profession which consisted mainly of women. She made a claim for equal pay with clinical psychologists and principal pharmacists, who were predominantly men, and who were being paid considerably more than she was earning.

The health authority's defence was based on a two-part material difference argument. Firstly they argued that the relevant rates of pay for each of the two groups had been established through separate collective bargaining procedures, and that these processes of collective bargaining had been carried out in a non-discriminatory manner. In addition, they argued that market forces obliged them to pay clinical psychologists and principal pharmacists higher rates of pay, as there was a shortage of suitably qualified job applicants for these posts.

Q Did this case represent a breach of the equal pay legislation, or was the material factor defence valid?

A This case was heard by the European Court of Justice in 1993. The Court stated that any difference in pay between two groups of workers who do work of equal value must be justified objectively.

The Court refused to accept the 'separate collective bargaining' argument, and pointed out that it was the result of the collective bargaining process, i.e. discriminatory rates of pay for jobs of equal value, which was the issue. The historical process by which the different rates of pay had come into existence explained the cause of the variation, but did not justify it.

The European Court did acknowledge, however, that market forces, namely shortage of candidates for a particular job, could justify the payment of different rates of pay for different jobs – at least to a proportional extent.

The case was referred back to the British Courts for resolution.

Based on the case *Enderby v Frenchay Health Authority*.

Equality legislation does not apply to the special legal entitlements given to women concerning pregnancy and childbirth. This means that male employees cannot claim that they have been less favourably treated (on the grounds of sex) because a female colleague has been paid maternity pay.

If you think that you are receiving unfavourable treatment with regard to your remuneration package on account of your sex, then you can make a claim to an industrial tribunal.

The process is, however, a long and arduous one, especially for claims under the heading of 'equal value'. Here an independent expert is appointed to look at the relevant jobs and provide a report on their comparative values. It has been known for equal value claims to go on for several years before being finally decided.

Sick pay – statutory and contractual

Contractual sick pay

There are two entirely separate types of 'sick pay' which may be paid to you. The first is company sick pay (sometimes called occupational sick pay) which is simply the continuation of your wage or salary during periods of sickness absence. Whether or not you are entitled to company sick pay is a contractual matter – there is no legal requirement for your employer to pay you if you are off sick. You should therefore examine your written terms of employment to establish what your entitlement is.

It is quite common for a contract of employment to say something like: 'If you are absent from work due to sickness, you will be paid company sick pay according to your manager's discretion'. Other more enlightened companies define clearly the time periods during which you will continue to be paid your wage or salary if you are off sick. Often this is service-related, meaning that the longer you have been employed by the company, the more sick pay you will be entitled to.

The only legal obligation which your employer has in this context is to state in writing what your sick pay entitlements are.

Statutory sick pay (SSP)

Unlike company sick pay, payment of statutory sick pay (SSP) is a legal requirement for all employers. There is no choice in the matter – all employers are obliged to pay SSP and to keep certain records (whether or not they pay company sick pay). Employers are liable to pay SSP to eligible employees who are absent from work due to sickness for four days or more for a maximum period of 28 weeks at a time.

Entitlement

Most employees are entitled to SSP as there is no minimum service qualification, and entitlement is not dependent on the number of hours worked. The following people are, however, excluded:

- Employees over state pension age.
- Individuals employed on a short-term contract for three months or less.
- Employees whose pay is less than the point at which National Insurance becomes payable (at the time of writing £58.00 per week).
- Employees who have received certain state benefits during the preceding eight weeks.
- Individuals who have not yet started their job. Where, however, the employee has started work, even for an hour or two, SSP will be payable.
- Employees who are taking part in a strike.
- Pregnant employees who are entitled to statutory maternity pay or maternity allowance, or who fall sick within six weeks of their baby being due.
- Where 28 weeks of SSP has been paid already.
- Employees outside the European Community (e.g. on holiday).
- Employees in legal custody.

If you are excluded from receiving SSP for one of the above reasons, your employer must issue you with an exclusion form, so that you are able to claim social security sickness benefit instead. If you have been off sick, and have not received SSP or an exclusion form, then you should raise the matter with your employer.

Qualifying conditions

The qualifying conditions for SSP are complicated – the most important of these are listed below. To qualify for SSP:

- You must notify your employer that you are sick in accordance with your company's rules.
- You must provide suitable medical evidence, such as a self-certificate (most companies use these for up to seven days' sickness absence), or a doctor's statement.
- You must be off sick for four or more calendar days in a row (this is known as a period of incapacity for work, or PIW for short). PIW's separated by eight weeks or less are linked and count as one PIW. Note that there is no payment for the first three days in any PIW – these are known as 'waiting days'.
- Your days of absence must be days on which you would normally have worked – known as 'qualifying days'.

The amount of SSP is based on rates laid down by the government which are reviewed each year. SSP is treated as pay, therefore income tax and national insurance contributions will be deducted in the normal way.

You cannot, of course, receive SSP and your normal salary as well – this would be illegal – you would end up being financially better off sick than at work! So if you continue to receive your normal pay during periods of sickness absence, your employer will offset SSP against your pay. This means that your take-home pay will be the same as usual, and only its make-up will be different. You should find that this is clearly itemised on your pay slip.

Holiday pay

You have no statutory right to holidays, paid or unpaid (despite rumours and myths to the contrary!). Most companies establish holiday entitlements and holiday pay according to what the competition is doing and what they feel is appropriate. Your entitlement should, however, be clearly laid down within your written terms and conditions. If not, you should ask to have the matter clarified.

Typically, companies will offer employees 4–5 weeks paid holiday per year. Sometimes entitlement to holidays increases after a period of service of five years or more.

Your company may also have rules regarding the timing of holidays, such as a clause along the lines of 'all holiday dates must be agreed in advance with your manager'. It is also common for there to be a clause restricting the carry-over of holiday entitlement from one year to the next.

If there are such rules, they must be written into your contract of employment or terms and conditions.

CASE STUDY

Mr Morley was financial director of a company called Heritage plc. His contract said he was entitled to 20 days paid holiday a year, plus public holidays, or the pro-rata equivalent for any period of less than a year. There was nothing in writing about what entitlement Mr Morley would have to pay in lieu of holidays not taken in the event of termination of his employment.

When Mr Morley resigned from his employment on 20 October, he had taken only two out of the 15 days' holiday which he had accrued for that year (i.e. his holiday entitlement for January to the end September – nine completed months). His employer refused to give him the 13 days pay in lieu of his unused holiday entitlement. Mr Morley subsequently sued Heritage for the outstanding amount.

(CASE STUDY CONTINUED)

Q Was payment in lieu of holidays on termination of Mr Morley's employment an implied term of his contract (since there was no express
term defining entitlement)?

A The Court of Appeal rejected Mr Morley's claim. Even although written statements of terms and conditions of employment should include
full information related to holiday pay entitlement, the Court would not
imply a term that Mr Morley was entitled to pay in lieu of holidays on
termination. For this to be a contractual right, the entitlement would have to
be specified in his written terms.

   This case demonstrates that payment for accrued holidays on termination
of employment depends on the terms of your contract, and, unless specified
in writing, is not an automatic right.

Based on the case *Morley* v *Heritage plc*.

For information about your entitlement (if any) to public holidays, please
refer to Chapter 5.

Questions and Answers

Q I have been offered a job in a local hotel on a part-time basis, but the
pay, which is based on an hourly rate, seems very low. I thought there
were minimum rates of pay defined by law?

A Not any more, since the abolition of Wages Councils in 1993. In any
event such minimum rates of pay applied only to certain industries
(although the hotel and catering industry was one of the industries
covered). Currently employers are free to offer employees any rate of pay
they wish, just as you are free to accept or reject what is offered.

Q For years my colleagues and I have received an annual bonus, usually
paid just before Christmas. This year, apparently because company
profits have been poor, we have been told that no bonus can be paid. I rely
on the extra cash, and am very upset at this news. Can I do anything about
it?

A It depends on whether the bonus is a contractual entitlement, or just a
discretionary payment. Check your contract of employment to see
what total remuneration (pay plus other benefits) you are entitled to. Unless
there is a clear statement that you are contractually entitled to an annual
bonus, there is nothing you can do if your employer decides not to pay the
bonus.

Q My contract says that if I work overtime, I will be paid only at 'single time'. Surely I am entitled to time and a half or double time, especially for weekend working?

A No, this is not the case. Employers are free to decide their level of pay for overtime working, and indeed are not obliged in law to pay you any additional wages at all for working extra hours.

As long as your contract makes it clear what your entitlement to overtime payment is, then your employer is acting legally.

Q Can my employer deduct money from my pay if I come to work late?

A No, not unless there is a clause in your contract of employment specifying that your employer has the right to do this, and explaining the conditions under which any deductions will be implemented.

Q Recently I accidentally dropped a cup of coffee, as a result of which a computer keyboard was damaged. My manager has told me he is going to deduct the cost of the equipment repair from my salary over the next few months. Can he do this?

A No, not unless you have already signed a statement agreeing to deductions of this kind from your salary. Your employer cannot legally put pressure on you to now agree to the deduction of the cost of the equipment repair. Any attempt to do so will not have any effect, as such consent (to be effective in law) must be given in writing in advance.

If your employer deducts the money anyway, you could apply to an industrial tribunal to recover the sum.

Q My employer has told me that, for the last six months, I have been receiving an allowance of £50 per month in my pay, to which I am not entitled. I had noticed the allowance, but assumed I was entitled to it. Now they want me to pay the £300 back by deducting it from my salary over the next six months. Must I pay the money back?

A No. Any attempt to recover the sum over-paid will probably be illegal, assuming the over-payment was not your fault. Provided you were genuinely unaware that your employer was likely to reclaim the money, and you have already spent it, then your employer would not be entitled to reclaim the £300 from you.

Q I have recently started a new job in a large department store, having previously worked in an office. My contract states that money can be deducted from my wages if cash or stock is short. Surely this cannot be legal?

A Such a clause is legal in the contracts of people employed in shops, provided you have received a copy of the clause before any deduction is made from your wages.

However, the law limits the amount of any deduction which is made from your pay to 10 per cent of your gross wage on any pay day.

Q I have discovered that a colleague who is doing the same job as I am is earning £3,000 per annum more than I am being paid. I have been with my firm for two years longer than my colleague. Can I claim equal pay?

A No, the concept of equal pay applies only under the sex discrimination legislation, meaning that employers are obliged to treat men and women who do the same work equally in terms of their pay.

Even then your employer is entitled legally to pay you a different amount from another employee based on factors other than gender. For example, you may be paid less if you have less experience, fewer qualifications, have performed less well than another employee, or just because the other employee negotiated a better deal than you. Length of service does not automatically entitle you to more pay.

Q What does my employer have to pay me if I am off sick?

A The only legal obligation on your employer is to pay you statutory sick pay. There is no law obliging employers to continue wages or salary during periods of sickness absence. However, you should check your contract of employment, because any terms relating to sickness absence should be stated in writing, and should be adhered to by your employer.

Q What are my rights if I wish to take unpaid holiday over and above my annual paid holiday entitlement?

A Normally you would not have any right to take holidays, paid or unpaid, over and above the holiday entitlement defined in your contract of employment. Of course there is nothing to stop you asking your employer for unpaid leave, but be aware that a refusal would be quite legal.

5

Hours of Work and Time Off

Your working hours are a matter for agreement between your employer and yourself. There is no legal minimum, nor maximum, number of hours which you may work (unless you work as a driver of a goods vehicle or public service vehicle). This position could change in the future, but at present in Britain employers are free to decide what number of hours they wish their employees to work.

Your hours of work must, however, be stated in writing within your terms and conditions of employment, which should also make clear to you whether or not you are required to work overtime. If so, the rate of overtime pay and any rules regarding overtime entitlement should also be stated in writing (please refer to the previous chapter for further information about overtime pay).

What if your employer asks you to work overtime, and you do not wish to do it? If your terms and conditions do not state that overtime is a contractual requirement (when asked for), then your employer cannot demand it, nor penalise you if you refuse to work extra hours. Equally, if overtime is a contractual requirement, and you refuse to work it, then your employer could take disciplinary action against you as you would be in breach of your contract of employment. It is important to be sure of your contractual entitlements and obligations on this matter. You should refer first to your written terms of employment, or else ask your employer to clarify your contractual obligations regarding overtime working.

CASE STUDY

Mr George worked under a contract of employment which required him to work overtime 'when the workload made this necessary'. His employer made demands on him to work 12 hours a day, seven days a week for long periods. Eventually Mr George refused to work such hours and was dismissed.

Q Could Mr George's employer legally insist that he should work such excessively long hours?

A In this rather unusual case, the tribunal said that there was an implied condition of reasonableness in the employer's contractual requirement for employees to work overtime. They concluded that the demands made on Mr George exceeded the bounds of what was reasonable, and consequently dismissal for refusing to work such hours was unfair despite the term in his contract requiring overtime working.

This case is unusual because tribunals do not normally imply a condition of reasonableness into the manner in which employers implement the written terms of a contract. In other words they concern themselves principally with what the contract says, rather than how the terms are applied.

Based on the case *George v Plant Breeding International (Cambridge) Ltd.*

It is obviously important to be clear as to the number of hours which you are contractually required to work, even though the Government has now removed all previous distinctions based on hours worked per week – see page 7. A statement on your hours of work is one of the items which must (by law) be provided to you in writing.

CASE STUDY

Mrs Roberts worked for her employer on a part-time basis, originally three hours a day for five days a week. Shortly after her appointment she was asked to work an extra half hour per day with the result that her average working week was 17.5 hours instead of 15.

(CASE STUDY CONTINUED)

When she was made redundant she made a claim for unfair dismissal, but the company challenged whether she was eligible to have her claim heard on the grounds that she had worked less than 16 hours per week. There was no written contract of employment. (At the time of this case it was necessary to have two years service working at least 16 hours a week to claim unfair dismissal or redundancy pay).

Q What were Mrs Roberts's normal hours of work in law?

A An industrial tribunal found that Mrs Roberts's contract was one for variable hours. In the absence of a written contract they examined the hours she had actually worked and concluded that her normal working week was more than 16 hours per week, thus making her eligible to make a claim for unfair dismissal.

Based on the case *Green* v *Roberts*.

The EC draft Directive on working hours, which originally proposed a 48-hour maximum working week, was amended to permit work in excess of 48 hours for employees who had no objection to working longer hours. But, in any event, the Directive (at the time of writing) is still at the draft stage, and Member States will have several years to implement the provisions. So it may be some considerable time before we see any legislation on this subject affecting us in Britain!

Sunday working

All restrictions on shop opening hours were abolished in December 1994. It is now legal for shops to open on Sundays in England and Wales, whilst it has been legal in Scotland for some time.

Whether or not you work on a Sunday is a matter for you to decide. Many people are happy to work on Sundays as the majority of the larger retailers pay premium rates equivalent to at least time and a half (although they are not obliged legally to do so).

A law introduced in 1994 in England and Wales (the Sunday Trading Act) introduced the concepts of 'protected shop worker' and 'opted-out shop worker.' If you fall into either of these categories, then you have the right to choose whether or not you wish to work on Sundays. However, this law does not apply in Scotland.

You will be a protected shop worker if you were employed as a shop worker when the new act came into force (26 August, 1994), provided you were not employed to work only on Sundays.

If you were not yet employed at that time, you can become an 'opted-out shop worker' by giving your employer three months written notice that you object to working on Sundays. Thus after the three months notice has expired, you cannot be obliged to work on Sundays, even if your contract of employment states that Sunday working is part of your duties. (This provision would not, however, apply to you if you were employed to work only on Sundays). Thus you have the choice (at any time) to opt out of Sunday working by giving the appropriate notice. Equally, you may opt back in again if you change your mind.

You are further protected by the Sunday Trading Act in that any dismissal of a protected shop worker or an opted-out shop worker for refusing to work on Sundays is automatically unfair in law, and you would have the right to take the case to an industrial tribunal irrespective of your age, number of hours worked, or length of service. It would also be illegal for your employer to dismiss you for proposing to give an opting-out notice (unless you are employed only to work on Sundays). Additionally it is illegal to penalise employees in any other way for refusing to do Sunday work, for example a refusal of promotion purely on the grounds that the employee will not work on Sundays.

Employers are allowed, however, to offer financial or other incentives to shop workers who are prepared to do Sunday work.

This means effectively that working on Sundays is entirely your choice, and your employer cannot legally penalise you, or dismiss you for refusing to work on Sundays.

If you are a shop worker, your employer has a duty to provide you with a statement explaining your right to opt out of Sunday work, and the consequences of such action. This should be provided within two months of the commencement of your employment.

Public holidays

There is no general legal right for employees to be granted public holidays, far less to be paid for them. The public holidays commonly recognised in England and Wales are those which are laid down in the Banking and Financial Dealings Act. This Act, however, only applies directly to banks and certain other financial institutions. The majority of employees are therefore not affected.

So it is likely that your employer is free to decide which public holidays, if any, are recognised, and whether or not you will be granted time off with pay on the nominated days. Again, your written terms of employment should provide the answer to your entitlement.

Your right to time off work

Employers have a legal obligation to allow employees reasonable time off during normal working hours for certain defined purposes, as follows:

● Time off to perform public duties.
● If you are pregnant, time off for ante-natal care.
● If you are an official of an independent trade union recognised by your employer, time off to carry out trade union duties or undergo training relevant to those duties.
● If you are a member of an independent trade union recognised by your employer, time off to take part in trade union activities (other than industrial action).
● If you are an appointed safety representative, time off to perform the necessary safety functions, or undergo relevant training.
● If you have been given notice of redundancy, time off to look for a new job.

In some, but not all cases, the time off must be paid. Further details are given in the following sections.

Time off for public duties

Employers are required under defined circumstances to allow employees who hold certain public positions reasonable time off to perform the duties associated with them.

These provisions cover positions such as:

● Justice of the peace;
● Member of a visiting committee to prisons, remand centres and young offender institutions;
● Member of a local authority;
● Member of any statutory tribunal;
● Member of certain health, education, water and river authorities.

It can sometimes be difficult to know how much time off would be seen as 'reasonable' in this context. Generally the amount of time off granted will depend on how much time is required to perform the duty, the circumstances of your employer's business and the effect your absence has on it. If in doubt, discuss the matter with your employer.

Jury service

Any employee who is between the ages of 18 and 65 may be called upon to do jury service. The duty is unavoidable unless there is real evidence that your absence from work would be seriously disruptive.

Paradoxically, there is no statutory obligation on your employer to give you time off for jury service. However, in practice, refusal to grant time off would place the employer in contempt of court, so the effect is really the same.

Your employer is not obliged to pay you for time off for public duties, but may choose to do so. In the case of jury service, you are entitled to put in a claim to the court for any loss of earnings, if you are not paid your salary when absent.

Time off for ante-natal care

A pregnant employee has the right to be granted time off with pay to attend medical appointments. This provision can include appointments with your doctor, midwife, health visitor or clinic.

This right is available to all female employees. No service qualification is needed, nor do you need to work any minimum number of hours a week to qualify.

Your employer is entitled, however, to ask you to produce a certificate of pregnancy and an appointment card.

CASE STUDY

Mrs Dhamrait, an employee of United Biscuits Ltd. was allowed time off work for an appointment connected with her pregnancy. The appointment lasted longer than expected as a result of which she missed the works bus (the only available means of transport). Consequently, instead of missing only the first hour of her shift, she missed the whole of it.

Q Was Mrs Dhamrait entitled to be paid for the whole of her shift in these circumstances?

A The tribunal decided that Mrs Dhamrait was entitled to be paid for the whole shift. The right to be paid is for the period of absence necessary for the employee to keep the appointment.

Based on the case *Dhamrait v United Biscuits Ltd.*

For further information on maternity rights, see Chapter 7.

Time off for trade union activities

If you are an official (shop steward or convener) of an independent trade union which is recognised by your employer, you are entitled to be granted reasonable time off with pay to carry out the duties associated with the position (i.e. duties which have to do with industrial relations within the company). This includes time off to attend training relevant to the necessary duties.

The right to time off exists only where the time involved falls within your normal working hours. Supposing you are a shift worker, and attend a union meeting (in the capacity of official of the union) during your own time just before or just after your shift. Are you entitled to receive additional pay? The answer is no, nor would you be entitled to time off in lieu.

CASE STUDY

Mr Hairsine gained permission from his employer, a local authority, to attend a union-organised course for shop stewards. The course was scheduled on a day when Mr Hairsine was due to work late shift from 3.00 – 11.00 p.m. The course itself ran from 09.00 – 4.00 p.m. When it finished, Mr Hairsine went to work, arriving at 4.40, but he left again at 7.00 p.m. His employer paid him for the hours from 3.00 to 7.00 p.m. but not for the hours from 7.00 to 11.00 p.m. which he did not work.

Mr Hairsine claimed that the course he attended was the equivalent of a normal shift, and therefore he was entitled to be paid for those hours, and not work the shift in the evening. He argued that the hours he had actually worked (from 4.40 to 7.00) were purely voluntary.

Q Was Mr Hairsine right in his claim?

A No, the tribunal rejected Mr. Hairsine's argument on the basis that the hours before 3.00 p.m. during which he attended the course were not part of his working hours, and the hours from 4.00 – 11.00 p.m. when he was required to work did not count because the course had ended by that time.

Based on the case *Hairsine* v *Kingston upon Hull City Council*.

If you are a member (but not an official) of a union recognised by your employer, then you must be allowed reasonable time off to take part in certain trade union activities, such as attending meetings, voting in elections, and holding discussions with union officials. Your employer is not, however, obliged to pay you for such time off.

The law clearly gives you the right to take part in the activities of an independent trade union at appropriate times – you must not be penalised in any way for doing so.

Time off as a safety representative

If your employer recognises an independent trade union, then the union is entitled to appoint safety representatives. If you have been appointed as a safety representative, then you are entitled to paid time off to carry out the duties associated with the position, including time off to attend relevant training.

Time off when under notice of redundancy

If you have been given notice that you are to be made redundant from your job, then you have the right to be allowed reasonable time off with pay to look for another job. This right, however, is technically only available to you if you have a minimum of two years continuous service with your employer. Time off in this context would include time spent attending interviews, visiting job centres or making arrangements for training, and travel time associated with these purposes.

Once again, the term 'reasonable' is not specified in law, probably because individual circumstances and needs always differ. However, tribunal cases have indicated that a maximum of two days per week would not be unreasonable.

If you are refused time off for any of the above purposes, or if your employer refuses to make the appropriate payment where you are entitled to be paid, you may make a complaint to an industrial tribunal.

Rights as a reservist

If you are a member of the Reserve Forces, and are called up for military service, then your employer must allow you to take leave for the period of time required. However, your employer is not obliged to pay you during your leave, as you will receive pay from the Forces. This right to time off does not, however, apply to any annual training which you may be called upon to attend.

Your employer is not obliged to preserve your contract of employment whilst you are on leave (although some do so), but they are obliged to reinstate you when you return from your military duties.

This means that, provided you make an application to your former employer to be taken back into employment, the employer must comply as soon as possible. Your right is to be reinstated into either:

- Your old job on terms and conditions not less favourable than before, or
- Another suitable job on the most favourable terms and conditions as are reasonable and practicable in the circumstances.

  If you are dismissed solely because you are, or are planning to become, a reservist, then your employer is guilty of a criminal offence.

Questions and Answers

Q Recently I have been working excessively long hours because of a shortage of staff and pressure of work. Is there a legal limit on the number of hours my employer can ask me to work?

A No, there is no legal minimum, nor maximum, number of hours which your employer may ask you to work (unless you work as a driver of a goods vehicle or public service vehicle).

Q Am I obliged to work overtime if my employer asks for it?

A It depends entirely on what your contract of employment says on the subject of your hours of work and overtime. If there is nothing in writing that makes it clear that you are required to work overtime, then it is likely that you would be quite entitled (contractually) to refuse.

Q I am employed in a branch of a national chain of DIY stores. There is a lot of talk about Sunday working. My contract defines my working hours as Monday to Friday from 09.00 – 17.00 hours each day. How do I stand if I am asked to work on Sundays?

A Your hours of work are clearly defined, and therefore your employer cannot just change them without your agreement. You would be entitled therefore to either agree or refuse Sunday working. Additionally, employees whose contracts of employment specify Sundays as part of the working week have the right to 'opt out' of Sunday working by giving three months notice in writing.

Q What public holidays am I entitled to by law?

A You have no legal right to be granted public holidays, unless you work in a bank or other financial institution. Your contract of employment should, however, state what public holidays (if any) your employer recognises, and whether or not you will be paid for them.

Q I have been called for jury service in a court case. Does my employer have to pay my wages for the time I have to be away from work?

A Your employer is not obliged to pay you for time off for jury service, although many employers do so. If you are not paid your salary during the time you are away from work, you are entitled to put in a claim to the court for loss of earnings.

Q I am a trade union representative with the union which is recognised by my employer. What time off am I entitled to in order to perform my trade union duties?

A The amount of time off you are entitled to is not defined in law. Your right (since you are an official of an independent trade union which is recognised by your employer) is to be granted 'reasonable' time off with pay to carry out the duties associated with the position. This includes time off to attend necessary training.

6
Discrimin-
ation

Sex discrimination

The Sex Discrimination Act 1975 defines that employers must not discriminate directly or indirectly against men or women on the grounds of sex.
Both men and women are equally protected. The Act also states that married people should not be treated less favourably than single people of the
same sex. Paradoxically it does not give similar protection to single people
if they are treated less favourably than married people! Single people might
perhaps be forgiven for coming to the conclusion that this is one of several
issues in Britain where they suffer a poor deal!

So the law means that you have the right not be treated less favourably
than a person of the opposite sex, if the reason for the unfavourable treatment is your sex.

The provisions on sex discrimination cover:

- Recruitment, interview arrangements and selection for employment;
- Pay (see Chapter 4 for more information);
- Fringe benefits, e.g. company car, sick pay, etc.
- Opportunities for training;
- Access to promotion and transfer;
- Termination of employment, including dismissal.

CASE STUDY

Miss Montgomery worked for a company who had a rule which forbad intimate relationships between staff members. Nevertheless she went on holiday to the USA with a male colleague, and on their return, both were dismissed.

Q Was Miss Montgomery the victim of sex discrimination?

A The tribunal decided that the company had breached the Sex Discrimination Act because they had treated Miss Montgomery less favourably than they would have treated a man on the grounds of her sex. The decision was based on the argument that if Miss Montgomery had been a man on holiday with a male colleague, she would not have been dismissed. Naturally this implies that her male colleague would also have had a claim for sex discrimination.

Based on the case *Brocks Explosives Ltd* v *Montgomery*.

Cases involving discrimination during employment are less common than those involving recruitment and dismissal, but discrimination on the grounds of sex at any stage before or during employment is liable to be illegal.

Sex discrimination may be direct or indirect. Broadly speaking direct discrimination would occur if you are personally treated less favourably than a colleague or job applicant of the opposite sex.

Indirect discrimination would occur if your employer applied a requirement or condition to all employees, male and female alike, but the proportion of women (men) who could comply with the requirement was considerably smaller than the proportion of men (women), and this resulted in you personally being disadvantaged in some way. This is explained further below.

Direct Discrimination

Direct discrimination is relatively easy to understand and recognise. If, on the grounds of your sex, you are refused employment, overlooked for promotion, denied a company benefit which is available to someone of the opposite sex, dismissed, or forced to retire early, then this will constitute direct discrimination.

Indeed any situation where recruitment or employment benefits are restricted to one sex, would constitute direct sex discrimination.

Some examples of direct discrimination are as follows:

- A job advertisement which uses sexist job titles, e.g. 'girl Friday wanted'.
- An employer who instructs an employment agency that he does not wish to interview any female candidates for a particular job.
- An interviewer asking a woman questions about child-minding arrangements, or worse, family planning intentions! (Despite the obvious unprofessionalism of this, it still appears to be a widespread practice amongst uninitiated interviewers!).
- A manager who decides not to promote a female employee on the grounds that she will probably leave to have children sometime in the future.
- A manager who refuses to employ a man on account of a view that a particular job is 'women's work', or who professes that people of one sex are better at a particular type of work.
- A company which transfers an employee because the department manager prefers to work with people of only one sex.

CASE STUDY

Mr Rewcastle worked for Safeway plc, and was subject to the company's strict rules with regard to hair length. The rules stated that men's hair had to be short and well-groomed and women were obliged to pin or tie back shoulder-length hair.

Mr Rewcastle had long hair and, although he was willing to tie it back, he refused to have it cut. He was dismissed.

Q Did Safeway breach the sex discrimination legislation in applying different rules to men and women regarding how hair should be worn?
A Yes, the tribunal judged that Safeway's rules regarding hair were based on conventional assumptions about the sexes and their appearance, and such assumptions could not be reconciled with the underlying principles of the sex discrimination legislation.

Based on the case *Rewcastle* v *Safeway plc*.

- Please refer to the section on Dress and Appearance later in this chapter for more information on this topic.

Indirect Discrimination

Indirect discrimination occurs where the following circumstances exist:

- The employer imposes a requirement or condition on everyone; and
- Because of the nature of the requirement, a smaller proportion of women than men (or men than women) can comply with it; and
- As a result of the requirement, you are disadvantaged in some tangible way (the legal jargon here is that you 'suffer a detriment'); and

- Your employer is unable to show that the requirement is justifiable irrespective of gender.

Thus indirect discrimination involves a rule or condition which has a greater adverse impact on one sex than on the other.

CASE STUDY

Mrs Briggs was a teacher in Northern Ireland who coached badminton during lunch hours. The education authority responsible for the school where she worked imposed a requirement that badminton coaching should be carried out after school hours. Mrs Briggs, who found it difficult to be available after school hours, claimed indirect sex discrimination, arguing that fewer women than men could comply with the requirement to be available after school hours, due to child-minding responsibilities.

Q Did this claim for sex discrimination succeed?

A No, ultimately the Court of Appeal found that, although the requirement to coach badminton after school hours did have a discriminatory impact on women, it was nevertheless justified on objective grounds due to the limited time available at lunchtimes.

So in this case, although the requirement was acknowledged as having a greater adverse impact on women, and although Mrs Briggs had been disadvantaged by it, the employer was able to demonstrate that the requirement was justifiable and thus Mrs Briggs lost her claim.

Based on the case *Briggs v North Eastern Education and Library Board*.

Some examples of indirect discrimination are as follows:
- A company which insists on recruiting within an age range of 25 – 35 (or thereabouts), whilst at the same time requiring that candidates must have a minimum of, say, five years experience. This could indirectly discriminate against women since more women than men of that age group would be out of the labour market due to family commitments (and hence unable to acquire the necessary experience).
- A requirement that employees wanting promotion must be able to spend time away from home, which might also discriminate against women for the same reason.
- A company which offers full-time employees a particular perk, e.g. provision of company sick pay, but does not offer the same benefit to part-time employees. This provision could be indirectly discriminatory if, for example, the majority of full-time employees are male, and the majority of part-time employees female.

- Insistence that a requirement for employment is that the employee must be able to perform heavy lifting, where physical lifting is not relevant to the job in question.
    Other types of sex discrimination can occur:
- Where men and women are deliberately segregated.
- Where a person is victimised because he has made, or plans to make, a complaint of sex discrimination, or has given evidence in a case of discrimination.
- Where a married person is subjected to less favourable treatment purely on the grounds of marital status.

Exceptions

Most of the restrictions which once applied to women at work have been removed. The Sex Discrimination Act does, however, retain some legislation which is considered necessary for the protection of women, as follows:

- Women within four weeks of childbirth are prohibited from working in factories.
- Pregnant women are restricted as regards working on ships and aeroplanes.
- Women are prevented from working in certain occupations which involve contact with lead, exposure to ionising radiation and in a range of processes in the pottery industry.

Genuine occupational qualifications (GOQ's)

There are a limited number of exceptions to the legislation on direct discrimination, known as a 'genuine occupational qualifications' (GOQ's). These include the following situations:

- Where the job involves 'living in' (e.g. on an offshore oil rig) and there is no separate sleeping accommodation and / or sanitary facilities. In such cases the employer may discriminate by employing only people of the same sex as those who are already there.
- Where for reasons of authenticity, either a man or woman must be hired (e.g. in entertainment). So, for example, the director of a play would be entitled to insist on hiring a male actor, if the part to be played was that of a man.
- To preserve decency or privacy, for example where the job involves close physical contact, or the employee is likely to be working in the presence of people who are in a state of undress, or using sanitary facilities. This could occur, for example, in the case of someone employed as an attendant in a public convenience.

- In a single-sex establishment for people requiring special care, where the character of the establishment is such that the job should be held by a man (or a woman). An example of this might be a nurse employed in a single-sex old people's home.
- Where the person is employed to provide 'personal services' which involve promoting the welfare or education of a particular group of people, and those services can be better provided by a man (or a woman). For example it is possible that a woman might respond more favourably to a female welfare worker than to a man doing the same job.
- Where the job is one of two to be held by a married couple.
- Where the job is based in a country whose law or customs are such that the duties of the job cannot be performed by a woman, for example a country where women are forbidden to drive.

Discrimination in recruitment

The protection afforded under the Sex Discrimination legislation applies to all, regardless of employment status.

CASE STUDY

Graham was a 16-year-old school leaver who answered an advertisement for a person to wash dishes in a local hotel. When he telephoned, to his surprise the manager told him the job was filled.

Later that day, Graham relayed this story to his sister. Out of curiosity, his sister telephoned the hotel manager and enquired whether the job of dishwasher was still available. She was told it was, and invited along for an interview.

Suspecting that he had been the victim of sex discrimination, Graham took the matter to an industrial tribunal.

Q What chance did Graham have of succeeding with his claim?

A Provided Graham could present some evidence of what happened, the tribunal would look to the hotel manager to provide an explanation of why he was denied the opportunity of applying for the job when a female applicant was later offered an interview. In the absence of a valid explanation, the tribunal could well decide, on the balance of probabilities, that Graham had been the victim of sex discrimination.

So if a company discriminates in any way within its selection procedures, and treats one sex more favourably than the other, then this will amount to illegal sex discrimination.

In recruitment, an employer could fall foul of the legislation by, for example, specifying different criteria for men and women in a particular job, or excluding (or discouraging) persons of one sex from applying for a job.

If you are attending a job interview, the interviewer should not on any account ask you personal questions of a sexist nature, including questions about who looks after your children while you are at work. The legal view of this is that if such questions are asked, then it demonstrates that the employer has an intention to discriminate.

One woman won £6,696 compensation (in 1992) following an interview with a regional council in Scotland where she was asked sexist questions (including a question about how she would feel about working alone with a man all day) and subjected to negative comments. She had applied for a post as a technical officer within the region's water services department, but the job was subsequently offered to a 17-year-old former postman who was considerably less qualified and experienced than she was. The industrial tribunal had no difficulty in concluding that the interview was discriminatory.

Discrimination against pregnant women

If you are a pregnant women, then you are in a very strong position in employment terms, in that any unfavourable treatment afforded to you because of your pregnancy will almost certainly constitute illegal sex discrimination.

Examples of sex discrimination could be where a pregnant woman is not nominated for a training course when male colleagues are offered training, where a pregnant woman's job responsibilities are removed from her for no reason other than pregnancy, or even where a woman is refused employment purely on the grounds that she is pregnant.

CASE STUDY

Mrs Dekker applied for a post as a training instructor with an organisation in Holland. She was clearly the most suitable candidate for the job, but she was not appointed. At the interview she told her prospective employer that she was pregnant. Under Dutch law, the employer would have had to pay her certain payments during her maternity absence, which they felt they could not afford. Mrs Dekker claimed sex discrimination, and the Dutch national courts referred the matter to the European Court in 1991 for a decision on certain points of principle.

Q Was the employer guilty of sex discrimination in refusing a job to a woman because she was pregnant?

A The employer argued that the true reason for refusing Mrs Dekker the job was financial – the maternity benefits which they would have had to pay to her would have been non-refundable, and they would have had to take on a replacement to cover for her maternity absence. The Court, how-

(CASE STUDY CONTINUED)
ever, rejected this argument and concluded that the refusal to recruit a
woman on pregnancy grounds was, of itself, discriminatory.

The legal position, following this ruling, is that any unfavourable treatment of a pregnant woman (including refusal to employ on the grounds of
pregnancy) will amount to direct sex discrimination. This conclusion was
reached on the simple basis that because only women (and not men) can be
pregnant, then any differing treatment must be discriminatory.

Based on the case *Dekker v Stichting Vormingscentrum voor Jonge Volwassen*.

Bear in mind, however, that if there is a genuine reason why your employer has treated you in a particular way, and this reason is based on real
and significant business needs or some reason completely unconnected with
your pregnancy, then the treatment would not necessarily amount to illegal
sex discrimination.

Sexual harassment

It has been well established that sexual harassment (of a woman or of a man)
constitutes illegal sex discrimination. This raises the emotive question as to
what makes particular behaviour at work harassment, as opposed to
friendly banter. Sexual harassment occurs when a woman (or a man) is
subjected to abuse, either physical or verbal, or to hostile behaviour because
of his / her sex.

Additionally, the European Commission has described sexual harassment
as conduct of a sexual nature which is 'unwanted, unreasonable and offensive' to the recipient. This can include physical, verbal or non-verbal conduct. Thus behaviour becomes harassment at the point where the person on
the receiving end does not welcome it, or finds it offensive.

Examples
Some examples of behaviour which could constitute illegal sexual harassment are:

- Insensitive jokes, or pranks of a sexual nature;
- Displays of sexually-oriented material, e.g. pin-up calendars;
- Fondling or touching;
- Lewd comments of a personal nature;
- Requests for sexual favours;
- Threat of dismissal, loss of promotion, or some other disadvantage, if
  sexual favours are refused.

CASE STUDY

Ms Johnstone worked alongside male colleagues in a turkey factory. She began to regard the behaviour of two particular men as obscene. After two incidents involving lurid conversations about menstruation and their private sexual habits, Ms Johnstone made her objections known to the men, and complained to the factory manager. She also requested a transfer to another department. Her manager, however, ignored her request and the offensive behaviour continued.

Q Could Ms Johnstone bring a claim to an industrial tribunal for sex discrimination?

A Yes, she did so and won her case. The tribunal ruled that the two men had treated her less favourably than they would have treated a man. This was direct sex discrimination.

A recent legal decision has shown that sexual harassment by a man towards another man can also be illegal sex discrimination. It is reasonable to assume that a similar view would be taken of harassment from a woman to a woman, provided the behaviour was of a sexual nature.

Another well-publicised case concerned a policewoman who was awarded £32,000 as an out-of-court settlement in December 1993 following her complaint of sexual and racial harassment. She had been passed over for promotion because she was pregnant, and complained also that pornographic magazines and a racially abusive note had been left on her desk.

If you have a genuine complaint of this nature, you should in the first instance explain clearly to the person who is harassing you that their behaviour offends you, and ask them to stop such behaviour. It is, after all always possible that the person is genuinely unaware that you are offended, and unless you say so, how are they to know?

If you feel uncomfortable with this idea, then you might consider asking a colleague to accompany you when you speak to the person, or alternatively write a note to the person concerned explaining that you regard their behaviour as offensive. If this does not work, or if you feel that you cannot talk to the person directly, then you should approach a senior person within your company whom you feel you can talk to, and explain your complaint in a factual way. The company is obliged to take your complaint seriously and to investigate and resolve the issue.

You should always tell someone in authority about the problem, otherwise you may not succeed in a subsequent complaint to an industrial tribunal. Although some conduct may be so obviously offensive that no tribunal would doubt that it amounted to harassment, other types of behaviour could be the result of a misunderstanding over whether or not you found it offensive. If, however, you have made it clear that you find a colleague's behaviour offensive, then repetition of the behaviour will almost certainly amount to illegal sex discrimination.

Equally if the company fails to take your complaint seriously, or refuses to investigate it, then you would have every right to complain of sex discrimination to an industrial tribunal. In addition, it is possible in the event of a genuine complaint which is not taken seriously, that you would have a breach of contract claim – because your employer would be in breach of the duty of trust and support (see Chapter 3, *Breach of Implied Terms*).

Another typical case which occurred in 1992 concerned a female employee in a store who alleged that her manager had made sexual gestures towards her when they were alone. No investigation took place for some considerable time. Eventually the company did investigate and subsequently offered the woman (not her manager) a transfer. The industrial tribunal awarded the woman £3,500 for sex discrimination, based on clear evidence that harassment had occurred and that the company had failed to handle the situation in a reasonable manner.

Victimisation

If you have made a valid complaint about sex or marriage discrimination, and your employer victimises you as a result, then this would constitute further illegal discrimination against you. Your employer must not treat you in any way less favourably following on from a genuine complaint which you have made in good faith.

Discrimination in retirement

In 1986 there was an amendment to the Sex Discrimination Act to extend discrimination provisions to men and women at retirement. Since the implementation of the amendment it has been illegal for companies to apply different retirement ages to men and women. The actual age for retirement is a question for the company to establish via its contracts of employment, and can be any age. Whatever age is applied, it must be the same for both men and women, and neither sex must be treated more favourably than the other.

CASE STUDY

Mrs Nicol worked as a secretary for the Ben Line Group. Shortly after the implementation of the 1986 amendment to the Sex Discrimination Act, the company introduced a common retirement age of 60 for both men and women. Previously they had operated a retirement policy whereby male employees retired at 65 and females at 60. In order to preserve existing

(CASE STUDY CONTINUED)

contracts of employment, they also introduced transitional arrangements whereby existing male employees could retire at 60, or continue to 65 if they wished. Female employees on the other hand had always had the expectation to retire at 60 and this remained unchanged. All new employees recruited into the company were to have a fixed retirement age of 60.

Mrs Nicol was obliged to retire when she was 60. She claimed sex discrimination.

Q Was the company in breach of the sex discrimination legislation in obliging Mrs Nicol to retire at age 60 (bearing in mind that this was her contractual retirement age)?

A The tribunal found that the company's transitional arrangements were clearly discriminatory. Mrs Nicol had been refused the choice to continue in employment until age 65, whereas a male colleague would have been given that choice. She was awarded £8,500 for sex discrimination, which was the maximum entitlement at the time.

Based on the case *Nicol v Ben Line Group*.

So if a woman is forced to retire because she has reached age 60, where a male colleague would be allowed to continue in employment until a later age, then this constitutes illegal discrimination.

A company may, however, operate different retirement ages for different jobs or different groups of employees, provided there is no inherent discrimination within the system used for differentiating between jobs or groups of jobs.

CASE STUDY

Mrs Bullock was one of 70 domestic staff (who, apart from one, were all female) in a school. Other staff groups in the school comprised some 70 teachers (nearly all women), a small administrative staff, 4 gardeners and 3 maintenance staff. The gardeners and maintenance staff were all men.

The school had introduced a policy whereby teachers, administrative staff and domestic staff would all retire at age 60, and the group comprising the gardening and maintenance staff would have a retirement age of 65.

Mrs Bullock, who had already worked one year beyond her official retirement age of 60, was refused when she made a request to continue working for another year.

Q Was Mrs Bullock discriminated against because the gardeners and maintenance staff (all men) had a retiring age of 65 whilst she was not permitted to work beyond age 61?

A No, the company was able to justify the later retiring age for the gardeners and maintenance staff on the basis that these jobs required

(CASE STUDY CONTINUED)

special skills and were difficult to recruit. They were entitled to operate separate retirement ages for the different groups of employees. There was no barrier to women being recruited into the jobs within the group comprising gardeners and maintenance staff, thus no sex discrimination had taken place.

Based on the case *Bullock* v *The Alice Ottley School.*

More recently, as a result of case law, it has been established that companies must also offer equal (company) pension benefits to men and women (where a company pension scheme is operated). This applies to pension benefits accrued since May 1990.

This is an area where, in the past, men rather than women have suffered discrimination. Traditionally, many company pension schemes had a five year gap between men and women's eligibility to receive a company pension. For example men might have had to wait until they were 65 to benefit, whereas female employees could have taken their company pension at age 60. This type of arrangement is now illegal.

It would also be illegal if your company's pension scheme provided for a widow's pension for male employees, but not a widower's pension for female employees. If you are in any doubt as to your company's pension scheme arrangements, then you should ask for a copy of your company's pension scheme booklet or terms and conditions.

Part-time staff now also have equal rights (with full-timers) as regards access to membership of company pension schemes and the provision of company pension benefits as a result of a European Court decision in 1994.

Note that these provisions apply only to company pension schemes, and not the state pension scheme. The Government has announced changes to the state pension scheme which will, in time, equalise the state pension benefits payable to men and women.

Instructions to discriminate

Illegal discrimination would occur if you are instructed (for example by your boss) to carry out a discriminatory act, or if attempts are made to pressurise you into taking illegal action contrary to the sex discrimination legislation. An example of this would be if you are instructed to interview only male (or only female) applicants for a particular job. You are perfectly entitled to refuse to carry out such instructions, and to state why. If you are dismissed for such refusal, you would win a case of sex discrimination. In this situation, oddly, it is you who are being discriminated against, regardless of your own or your boss's gender!

Positive action

Employers are permitted in certain circumstances to take positive action to promote equal opportunities in the workplace. An example of this could be where an employer elects to provide special facilities for management training for women. This would be quite legal provided that the existing proportion of women in management positions within the company was small in comparison to the number of men.

Complaints of sex discrimination

Complaints of sex discrimination may be made to an industrial tribunal within three months of the discriminatory act taking place. Note that you do not require any length of company service to complain of sex discrimination – indeed you are protected even before you are employed, for example during a recruitment interview.

Technically, the burden of proof is on the person making the complaint to show that discrimination has occurred. This can be difficult to prove, as conclusive evidence is rarely available. Because of this, what actually happens in practice is that (provided you have some evidence) tribunals will look to the employer to demonstrate valid reasons for the action taken. Then, if the employer cannot provide a tangible defence against the discrimination claim, the tribunal may 'draw an inference' that discrimination took place, if they believe it is fair to do so. This may occur even where there is no conclusive evidence. This means effectively that you do not need absolute proof to win your case at an industrial tribunal, only a reasonable amount of evidence.

The maximum amount of compensation available from an industrial tribunal on account of sex discrimination was, until 1993, £11,000, an amount which was subject to annual review. The European Court declared in 1993 that this upper limit was illegal and individuals must be compensated in full for the damage and loss they suffer as a result of their employer's discrimination. Following on from this decision, the Government enacted the Sex Discrimination and Equal Pay (Remedies) Regulations to remove the upper limit. This means that there is now no limit on the amount of money which may be awarded in cases of sex discrimination!

It is interesting to note also that compensation may include an amount for injury to feelings, according to the discretion of the tribunal. Awards for injury to feelings are likely to be particularly high in cases of sexual harassment. This would be so especially in cases where discrimination was deliberate, where harassment went on over a protracted period of time or where the woman was highly distressed by it. Three examples are as follows:

- When an employee was sexually harassed for over two years by a colleague, and where the company's response was to move her colleague to another floor where she could still come into contact with him, the award for injury to feelings was assessed at £6,235.
- Where an employee was physically assaulted but the employer nevertheless refused to move the harasser (having exonerated him), the tribunal awarded £8,925 for injury to feelings in view of the company's poor handling of the case.
- A woman who had been the victim of a long campaign of unpleasant sexual harassment was awarded £3,000 as compensation for emotional stress, strain on her domestic life, damage to her health and emotional distress. The campaign against her was aimed at forcing her to transfer to another work location because she was disliked. The harassment had included suggestive remarks and situations where she had been forced to brush against her male tormentors in order to pass them by.

Awards for injury to feelings in cases of sex discrimination may well increase in the future since the abolition of the upper limit on the level of compensation which may be granted.

Race discrimination

The Race Relations Act follows very similar principles to the Sex Discrimination Act wherein discrimination can be direct or indirect.

The law states that is unlawful to discriminate against a person on the grounds of:

- Colour
- Race
- Nationality (including citizenship)
- Ethnic origin
- National origin

'Ethnic origin' is perhaps the most difficult category to define here. For a group to be of separate ethnic origin, it must be regarded as a distinct community by virtue of characteristics which are unique or specific to that group. Factors like a long shared history, identifiable culture and language would be relevant.

It is perhaps strange that the Act does not cover religion, although in Northern Ireland there is a separate piece of legislation, called the Fair Employment (Northern Ireland) Act, which specifically outlaws discrimination on the grounds of religious beliefs and / or political opinions. This Act came into force in 1976, its purpose being, quite specifically, to prevent discrimination in employment between Protestants and Catholics. There is no similar legislation in other parts of Britain.

CASE STUDY

The St Matthias Church of England School wished to recruit a head teacher and imposed a requirement that the appointee must be a 'committed communicant Christian'. An Asian applicant for the post claimed discrimination on the grounds of race.

Q Was the Asian applicant discriminated against in being deemed ineligible for the post on account of not being a Christian?

A The tribunal accepted that the requirement for the head teacher (who was expected to assist in Christian worship in the school) to be Christian was justifiable. The religious 'discrimination' in this case did not amount to discrimination on the grounds of race, and was thereore not illegal.

Based on the case *Board of Governors of St Matthias Church of England School* v *Crizzle*.

The provisions on race discrimination generally cover the same areas as the law on sex discrimination:

- Recruitment, interview arrangements and selection;
- Pay;
- Fringe benefits;
- Opportunities for training;
- Access to promotion and transfer;
- Termination of employment including dismissal.

Like sex discrimination, race discrimination may be direct or indirect. Some examples of direct race discrimination are as follows:

- Where you are refused an interview because you happen to have a foreign surname.
- Where you are refused employment because the interviewer thinks that someone in the company would object to working alongside a black person.
- Where you are not selected for promotion on account of your nationality.
- Where an employment agency declines to put you forward for a particular job on account of your racial group.

CASE STUDY

Mr Sharifi, a British subject of Iranian origin had a number of degrees including a PhD in biology and microbiology. He applied in 1990 for a job as divisional scientist with Strathclyde Regional Council and subsequently applied twice more for employment (during the same year) to the Council. Each time he was rejected without interview, despite his qualifications. He made a claim for race discrimination.

Q Was Mr Sharifi's claim for race discrimination likely to succeed?

A It did succeed. Evidence was heard that there had been about 90 applications for the three posts, five of which were from members of ethnic minorities. None of these was short-listed even although three of them had distinguished qualifications. The tribunal found that selection for the short-list was not made in accordance with either the job description or the personnel specification. The candidates who were selected for the short-list had been chosen because of previous connections with the Council or association with the people responsible for making the selection.

The industrial tribunal inferred from this evidence that outsiders and foreigners were not welcome and were excluded regardless of their suitability for the job.

Based on the case *Sharifi v Strathclyde Regional Council.*

Indirect discrimination occurs where the following circumstances exist:

- The employer imposes a requirement or condition on everyone; and
- Because of the nature of the requirement, a smaller proportion of persons of a particular race (or colour, nationality, ethnic or national origin) can comply with it; and
- As a result of the requirement, you are disadvantaged in some tangible way, and
- Your employer cannot show that the requirement is justifiable irrespective of your racial group.

Some examples of indirect discrimination are as follows:

- An employer who uses an English language test as a pre-employment requirement where the ability to speak or write fluent English is not really a requirement of the job. Such tests could obviously discriminate against those whose first language is not English.
- A company which insists on a ruling that employees must not have beards and/or long hair. Once again, provided there is no objective

job-related reason for the rule, then this could indirectly discriminate against people of certain races whose beliefs mean that they do not cut their hair or shave.

If on the other hand, the company can demonstrate that there is a genuine job-related reason for the rule (for example hygiene regulations), then it will be quite legal to apply it.

CASE STUDY

Ms Wetstein was a Jew who observed the Jewish Sabbath from sunset on Fridays to nightfall on Saturdays. She registered for work as a secretary with an employment agency and was put forward for a post to a prospective employer. During the interview she indicated that she would have to leave early each Friday in winter. Thereafter she was told by the agency that she would not be given further interviews because employers wanted workers who could work a full week. She raised a claim for race discrimination.

Q Did the agency's conduct amount to indirect race discrimination?

A The tribunal rejected Ms Wetstein's claim. Their rejection was based on their findings that only 5–10 per cent of Jews were strict observers of the Sabbath which meant that 90–95 per cent of Jews would be able to comply with the agency's requirement that prospective employees should be available for a full week's work. Thus the proportion of Jews who could comply with the requirement was not considerably smaller than the proportion of non-Jews who could comply.

Based on the case *Wetstein v Misprestige Management Services Ltd.*

Other types of race discrimination occur:

● Where people of one racial group are deliberately segregated from others.
● Where a person is victimised on account of race. This would occur if the person was treated unfavourably because he had made, or planned to make, a complaint of race discrimination, or had given evidence in a case of discrimination.

The actual race of the individual being victimised is irrelevant – the key factor is whether the person has been treated differently on account of having complained or given evidence in a case of race discrimination.

Exceptions

The Race Relations Act does not cover discrimination in employment within a private household, except for victimisation.

Other exceptions to the legislation on direct race discrimination, known as 'genuine occupational qualifications' (GOQ's) include the following situations:

● Where the job is in entertainment and, for reasons of authenticity, a person of a particular racial group must be hired.
● Similarly where the job involves modelling and, for reasons of authenticity the model must be of a particular racial group. This could occur, for example, where a photographer requires a person whose appearance is associated with a particular ethnic or national group.
● In restaurants, for example Chinese restaurants, where, for authenticity in the particular setting, the waiting staff must be of Chinese origin.
● Where the person is employed to provide 'personal services' which involve promoting the welfare or education of a particular racial group, and those services can most effectively be provided by a person of the same racial group.

CASE STUDY

Mr Hartup, who was white, applied for a local authority post as a home help despite the fact that the advertisement specified that the post was only open to Afro-Caribbean/Asian candidates. This requirement was because there was an increasing number of elderly Afro-Caribbean and Asian people in the area who needed home help services, and these elderly people preferred home helps with the same racial background as themselves. Mr Hartup was unsuccessful in his job application and brought a claim of race discrimination.

Q Was the requirement for the job holder to be Afro-Caribbean or Asian a genuine occupational qualification for the job?

A Yes, the tribunal accepted the employer's argument and decided that the home help services (the G.O.Q of 'personal services') could be most effectively provided by members of the same racial groups. Mr Hartup therefore lost his claim.

Based on the case *Hartup* v *Sandwell Metropolitan Borough Council*.

Ethnic monitoring

Some employers carry out ethnic monitoring, to ensure that their employment practices do not discriminate against particular racial groups. Similarly sex monitoring may be carried out.

It is considered good practice with regard to the elimination of discrimination in employment for companies to monitor both job applicants and existing employees on the basis of their sex and ethnic group.

This could involve, for example, questions on a company's application form asking you to state your ethnic background. This information would enable the company to carry out an analysis of the sex and ethnic composition of its workforce and of all job applicants, with a view to ensuring that discrimination was not taking place. It may be in your own interests therefore not to refuse to answer such questions.

Complaints of race discrimination

Complaints of race discrimination may be made to an industrial tribunal within three months of the act being complained of. As for complaints of sex discrimination, you do not require any minimum length of service to make a complaint.

The maximum amount of compensation available from an industrial tribunal on account of race discrimination was, until recently, £11,000. In 1994 this upper limit was removed, meaning that there is now no limit on the amount of compensation which can be awarded for race discrimination. In Northern Ireland, compensation for religious discrimination also has no upper limit.

Complaints of race discrimination are likely to produce an element of compensation for injury to feelings. One recent case centred around an Irish employee who was subjected to constant derogatory Irish jokes at work, and then dismissed just a few days short of two years service. He had complained to management of constant racist comments which he regarded as racial harassment, and had also taken time off work for stress. His management had failed to support him when he complained, and his award of compensation from an industrial tribunal totalled £5,902.

Legislation covering other aspects of race discrimination, namely harassment, victimisation, instructions to discriminate and positive action follow parallel lines to the sex discrimination legislation described earlier in this Chapter.

Age discrimination

There is no age discrimination legislation at present in Britain, despite the introduction (and defeat) of seven Parliamentary Bills since 1979. However, companies who place upper age limits on job applicants could, in some instances, fall foul of the sex discrimination legislation. This can happen because fewer women in certain age groups are available for full-time employment than men in the same age groups, due to child-rearing responsibilities. However strange this may sound, age limitations have been shown in several legal cases to be indirectly discriminatory against women.

To repeat the example quoted earlier in this chapter under 'Sex discrimination', a company which insisted on recruiting within an age range of 25–35 could be indirectly discriminating against women, since more women than men of that age group would be out of the labour market due to family commitments.

Dress and appearance

Employers have considerable freedom to impose rules regarding dress and appearance on their employees. However, a purely subjective approach based on the employer's own taste or preferences is not sufficient reason to impose such requirements. There must be a convincing reason for rules regarding dress or appearance, for example where the employees come into contact with the public or customers, or the company wishes to project a particularly company image. Once again, however, such rules could be discriminatory if they impose differing standards on men and women.

CASE STUDY

Miss Cresswell worked in a clerical capacity for Stoke-on-Trent Community Transport, a charity. The organisation operated a dress code which included the rule that female office staff should not wear trousers to work. After a number of disciplinary warnings, Miss Cresswell was dismissed in 1992 for wearing trousers to work.

Q Was Miss Cresswell's dismissal discriminatory under the Sex Discrimination Act?

A Yes, Miss Cresswell won her case and was awarded £4,669 compensation. The tribunal said that sacking a woman for wearing trousers was contrary to the Sex Discrimination Act. The organisation could provide no objective reason for imposing such a dress code.

Based on the case *Cresswell v Follett & Others*.

This does not mean, however, that your employer must have identical rules of dress for both men and women! If you are a woman and are prevented from wearing jeans to work, this could well be justified on the grounds of company image, especially if your job involves contact with the public. But the standards for one sex should not be more restrictive than the standards set for the other.

CASE STUDY

Ms Burrett was employed as a staff nurse in the casualty department of a hospital. Although both male and female nurses were required to wear a

(CASE STUDY CONTINUED)
uniform, only the female nurses had to wear a cap. Ms Burrett decided after
four months of employment that she did not wish to wear a cap as she took
the view that it was demeaning and undignified.

Consequently Ms Burrett was disciplined and transferred to another job, as
a result of which she lost the chance of being regraded and was unable to
work paid overtime. After an unsuccessful internal appeal, she commenced a
sex discrimination claim with an industrial tribunal.

Q Was Ms Burrett unlawfully discriminated against?

A The tribunal established that the uniform requirement applied to both
men and women, and even although the type of uniform differed for
male and female nurses, that did not amount to less favourable treatment of
female nurses. A male nurse would have been equally disciplined for refusing
to wear the nurses' uniform. Thus Ms Burrett lost her claim.

Based on the case *Burrett* v *West Birmingham Health authority*.

Rights of disabled people

Disabled people often face prejudice and discrimination in obtaining and
retaining employment. Until recently disabled people were not covered by
anti-discrimination legislation, despite various Bills having been introduced
to Parliament over the years.

In 1995, new legislation (the Disability Discrimination Act) was introduced. This replaced the previous legislation covering disabled people in
Britain (the Disabled Persons (Employment) Act) which dated back to 1944.
The old law imposed a 'quota' of (registered) disabled persons on all employers with more than 20 employees, so that employers had to ensure that
3 per cent of their workforce were registered disabled people. Compliance
with this Act had become impossible, because only about 3 per cent of the
total working population in Britain was disabled, and only about one per
cent actually registered. In practice there were only ever about 10 prosecu-
tions under the Act.

The new law has created a statutory right for disabled people not to be
directly discriminated against on the grounds of disability. A disabled
person is defined as someone who 'has a physical or mental impairment
which has a substantial and long-term adverse effect on his ability to carry
out normal day-to-day activities'. The definition of 'long-term effects' in this
context is stated as effects which have lasted, or can reasonably be expected
to last, at least 12 months. As regards the 'effect on normal day-to-day
activities', this is defined as an impairment which affects mobility; manual
dexterity; physical coordination; continence; ability to lift, carry or other-

wise move everyday objects; speech, hearing or eyesight; memory or ability to learn or understand; perception of the risk of physical danger; or severe disfigurement.

It is worth noting that people who were registered as disabled in January 1995 (and still registered on the date the legislation was introduced) are deemed to be disabled for the purposes of the new Act.

The Disability Discrimination Act gives disabled people rights in all areas of employment namely recruitment, terms and conditions of employment, transfer, training, career progression, dismissal and general treatment at work.

Employees' rights under this Act are largely parallel to those under the sex and race discrimination legislation, except that there is no concept of indirect discrimination in the disability legislation. Also, protection under the Act applies only where your employer has 20 employees or more.

The procedures and time limits for complaints to an industrial tribunal are the same as those which apply to sex and race discrimination.

The procedures and time limits for complaints to an industrial tribunal are the same as those which apply to sex and race discrimination. This means that where an employee believes he has been discriminated against on the grounds of disability, he may make a complaint to an industrial tribunal within 3 months of the discrimination taking place. There is no minimum service requirement.

Rights of ex offenders

The Rehabilitation of Offenders Act (1974) was devised to protect people from being discriminated against as a result of an offence committed many years ago. The effect of the Act is that after a certain period of time (which depends on the seriousness of the offence and the type of the punishment), a person is deemed to be 'rehabilitated'. This means that for employment purposes, they must be treated as if their conviction had never occurred.

The factors that govern whether a conviction has become 'spent' (and the offender therefore, a 'rehabilitated' person) are:

- The sentence imposed for the conviction;
- Whether any other offences have subsequently been committed; and
- The period of time that has elapsed since conviction.

As mentioned above, the rehabilitation period depends upon the sentence imposed. The Act sets out the applicable periods:

Sentence	Rehabilitation period
Serious offences, e.g. imprisonment for more than 30 months	No rehabilitation
Imprisonment for more than six months, but not more than 30 months.	10 years
Cashiering, discharge with ignominy, or dismissal with disgrace from Her Majesty's Service	10 years
Imprisonment or youth custody for a term not exceeding six months	7 years
Dismissal from Her Majesty's Service	7 years
Any sentence of detention in respect of a conviction in service disciplinary proceedings	5 years
A fine or any other sentence subject to rehabilitation under the Act.	5 years
Conditional discharge, or probation	1 year
Absolute discharge	6 months

In certain cases, if the sentence is imposed on someone who was under 17 years old at the date of the conviction, the rehabilitation period is cut by half.

Under the Rehabilitation of Offenders Act, an employee or prospective employee is allowed to conceal information relating to a 'spent conviction'. The law's effects are similar to discrimination provisions. This means that concealing a spent conviction, or the conviction itself are not proper grounds for you to be refused employment, or to be dismissed.

An employer may therefore not ask you about spent convictions, and if he does so, then you need not provide any information about them.

There are, however, certain professions and employments for which exceptions are made under the Act. This means that for certain types of employment, it is still lawful for the employer to ask questions regarding previous convictions, even where they have become spent. In these cases the prospective employee must disclose any spent convictions.

The excluded professions include medical practitioner, barrister / advocate, solicitor, chartered or certified accountant, dentist, veterinary surgeon, nurse, optician, chemist and (in Scotland) registered teacher.

Other excluded employments include probation officers, social services personnel, police constables, traffic wardens, court clerks, prison personnel, and any employment concerned with dealings with young people under the age of 18.

There are also exceptions in respect of crown employment, employment by the UK Atomic Energy Authority, the Civil Aviation Authority and the Post Office, where questions may be asked about spent convictions in order to safeguard national security.

Where, however, you have a conviction which is not yet spent, and you conceal it from an employer or prospective employer, you risk being dismissed (fairly), even although you may have been working satisfactorily for a period of time. An example of this was a British Rail guard who had lied about a conviction, and who, when the conviction was discovered, was fairly dismissed despite having 16 months satisfactory service.

Employer's right to search

Certain companies, such as those which produce or sell expensive goods, or those where employees handle large amounts of cash, may wish to carry out routine searching of employees as part of company security procedures. The searching may include employees' bags, outer clothing, pockets and motor vehicles.

For searching to be legal, there must be a clause in your contract of employment requiring you to consent to specific types of searches. Even so, each time a search takes place, you must be asked for your permission, otherwise the search could still be unlawful.

Bear in mind, however, that if your contract contains a 'permission to search' clause, and you subsequently refuse to agree to being searched, then your employer could take disciplinary action against you on account of your refusal.

Discrimination on account of trade union membership

All employees have the right to belong to an independent trade union of their choice. You also have the right to refuse to belong to a trade union or staff association.

Your employer is under no obligation to recognise, or continue to recognise, a trade union, regardless of how many employees are members. Nevertheless it is illegal to penalise employees on account of trade union membership/non-membership, or trade union activities. More specifically you have the right not to be penalised or disadvantaged in any way for the purpose of:

● Preventing or deterring you from being a member of an independent trade union;

- Compelling you to become a member of a trade union;
- Forcing you to make payments to a union which you have not joined, or which you have left;
- Preventing or deterring you from taking part in the activities of an independent trade union at an appropriate time;

    'An appropriate time' means either time outside your working hours, or else inside working hours in accordance with an agreement with your employer.

CASE STUDY

Mr O'Shea worked for the Department of Trade. An unfairly adverse report was made about him because of his union activities, as a result of which he was not considered for promotion.

Q Did the Department of Trade's report constitute 'action short of dismissal' under trade union legislation?

A Yes, the tribunal heard that the opportunity for promotion would not arise for another year and thus awarded Mr O'Shea a sum equivalent to the difference between his current net annual pay and the net pay he would have received if he had been promoted.

Based on the case *O'Shea* v *Department of Trade*.

It is also unlawful to dismiss a person because he is, or is not, a member of a trade union or has refused to join one.

Furthermore, as a result of more recent amendments to legislation in this area, it is now illegal for an employer to refuse employment to an individual on the grounds of membership or non-membership of a trade union. If therefore you believe that you have been denied a job either because you are a member of a trade union, or because you are unwilling to join a union, then you have the right to complain to an industrial tribunal. As a result of these amendments to legislation, closed shop agreements are now unenforceable in Britain.

You may make a complaint to an industrial tribunal if you have in any way been discriminated against on account of trade union membership. You must claim within three months, and you may do so regardless of the period of time you have worked for your employer, or the number of hours you work.

More detailed information about trade union rights is given in Chapter 11.

Discrimination on account of health and safety activities

The Trade Union Reform and Employment Rights Act, passed as law in July 1993, has given new protection to all employees involved in health and safety activities, whether officially or unofficially. The protection given is similar to the provisions regarding trade union activities outlined in the last section.

All employees have the right not to be treated unfavourably, discriminated against or dismissed on account of health and safety activities. The protection covers not only officially nominated safety representatives, but all employees who are taking reasonable steps to promote health and safety. You are protected in the following circumstances:

- Where you are nominated by your employer as a health and safety representative and you are carrying out your duties and activities in this respect.
- Where you have been asked by your employer to carry out activities connected with the prevention or reduction of risks, and you are fulfilling this function.
- In a situation where there is no official safety committee or representative, you raise a health and safety issue with your employer personally.
- Where you leave your place of work, or refuse to return to work because you reasonably believe there is a serious danger to health and safety.
- Where you take appropriate and reasonable steps to protect yourself or other people from serious danger.

If you are dismissed in any of the above circumstances, you may take your complaint to an industrial tribunal (within three months of your dismissal) regardless of your length of service. Levels of compensation could well be high for such dismissals in the future.

Questions and Answers

Q I am a woman wishing to return to work after spending several years looking after my three children at home. Recently at a job interview, the interviewer asked me questions about my arrangements for having my children looked after when I start working. He also asked me how much time off I thought I would need to look after my children if they were sick. I thought such questions were not allowed at interviews?

A You are right in thinking so. Questions such as you describe are discriminatory, because, in the eyes of the law, they indicate an intention to treat you less favourably than a man would be treated. You could, if you wished, make a complaint to an industrial tribunal (within three months of the interview) for sex discrimination.

Q I have applied for a promotion to a post for which I have all the necessary qualifications and experience. However, my manager has informed me that a male colleague is to be appointed to the post, because he is 'more suitable'. My manager will not give me any other reason. I know that my colleague is less experienced than I am, and has fewer qualifications. I am convinced that the real reason for the choice is that my boss wants a man in the particular job (rather than a woman), but I have no proof of this. What chance of success would I have if I make a claim for sex discrimination to an industrial tribunal?

A You do not need absolute proof of sex discrimination to win a case at tribunal, merely some positive evidence. If your qualifications and experience are in fact greater than your colleague's, then this constitutes positive evidence. Your employer would be required, at tribunal, to provide justification for appointing your male colleague to the promoted post in place of you. If there is no such justification, then your chances of winning your case would be high.

Q Not long ago, I was transferred to a more senior job in another department. I am very happy in my work, but the problem is that one of my male colleagues keeps pestering me to go out with him. I have made it clear to him that I am not interested, but his attentions are becoming embarrassing. Now he has started making crude remarks to me when we are alone. Is this sexual harassment?

A Yes, it is, because you genuinely find your colleague's attentions unwelcome. You should explain to him in a firm manner that you find his attentions and crude remarks offensive, and ask him to stop. If this does not work, you could raise the matter with your boss or another manager to complain officially.

If, ultimately, the problem does not cease, then you would have the right to make a claim of sex discrimination at industrial tribunal – it has been well established that sexual harassment constitutes illegal discrimination.

Q I am a 59-year-old woman working for an engineering company. My company has a retirement policy whereby women retire at age 60 and men at 63. I would like to continue working after age 60, but my employer has told me that I cannot do so. Is this right?

A Your employer's policy on retirement is illegal. Companies are obliged by law to operate equal retirement ages for men and women. It follows, therefore, that if your male colleagues have the opportunity to continue working until age 63, then you must be offered the same. If you fail to convince your employer, and are forced to retire at age 60, then you could take a claim to an industrial tribunal for sex discrimination and unfair dismissal. Your chances of success would be high.

Q There seems to be a great deal of legislation these days protecting women from unfair sex discrimination. What about men – don't we have any advantages?

A The sex discrimination legislation protects both men and women equally. You would have the same rights as any woman to make a claim for sex discrimination if you had been afforded unfavourable treatment on the grounds of your sex. It's true that the majority of cases which come before tribunals are raised by women, but this does not change the fact that both men and women have the same protection in law. Neither sex has any 'advantage' over the other in this respect.

Q I worked for my employer for 14 months before being dismissed last month. My boss said that the reason for my dismissal was that I 'didn't fit in'. I know that my work was satisfactory, and I have grounds to believe that the true reason for my dismissal was that I am black. Bearing in mind that I have less than two years service, is there any legal remedy open to me?

A Yes, you could make a claim for race discrimination to an industrial tribunal (within three months of the date of your dismissal). You do not require to have any minimum length of service to make such a claim. At the tribunal hearing, you would need to provide some evidence that your employer discriminated against you in dismissing you, i.e. that the true reason for the dismissal was based on your colour, race or nationality.

Q I notice that a lot of the job advertisements in our local newspaper state an upper age limit, typically 35 or 40. Is this legal?

A Yes, there is no legislation preventing employers from 'discriminating' on the grounds of a person's age, provided there is no implicit sex discrimination within the age limits imposed.

Q My employer operates a dress code which rules that women must not wear trousers to work. I could understand it if the rule referred to jeans, but women are not allowed to wear trousers of any description, even although the majority of jobs are office based and do not involve meeting the public. Is such a ruling legal?

A Your company's policy on trousers is discriminatory, and certainly open to challenge under the sex discrimination legislation. Whilst employers are within their rights to operate a dress code, the rules must not impose more stringent restrictions on women than on men (or vice versa).

Q I am registered disabled and have worked for my present employer for five years. Now the company is talking about the possibility of redundancies. How will this affect me?

A Under the new disability discrimination legislation, you are entitled not to be discriminated against on the grounds of disability. This includes protection against being selected for redundancy on account of your disability. In other words you must be treated in the same way as all other employees during a redundancy programme, and not picked out because you are disabled. Your employer must use criteria for selecting people for redundancy, which are objective, fair and reasonable.

Q I recently joined a trade union which is actively recruiting in my work-place. I have attended several meetings in my own time and have also become involved in helping the union recruit more new members.

My boss has hinted to me that he disapproves of the union, and of my active part in its recruitment campaign. I am concerned that this will affect my chances of promotion next month when two vacancies will become available. Can my boss legally deny me a promotion on the grounds of my trade union activities?

A No, it would be illegal for your employer to penalise you, or treat you in any way less favourably, on account of your trade union member-ship, or because you have taken part in the activities of a trade union in your own time. If you are in fact denied a promotion, and have solid grounds to believe that your trade union activities are the reason for this, then you could make a claim to an industrial tribunal.

7
Maternity Rights

A woman who is pregnant has certain rights under the law as follows:

- The right to have time off work for ante-natal care;
- The right to be paid statutory maternity pay (subject to a minimum of six months' continuous service);
- The right to take maternity leave and return to work;
- The right not to be dismissed on account of her pregnancy.

These rights are generally available to all female employees, married or unmarried. The rights are examined in more detail in the following sections.

Time off work for ante-natal care

Irrespective of length of service or the number of hours worked, pregnant women are entitled to reasonable time off during working hours for ante-natal care. Such time off must be granted with pay.

Pregnant women are not obliged in any way to arrange medical appointments outside working hours, or to make up for lost time by working extra hours in lieu of time spent at appointments.

CASE STUDY
Mrs Sajil needed time off work for clinic appointments when she was pregnant. It was arranged that on the days of her appointments she would take

(CASE STUDY CONTINUED)
the whole day off and work on a Saturday instead. Her employer normally paid higher rates of pay for Saturday working.

Q Would Mrs Sajil be entitled to be paid for the days on which she attended clinic appointments, as well as for the Saturdays she worked?
A The tribunal decided that Mrs Sajil was entitled to be paid for the time spent at her appointments as well as for the Saturdays she worked. Saturday was not a normal working day and her statutory right was to be allowed paid time off during working hours.

Based on the case *Sajil v Carraro, t/a Foubert's Bar*.

Except on the first occasion on which time off is requested, your employer is entitled to ask you to produce a certificate stating that you are pregnant and an appointment card, prior to granting you time off.

Statutory maternity pay (SMP)

Entitlement to statutory maternity pay (SMP) depends on your length of service as at the fifteenth week before the expected week of your confinement. All women who at that time have at least 26 weeks continuous employment with the same employer qualify for SMP, regardless of the number of hours they work per week.

SMP is paid for a maximum of 18 weeks. This period of 18 weeks is known as the maternity pay period. Payment is based on a two-tier system as follows:

The higher rate of SMP is paid to women for the first six weeks of the maternity pay period. The higher rate is equivalent to 90 per cent of your normal earnings.

The standard rate of SMP is a flat-rate payment, currently £52.50 per week, and is paid for a further 12 weeks.

To qualify for SMP, you must:

- Have at least 26 weeks' service by the 'qualifying week' – which is 15 weeks before the expected week of confinement;
- Earn more than the lower earnings limit for national insurance (this limit is reviewed each year – the current level is £58 per week);
- Provide evidence of the expected date of your confinement;
- Provide notification of your intended maternity absence in accordance with your employer's rules;
- Have actually stopped work;

● Have reached the 11th week before the expected week of confinement, or have been confined earlier.

Entitlement to SMP does not depend on your returning to work after having your baby. You will be excluded from receiving SMP if:

● You are not employed by the company during the qualifying week;
● You are outside the European Community during the first week of the maternity pay period (e.g. abroad on holiday);
● You are taken into legal custody during the first week of the maternity pay period;
● You work for another employer after the confinement and during the maternity pay period.

If you are excluded from SMP, your employer must provide you with an exclusion form (Form SMP 1), so that you can claim state maternity allowance instead. If you think you are entitled to SMP, and you are not receiving it, and you have not been given an exclusion form, then you should ask your employer to clarify your entitlement.

SMP is treated as pay, therefore tax and national insurance contributions will be deducted in the usual way. Note that you cannot be paid SMP over and above your salary.

SMP is the legal minimum that employers can pay to female employees who take maternity leave. However many employers elect to pay higher amounts, or to continue paying actual salary for all or part of the woman's maternity leave. Your contract of employment should tell you if you are entitled to such enhanced payments.

Right to return to work

All pregnant employees now have the right to take 14 weeks maternity leave, and resume work. More specifically, the Trade Union Reform and Employment Rights Act gives employees who are pregnant the right to the continuation of all terms and conditions, apart from pay, during a period of 14 weeks maternity leave. This provision was brought into effect in October 1994. This right applies to all female employees regardless of their length of service or the number of hours they work per week. So, even if (for example) you are engaged on a part-time basis and have only worked for your employer for a few months, you are automatically entitled to this 14 weeks' maternity leave.

During this maternity leave period, the employer has to maintain all your contractual rights except for pay. This could include retention of a company

car, entitlement to pension or insurance benefits, accrual of holiday entitlement or even free lunches! Essentially, your contract of employment must
remain in force for this period of 14 weeks, except that you will not receive
your normal salary. (You will receive SMP instead provided you meet the
qualifying requirements).

You have the right to choose when you commence your maternity leave,
provided it does not begin prior to 11 weeks before your baby is due. You
may even elect to work right up to the day your baby is born. However, one
restriction is that if you are off sick on account of pregnancy at any time
after the beginning of the 6th week before your due date, then your maternity leave period will be triggered automatically. This means that you may
be obliged, whether you wish it or not, to start your maternity leave period
if you are absent from work on account of sickness associated with your
pregnancy, even if, for example, your sickness absence lasts only one day.

If you wish to return to work before the end of the 14 week period, then
you must give your employer at least seven days' notice of the date on
which you intend to return, otherwise no notice is required. Your employer
is not allowed to delay your return beyond the end of the 14-week period.

Women with two years or more continuous service have additional
rights over and above the rights described in the preceding paragraphs. If
you have two years service (here service is calculated as at 11 weeks before
the expected week of your confinement), you have the right to return to
work at any time between the end of your 14-week maternity leave and 29
weeks after your baby was born. You can choose when to return, provided
it is within the 29 week period.

Your right is to return to a job under the same contract of employment
and on terms and conditions not less favourable. Normally this will be the
same job as you left, but if it is not reasonably practicable for your employer
to permit you to return to your original job, you may be offered alternative
employment.

If, during the period of your maternity leave, your employer has instituted a pay review, then you have the right to benefit from any pay increase
as if you had not been absent.

If, during your maternity leave, your job becomes redundant, your employer is obliged to offer you any suitable vacancy which is available within
the organisation. The alternative employment must be suitable for you and
must carry terms and conditions which are not substantially less favourable
than those of your previous contract.

Your right to be offered alternative employment in these circumstances
starts as soon as you have given notice that you intend to take maternity
leave and return to work. This means in effect that if any suitable job
becomes available at any time during your maternity leave, then you are

entitled to be offered it in place of your old job. If, instead, your employer appoints someone else on a permanent basis to the vacant position, then your redundancy would be automatically unfair.

CASE STUDY

Ms Holmes had been employed for some years with the Home Office as an executive officer. She had already had maternity leave during the course of her employment, and was finding it difficult to look after her child whilst working full time, as she was a single parent.

Following a second period of maternity leave Ms Holmes asked if she could return to work on a part-time basis. The Home Office refused, saying that her right was to return on the same conditions and same job as before. They also stated that, as a matter of policy, they would not employ any part-time officers in her grade.

After returning to work on a full-time basis, Ms Holmes raised a claim for indirect sex discrimination.

Q Was Ms Holmes' claim likely to succeed?

A It did succeed, but the circumstances were unusual. The industrial tribunal agreed that the Home Office had applied a requirement to all executive officers – namely the requirement to work full-time. They also supported the view that fewer women than men could comply with this requirement due to child-minding responsibilities. Ms Holmes had therefore been subjected to a 'detriment' (disadvantage) by being refused the opportunity to work part-time. Consequently the case centred around the question as to whether the Home Office could justify the requirement that executive officers must work full-time.

The Home Office might have won the case had it not been for the fact that they had previously undertaken feasibility studies to see whether part-time working could be introduced more widely into the organisation, the results of which suggested that it could be. Consequently the Home Office was unable to show that the requirement to work full-time was justified, and Ms Holmes won her case.

It is important to note that this case does not imply that women automatically have the right to choose to return after maternity leave on a part-time basis instead of full-time. The law on contracts of employment still applies, and consequently any change to working hours has to be agreed by both parties. There is, of course, no harm in asking, and from the Holmes case it can be inferred that the onus is then on your employer to justify any refusal.

Based on the case *Home Office* v *Holmes*.

One exception to the right to return (within the 29 week period) is where you work for an employer with fewer than six employees. Here, if it is not reasonably practicable for your employer to give you your original job back, and there is no suitable alternative work, then your employer need not re-employ you at all.

To qualify for the right to return to work as described above:

- You must have at least two years service by the 11th week before the expected week of confinement it does not matter how many hours a week you work, as part-timers have the same rights as full-timers;
- You must still be employed (whether or not you are actually at work) at the beginning of the 11th week before the expected week of confinement;
- You must inform your employer, in writing, at least 21 days before your absence begins that you will be absent from work to have a baby and that you intend to return to work after your absence;
- You must provide a certificate of the expected week of your confinement, if asked;
- You must reply in writing (within 14 days) to any written request from your employer confirming that you still intend to return to work. Such a request from your employer cannot legitimately be made earlier than three weeks before your 14-week maternity leave period is due to expire.
- You must give your employer 21 days written notice of the date on which you intend to return to work. Your employer may postpone the date of your return by a maximum of four weeks, provided there are sound business reasons for doing so;

If you are sick when you are due to return to work, then you may postpone the date of your return for up to four weeks, provided you give your employer a doctor's certificate.

To sum up both sets of provisions, all pregnant employees have the right to take 14 weeks maternity leave (and resume work), whilst those with two or more years service have the right to take up to 29 weeks leave after the baby is born. Note that the 14 week period falls within the 29 weeks, so you would not of course have the right to 14 weeks leave plus an additional 29 weeks.

One further point is that there is a compulsory period of maternity leave of two weeks after the date of birth. If your baby arrives later than expected, and you have exhausted your maternity leave, your entitlement will be automatically extended to allow for this compulsory period of leave. Thus you will not lose out on your right to return just because your baby is late.

One other point of interest is that there is no limit to the number of times which women are entitled to claim maternity rights. Each time you become pregnant, all the rights described in this chapter would apply. Equally, there is no minimum or maximum time limit between one period of maternity leave and the next.

If your employer does not allow you to return to work after a period of maternity absence, then this constitutes a dismissal in law. For further information on the law on dismissals, please refer to Chapter 13.

Rights during maternity leave

A tricky question which often arises is whether or not a woman on maternity leave is entitled to continue to receive company benefits and perks, eg a company car.

During the period of 14 weeks' maternity leave to which all pregnant women are entitled, you have the right to the continuation of all terms and conditions, apart from pay. Essentially, your contract of employment remains in force during this 14-week period, which means that you must be allowed to continue to benefit from any 'perks' to which you are contractually entitled, e.g. company car, medical insurance, accrual of holiday entitlement and occupational pension benefits.

During the longer period of maternity leave to which women with two or more years service are entitled, the current legal position in Britain is unclear. In the first instance, if you are in doubt about this, you should refer to your contract of employment, or company policy document on maternity leave (if there is one). Essentially your rights during your maternity leave will depend on what your contract of employment says on the subject.

If there is nothing in writing to clarify the situation and you are still in doubt, or if you are refused the right to retain, for example, your company car during the whole period of your maternity leave, then you could possibly have a claim for illegal sex discrimination (depending on the circumstances).

All periods of time which you take off work as maternity leave must subsequently be counted as continuous service for the purposes of calculating any statutory rights which are service-related.

This means that, once you have returned to work, your length of service with your employer must be calculated as if you had never been absent.

Right not to be dismissed on account of pregnancy

It is automatically unfair to dismiss a woman because of pregnancy, or for any reason connected with pregnancy. Dismissal on account of pregnancy is also likely to amount to sex discrimination. Female employees are well protected during pregnancy against dismissal.

If, as a result of pregnancy you are discriminated against in some way other than dismissal, this too is likely to be illegal.

CASE STUDY

Ms O'Mara worked for the Scottish Agricultural College. She was pregnant at the time she applied for promotion. Her employer passed her over for the promotion, and appointed a man who had inferior qualifications and less service than she had.

Q Was the treatment of Ms O'Mara discriminatory?

A Yes, the tribunal found that Ms O'Mara had not been considered seriously when she was interviewed for the promotion, and the fact that she was pregnant at the time she applied for the promotion had counted against her.

Based on the case *Scottish Agricultural College* v *O'Mara.*

If during your pregnancy, you become unable to do your job, or if your work would put you in any way at risk while you are pregnant, then your employer is obliged to either adjust your working conditions and / or hours, or else move you to another job. If neither of these is possible, then you have the right to be placed on paid leave. Note that these provisions do not apply where you are signed off sick by your doctor, but rather where you are able to come to work, but unable to perform your particular job duties. An example of this could be where a woman's job involved heavy lifting – here the employer might be able to move the woman into lighter work for the period of her pregnancy.

If you believe that any of your maternity rights have been breached, you should raise the matter with your employer. Ultimately you have the right to raise a complaint with an industrial tribunal if you believe that you have been unfairly treated or denied your legal rights.

Paternity rights

Despite all the legislation in Britain to protect pregnant mothers, there is, as yet, no legislation offering prospective fathers any benefits.

Men have no legal right to time off work, with or without pay, when their partners have a baby, or to any subsequent period of paternity leave. Some enlightened employers allow such time off as a contractual right, but they are not compelled to do so by law.

Questions and Answers

Q I have recently discovered I am pregnant. My boss usually expects employees to arrange medical appointments outside working hours, but I have heard that I am entitled to take time off work to attend ante-natal appointments. Is this true?

A Yes, you are entitled to take reasonable time off work to undergo ante-natal care. Pregnant women are not obliged to arrange medical appointments outside working hours, nor to make up for lost time by working extra hours for time spent at appointments.

Q I am planning to resign from my job in a few months time, about eight weeks before my first baby is due. Will I be entitled to statutory maternity pay, since I am not planning to return to work?

A Yes, entitlement to statutory maternity pay does not depend on a woman returning to work after she has had her baby. You qualify for statutory maternity pay providing you have at least six months service.

Q Do I have to pay tax on my statutory maternity pay?

A Yes, unfortunately! Statutory maternity pay is regarded as 'pay' and therefore is liable for tax and national insurance deductions in the normal way.

Q I believe that there has been legislation introduced quite recently giving women the right to keep their jobs through maternity leave. Is this true?

A Yes, all pregnant employees now have the right to take 14 weeks maternity leave, and resume work. This right applies to all female employees regardless of their length of service or number of hours they work per week.

Q I am confused over my right to return to work after having a baby. I thought that I could return at any time within 29 weeks after my baby is born, but someone has told me that maternity leave can only last 14 weeks. Can you clarify this please?

A There are two different levels of maternity leave benefit: all pregnant employees have the right to take 14 weeks maternity leave (and resume work), whilst those with two or more years service have the right to take up to 11 weeks before, and 29 weeks after the baby is born.

So, if you have less than two years service (calculated as at the 11th week before your baby is due) then you qualify for the shorter period of leave, and if you have two years service or more, you qualify for the longer period.

Q I am due to return to work in a few weeks time, after having had a baby. Three months ago, whilst I was on maternity leave, there was a pay rise in my company. Will I be entitled to get the pay rise when I return?

A Yes, if the pay rise has been applied generally, you are entitled to receive it.

Q I am pregnant and due to start maternity leave in three months time. I have not decided yet whether or not I will return to work. My company has been conducting a lot of training lately, and most of my colleagues have been offered the opportunity of going on at least one training course. However, I have not been offered any training – does the fact I am pregnant mean that I am not entitled to training?

A On the contrary, you should not be treated any differently because you are pregnant. If your employer refuses you some benefit, like training, on account of your pregnancy, then this amounts to illegal sex discrimination.

You should ask your employer about the training which interests you. If you are refused access to training, and it appears that your pregnancy is the reason for the refusal, you would have the right to make a claim for sex discrimination to an industrial tribunal.

Q I am due to return to work soon after taking maternity leave. I would like to work part-time. Is this possible?

A Your right to return is to a job under the same contract of employment as the one you left. A change from full-time to part-time work would be a major contractual change. Consequently you have no automatic right to return to work part-time, where the job is a full-time job, unless there is clear evidence that the job does not require to be done on a full-time basis. This would be difficult to prove.

Of course there is nothing to stop you from asking your employer about part-time working. There may be the opportunity of job-sharing, or some other arrangement which your employer may be willing to consider.

Q My wife is due to have our first child soon. Am I entitled in law to time off work when she has the baby?

A No, there is no law in Britain compelling employers to give expectant fathers time off work (yet!)

8
The Law and Your Health

The Access to Medical Reports Act, which came into effect in January 1989, gives you the right to have access to any medical report (about yourself) prepared for employment or insurance purposes, provided it has been compiled by your own doctor, or someone who has been responsible for your clinical care.

In employment terms this means that if your employer asks for your permission to obtain a medical report from your GP, you have the right to apply to your doctor to see the report before it is sent to your employer. Furthermore, your employer must notify you of your rights under the Act before applying to your doctor for a medical report. If, therefore, your employer indicates an intent to obtain a medical report, then you should ask to have your rights clarified and respected. You also have the right to:

● Refuse to allow your employer to apply to your doctor for a medical report;

116

- Ask your doctor to amend the report, if it is inaccurate or misleading, or, if your doctor refuses to amend it, to ask for your objection to be attached to the report;
- Refuse to allow the report to be passed to your employer.

CASE STUDY

Sally worked as a secretary for a small oil-related company. Over a period of a year she had taken 23 days sick leave, most of which were due to symptoms associated with stress and depression, which had been brought on by personal problems. The majority of her absences were between one and three days.

One day Sally's manager informed her that the company had a new policy regarding sickness absence. The policy stated that an employee with more than 20 days sick leave in any period of 12 months was required to provide the company with a GP's medical report if requested to do so. Sally's manager asked her to agree to let the company have a medical report regarding her frequent absences.

Q Must Sally comply with her manager's request?

A The company is not legally entitled to insist that employees agree to provide a GP's report. The Access to Medical Reports Act gives Sally the final choice to agree or refuse such a request, regardless of company policy.

The Access to Medical Reports Act does not apply to medical reports prepared by company doctors or specialists, so if you are examined by a company doctor, who is not your normal doctor, then you have no right of access to any subsequent medical report prepared by that person. You may, of course, ask for access, and the doctor may comply with your request, but you have no legal right of access.

Access to health records – your rights

Following the Access to Medical Reports Act, a further piece of legislation, called the Access to Health Records Act was introduced in November 1991. This law gives you the right of access to your personal health records on written request. However the Act does not entitle you to obtain access to any record made before November 1991, although there is nothing to prevent your doctor from supplying such information to you if he / she wishes.

This Act, unlike the Access to Medical Reports Act, covers medical records held by company doctors as well as general practitioners. In fact this

Act covers records held by a range of medical professionals, for example dentists, opticians, health visitors, chiropodists and various other practitioners.

Upon access to your health records under this Act, you may apply for corrections to be made if you think the record is incorrect, misleading or incomplete.

Medical examinations by a company doctor

Many employers include a statement in employees' contracts of employment requiring them to agree to attend medical examinations with a company doctor at the company's request. This may include differing types of specialist medical examinations according to the particular type of industry in which you are working.

It is common for employers to carry out a pre-employment medical examination, and for any offer of employment to be 'subject to a satisfactory medical'. This is perfectly legal, and if you refuse, then you probably won't be offered the job! Equally it is common for employers to require employees to attend a company medical prior to returning to work after a period of sickness absence or maternity leave.

Your contract of employment is the source of your rights here. If your contract stipulates that you must comply with any request to attend a company medical, then you are contractually bound to do so. If you refuse, then you may face disciplinary action because you would be in breach of your contract.

If, however, nothing is stated in writing within your contract, then basically your employer has no authority to demand that you attend a company medical. It would be up to you to consent, or refuse, as you saw fit.

Nevertheless it may be in your interests to agree to be medically examined, for instance if you have had a considerable amount of sick leave and the employer wishes to make a genuine investigation into the reasons for your absences.

CASE STUDY

Mr McIntosh was a site engineer working overseas. After five years he had a nervous breakdown and was treated for anxiety. He was examined by the company doctor and returned to work. Subsequently when the company conducted an exercise to ensure overseas staff were medically fit, Mr McIntosh refused to be examined by the company doctor, to allow his employer to keep a report prepared by his own doctor, and to be examined by an independent medical specialist. The company eventually dismissed Mr McIntosh and his claim for unfair dismissal failed. The tribunal felt that the

(CASE STUDY CONTINUED)
employer acted reasonably in dismissing Mr McIntosh in the face of his
uncooperativeness.

Based on the case *McIntosh* v *John Brown Engineering Ltd.*

Company medical examinations must of course be dealt with in confidence, and if you have any doubt about this, you are perfectly entitled to ask either your company doctor, or the personnel manager, what happens to the information gained by the doctor at the medical examination.

Medical suspension

Certain employees may be suspended from their normal work on medical grounds, in circumstances where their health would be endangered because they could be exposed to a dangerous substance. The relevant substances in this context are lead, ionising radiations and other 'substances hazardous to health'.

Employees who are suspended in this way are entitled to be paid (within financial limits) during their suspension for up to six months at a time, provided they have a minimum of one month's service.

You may, however, be offered alternative work to do, and if you unreasonably refuse this, then you will lose your right to medical suspension pay. If you are entitled to medical suspension pay, and do not receive it, then you can make a complaint to an industrial tribunal within three months. If the tribunal finds the complaint justified, it will order your employer to pay you the appropriate amounts of money.

Note that this provision has nothing to do with absence due to personal sickness, but rather has to do with the working environment.

Statutory sick pay

All employees are potentially eligible to receive Statutory Sick Pay (SSP) when absent from work for four days or more because of sickness. This right exists regardless of length of service or number of hours worked, although there are certain exclusions.

Full details of the exclusions, qualifications for benefit and your rights and obligations are set out in Chapter 4, *Statutory Sick Pay*.

The working environment – health requirements

There are many provisions related to health and safety at work, full details of which are beyond the remit of this book. However certain requirements and rights regarding the working environment are perhaps of special interest, and therefore worth mentioning.

The Offices, Shops and Railway Premises Act 1963 lays down clear rules regarding the working environment, as follows:

- Employees in offices, shops and railway premises have the right to 40 sq ft of floor space (per person), or, where the ceiling is lower than 10 ft, a volume of not less than 400 cubic ft.
- Ventilation and lighting must be adequate and suitable.
- Your employer must maintain a temperature in the workplace of not less than 16 degrees centigrade (F60.8 degrees) after the first hour of work. A thermometer must be provided in a conspicuous place on each floor.
- Provision must be made for adequate sanitary conveniences, washing facilities, drinking water, places for outdoor clothing to be hung and proper seating arrangements.

Similar provisions are contained within the Factories Act 1961.

Noise at work

People at work must be protected from loud noise under the Noise at Work Regulations 1989, which came into force on 1 January 1990. These regulations cover all workplaces in Britain and are designed to protect workers from damage to their hearing.

If the noise level in your workplace is between 85 and 90 decibels, then you have the right to ask for suitable ear protection if you wish it. You must also be given information about the risks of noise at work, and offered hearing checks.

Where the exposure level reaches 90 decibels or above, then your employer must provide you with suitable ear protection and both you and your employer have a legal duty to ensure that the protection is properly used. If you are in any doubt about the level of noise in your workplace, then you should ask your manager or safety representative (if there is one) for information.

VDU users

If your job involves working with display screen equipment on a habitual basis, then your employer has certain obligations towards you under the

Health and Safety (Display Screen Equipment) Regulations 1992. These regulations came into effect in January 1993 for new equipment and will come into effect for all other work-stations by the end of 1996.

Your rights include the following:

- To have your work station assessed for risks, and to have any risks that are found minimised;
- To have regular breaks from your screen, or periodic changes of activity;
- To be provided with information and training on health and safety matters relating to your work-station;
- To have eye tests at appropriate intervals (paid for by your employer) if you request them. Your employer is obliged subsequently to pay for basic glasses to correct any vision defect if it is caused by VDU work.

Your employer is also obliged to pay attention to various aspects of design, layout and lighting of work-stations where VDU's are used.

CASE STUDY

Brenda was employed as a computer/filing clerk in a large accountants' office. Over the 15 years she had been there, her job had altered considerably and now about 80 per cent of her work consisted of key-board input to the computer. She was still required to maintain the company's manual files up-to-date and to complete certain paperwork, but computer work formed the key element of her job.

Brenda's manager, Charles, began to notice that she was taking frequent breaks from her work – every hour she was to be found in the coffee room for between 5–10 minutes. One day Charles confronted Brenda and suggested to her that she was spending too much time away from her work and that she should take fewer coffee breaks. Brenda replied that, in accordance with the new regulations for VDU users, she was entitled to have regular breaks from work, and the time off she was taking was the minimum she was entitled to under the law.

Q Is Brenda entitled to take time off work every hour because she is a regular VDU user?

A No, Brenda has misinterpreted the regulations. The law gives VDU users the right to take regular breaks from their screen. This does not mean that employees are entitled to stop work during such breaks, but rather that they are entitled to a change of activity on a regular basis. Charles would be entitled to ask Brenda to organise her work so that she undertook paperwork or manual filing activities on a regular basis, thus giving her regular breaks from her screen.

It is natural for employees working with VDU's to be concerned about their health. Although VDU work can lead to muscular fatigue and eye stress, it is not generally regarded as a high risk activity. Furthermore, scientific research has concluded that there is no risk of radiation emitted by display screen equipment, and there is therefore no evidence that there is any danger to women who are pregnant.

If you are in any way concerned, however, it makes sense to talk to either your own doctor, or a company doctor, in order to obtain reassurance.

Upper limb disorders and repetitive strain injury

Certain medical problems can occur in association with repeated work movements such as consistent key-board input work. The official view, however, is that repetitive strain injury (known as RSI) is not a precise medical term, as it suggests that the injury or pain has been caused only by repetitive movements. The concept of RSI has been questioned in the courts, and in one case, dismissed as having no place in the medical books.

The Health and Safety Executive uses the term 'upper limb disorder' (ULD) rather than repetitive strain injury. Upper limb disorders encompass a range of conditions affecting the fingers, hands, wrists, elbows and shoulders. Typically the tendons, muscles and the associated nerve supply are affected. Symptoms may range from occasional aches, pains and discomfort, to restriction of joint movement and soft tissue swelling. Often the onset of symptoms is gradual. Eventually there can be serious disease or injury.

Upper limb disorders are not specific to one particular industry or type of job. Some jobs and working practices, however, may impose undesirable demands on muscles, tendons and joints. The key factors causing upper limb disorders are now known to be use of excessive force, bad posture, and frequent repetitive movements (this latter is what repetitive strain injury is all about).

Activities associated with upper limb disorders may include forceful gripping, awkward twisting or reaching, and repeated movements. What makes these activities hazardous is their prolonged repetition, especially if they are done in a forceful and awkward manner, or carried out without sufficient rest or recovery time.

The Health and Safety Executive's view is that upper limb disorders can and should be prevented by employers. If you think you have an upper limb disorder, you would need reliable medical evidence to back any legal case against your employer. The court would require clear evidence that your injury or pain was the direct result of the negligence of your employer, and not caused by some other factor.

Rights of smokers / non-smokers at work

It is perfectly legal for employers to 'discriminate' against smokers in most situations. Job advertisements may state that 'only non-smokers need apply' or you may be refused employment on the grounds that you smoke (or do not smoke!). You would have no basis in law to complain of such actions.

Furthermore if you breach your employer's rules on smoking, for example, by smoking in an area where smoking is banned, then you may be liable to have disciplinary action taken against you (including dismissal) depending on your company's policy on smoking.

If your employer has not previously operated a no-smoking policy, and decides to introduce a complete or part smoking ban, then this too is perfectly legal. Your employer's only obligations are to ensure that all employees are properly informed of the ban and the penalties for its infringement, and to give reasonable notice of its introduction.

CASE STUDY

Greater Glasgow Health Authority operated a policy which permitted smoking in certain areas of their hospitals which were set aside for that purpose, although it was banned in public areas. The Authority wished, however to strengthen its no-smoking policy and in 1991 introduced a total no-smoking ban to be effective from July that year. Prior to implementation of the ban, they consulted trade unions and staff interest groups. They offered assistance, including counselling, to staff who had a problem giving up smoking and gave over three months notice of the introduction of the new policy.

Mrs Dryden was a nursing auxiliary working in an operating theatre. She was a heavy smoker and had not succeeded in giving up the habit. The ban meant that she would no longer have access to a 'smoking area'. Three days after the ban commenced, she found the situation intolerable and resigned. She claimed that the Authority was in breach of her contract in introducing the smoking ban.

Q Did Mrs Dryden have a contractual 'right to smoke', in which case the Authority could be said to be in breach of contract in withdrawing facilities where she could smoke?

A The industrial tribunal found that there was no express or implied term in Mrs Dryden's contract of employment entitling her to smoke at work. Thus she lost her case.

Based on the case *Dryden v Greater Glasgow Health Authority*.

So there is no legal 'right to smoke' at work, nor to have smoking breaks, nor to have a 'smoking room' available.

Furthermore, because of the provisions of the Health and Safety at Work Act, employers are obliged to ensure, as far as is reasonably possible, the health, safety and welfare at work of all employees. It is therefore quite possible that if you are a non-smoker and you are forced to work in an environment where many of your colleagues smoke, you could claim (in the light of recent evidence on the effects of passive smoking) that you were being subjected to a hazard. Such claims are becoming more frequent in Britain.

If you have a problem due to smoking colleagues at work, then you would be well advised to raise the issue with your management and express your concerns.

Questions and Answers

Q I have been off sick a lot lately. Now my employer has told me he wants to obtain a medical report from my GP. Do I have to agree to this?

A No, you have the right in law to refuse your consent for your employer to apply to your GP for a medical report.

Q My manager has asked me to agree to allow him to apply for a medical report from my own doctor. I have no objections to this, but would like to see the report first. Do I have this right?

A Yes, you have the right to apply to your doctor to see the report before it is sent to your employer. Having seen the report, you then have the right, if you wish, to change your mind and refuse to allow it to be sent to your employer.

Q My boss has asked me to make an appointment with the company doctor to check up on my fitness to work. I am not keen on this idea. Does my boss have the right to insist?

A It depends on what your contract of employment says on the subject of medical examinations with company-nominated doctors. If your contract stipulates that you must comply with any request to attend a company medical, then you are contractually bound to do so.

If, however, nothing is stated in writing within your contract, then your employer has no authority to demand that you attend a company medical. It would be up to you to consent, or refuse, as you wished.

Q My employer operates a policy whereby personnel in the first year of employment do not get any sick pay if they are absent from work due to sickness. Does this mean that I would get nothing at all if I am off sick?

A You are entitled to statutory sick pay, whatever your length of service, and whatever the policy of the company. The amount payable is a rate prescribed by the government, and you are entitled to start to receive it on the fourth day of sickness absence. Full details are given in Chapter 4.

Q The office where I work is often very cold in winter. Is it true that if the temperature falls below a certain level, I can refuse to work?

A Your employer must maintain a temperature in the workplace of not less than 16 degrees centigrade (F60.8 degrees) after the first hour of work. Failing this, you would be entitled to refuse to work in that particular location.

Q I am a word processor operator and work in front of a screen virtually all day. I thought that new legislation entitled me to take a break from work every hour, but my employer says I should do other work during these so called breaks. Surely this can't be right?

A Your employer is correct. The law gives you the right to take regular breaks from your screen. This does not mean that you are entitled to stop work during such breaks, but rather that you are entitled to a change of activity on a regular basis.

Q My employer has recently introduced a complete smoking ban at work, even in the staff canteen. Surely there has to be some place for smokers to have a cigarette during breaks?

A No, your employer is acting legally. There is no contractual 'right to smoke' at work, nor to have smoking breaks, nor to have a 'smoking room' available.

9

Data

Protection

The purpose of the Data Protection Act 1984 is to protect individuals against misuse of information held about them on computer. The Act uses the term 'personal data' to mean information relating to an individual who can be identified (directly or indirectly) from the information held. Both facts and opinions constitute 'personal data'. One aspect of information, curiously, which is not classed as personal data is the indications of any future intentions of the person or company holding the data. An example of this might be a recommendation for promotion which has been input to the computer.

The introduction of this Act meant that people had the right of access to information held about them on computer from any company which held such information, including their employer.

More specifically, your rights under this Act are:

- To gain access to information held about you on computer, on request;
- To have inaccurate information corrected or erased;
- To claim compensation (via the courts) for any personal loss caused by the use of inaccurate information, the unauthorised use of information, or the loss or destruction of information. Compensation may also be paid for any distress caused to you because of the inaccuracy of data or its unauthorised disclosure.

There are certain exemptions under the Act, the most important of which are payroll and pensions information. Provided such information is held purely for the purpose of calculating pay or pensions, making the payments and calculating deductions, then the Data Protection Act does not apply. This means that you have no legal right of access to such information.

It is important to note that there is no right in law for you to be allowed access to information held manually, for example in personnel files. Some employers, may however, allow you to view your personnel file, depending on their policy, but it is not a legal requirement that they should do so. This position may change in the future as a result of a Directive (at the time of writing this is at the discussion stage) from Europe. The draft Directive proposes that data protection would cover both computerised and manual files.

Your right of access to data held about you on computer

For the majority of employees, the most important aspect of the Data Protection Act is their right of access to information held about them on a computer file. Naturally you cannot gain access under the Act to information held about someone else on computer.

So, what if you believe that your employer holds information about you on computer, and you wish to see the information to check that it is accurate? You have the right, on request, to be told whether your employer holds any computerised data about you, and, if so, to be supplied with a copy of the information held in a form which you can readily understand. The employer is not allowed to tamper with the information, or alter it (apart from updating it) before providing it to you. The information must be given to you within 40 days.

Your request must be in writing, and your employer may charge a fee for access to personal information, and the amount of this fee is limited in law to a reasonable amount, prescribed from time to time by the Data Protection Registrar. The current maximum fee is £10.

Data protection principles explained

The Data Protection Act laid down certain principles to guide employers through the maze of the Act. The principles which your employer must comply with, when considering personal data held and processed on computer, are as follows:

● The information contained in personal data must be obtained and processed fairly and lawfully.

- Personal data must only be held for specified and lawful purposes.
- Personal data must not be used or disclosed in any manner incompatible with those purposes.
- Personal data must be adequate, relevant, and not excessive.
- Personal data should be accurate and, where necessary, kept up to date.
- Personal data must not be kept for longer than is necessary.
- Individuals are entitled to be informed whether any personal data is held about them, and to access any such data at reasonable time intervals and without undue delay. Additionally individuals have the right to have inaccurate data corrected or erased.
- Appropriate security measures must be taken against unauthorised access to, or alteration, disclosure or destruction of personal data, and against accidental loss or destruction of data.

Questions and Answers

Q I believe that I have the right to gain sight of whatever information my employer holds about me on computer. Am I correct?

A Yes, you can make a written request to your employer asking him to give you a copy of the information which is held about you on computer. Your employer must comply with your request within 40 days.

Q Do I have the right to see my personnel file?

A No, there is presently no right in law for you to be allowed access to information held manually, for example in personnel files. There is nothing to stop you from asking your employer to see your file, but he has the right to refuse.

Q I have requested access to my computer file from my manager. He has agreed, but says I must pay a fee of £10. Can he force me to pay for this?

A Yes, employers are allowed to charge a reasonable fee, if they wish, for giving you access to the information held about you on computer. The maximum fee in law is currently £10.

Q What can I do if I find that my employer holds computerised information about me which is inaccurate?

A You have the right to insist that your employer corrects or erases the inaccurate information. If this is not done, and if you suffer damage as a result of the inaccuracy of the information, then you can claim compensation from the courts.

Q I am concerned that information is being held about me on my employer's computer system, and that this information could be seen by anyone. What protection do I have?

A One of the primary aims of the Data Protection Act is to ensure that your right to privacy is respected. The Act protects you against unauthorised disclosure of information held about you on computer.

Your employer is obliged under the Act to take appropriate security measures to ensure there is no unauthorised access to, or disclosure of such computerised information. Your employer must also take proper steps to prevent accidental loss or destruction of the information.

If, despite your employer's security measures, you find out that information has been improperly disclosed or used, then you can claim compensation from the courts for any financial loss or distress which you have suffered.

Q I work as a data input operator in our company's personnel department. I have heard a lot of talk about the Data Protection Act, but do not know precisely what my obligations are under it. Can you explain?

A The Data Protection Principles are explained in this chapter. The most important responsibility you have is to ensure you process all the personal information you receive through your job accurately, and to ensure you do not at any time (accidentally or deliberately) disclose any of it to an unauthorised person.

You should ask your employer to clarify any company rules on data protection to you, and how they affect you in your job.

10

Disciplinary
and
Grievance
Issues

Most employers have written disciplinary rules, a disciplinary procedure and a grievance procedure which are available to all employees. Indeed it is a legal requirement for employers with 20 or more employees to make available (in writing) to all employees the following information:

- Any disciplinary rules which apply to you;
- The person to whom you should apply if you are dissatisfied with a disciplinary decision (for example if you are given a written warning for misconduct which, in your view, is unfair);
- The name of the person to whom you should apply if you have a

work-related grievance (i.e. any serious work-related problem or complaint);
● How you should go about raising such a grievance.

You should also be clearly told where you can gain access to both the disciplinary procedure and the grievance procedure. If this information is not readily available to you, then you should ask to have the position clarified, and to be given copies of any written disciplinary and grievance procedures.

Disciplinary rules and procedures

Generally a company's disciplinary rules and procedures are aimed at ensuring that disciplinary decisions are always fair, and procedures are applied consistently.

It is extremely important, from the employer's point of view, to apply disciplinary rules and procedures properly. It has been well established in law that failure to follow correct procedure can lead to claims of unfair dismissal (and also claims of breach of contract) from employees who have been dismissed.

The reason for this is that in claims for unfair dismissal, an industrial tribunal will consider not only the reason you were dismissed, but also whether the employer acted reasonably in all the circumstances in dismissing you. This involves consideration of the manner in which the dismissal was carried out, i.e. the procedure which was followed.

This has been the case since 1987 when a case for unfair dismissal was brought by a Mr Polkey following a redundancy situation. As a result of a company reorganisation, Mr Polkey and two of his colleagues had been dismissed on account of redundancy without consultation, without any attempt to find them alternative work and without warning. Thus proper procedures were not followed. It was as a result of this very important case that the House of Lords (to whom the case was eventually appealed) stated: 'Any procedural shortfall will make a dismissal unfair'. There are today very few exceptions to this principle, and employers must follow procedures correctly or risk claims of unfair dismissal against them succeeding.

This means that (in the event that you are dismissed by your employer) you have the right to have the company's disciplinary procedure complied with in all respects. Ultimately, if you are dismissed from your job, and your employer has failed to follow his disciplinary procedure, you will be likely to succeed in a claim for unfair dismissal in an industrial tribunal.

Further information about unfair dismissal is provided in Chapter 13.

CASE STUDY

Mr McLaren was a miner at the time of a miners' strike. During the course of a disagreement, he assaulted another miner and was subsequently convicted in court of assault, and fined. The colliery manager, who took the decision to dismiss Mr McLaren, acted on the outcome of the court proceedings, rather than interviewing Mr McLaren prior to his dismissal. Thus the employer's normal disciplinary procedure was not followed.

Q Did the employer act reasonably in deciding not to follow the disciplinary procedure in these circumstances?

A The Court of Appeal ruled that, despite the circumstances, there could be no justification for a failure to give an employee the chance to explain his conduct.

Based on the case *McLaren v National Coal Board.*

Disciplinary rules

The intent of disciplinary rules at work should be to set standards of conduct and promote fairness and order in the workplace.

If your company has a set of disciplinary rules, then you must either be given a copy, or told where you can see them. Generally, rules cover conduct and behaviour, use of company resources and facilities, timekeeping, absence from work, smoking and safety.

CASE STUDY

Mr McNee worked for Scottish Grain Distillers . The employer had a rule that any unauthorised possession of alcohol at work would lead to summary (immediate) dismissal. One day during a locker search the employer found jars with small amounts of a liquid containing (on analysis) one per cent of ethyl alcohol in the lockers of two employees, one of which was Mr McNee. Both employees were summarily dismissed.

Q Did the company act correctly in enforcing their rule on alcohol in this case?

A The tribunal considered that, even if the liquid could fairly be described as alcohol, the breach of the rules was trivial. Thus the dismissal was unfair.

Based on the case *Scottish Grain Distillers Ltd v McNee & another.*

Disciplinary procedures

Whilst rules set the standards for conduct, disciplinary procedures help the employer to ensure that standards are adhered to, as well as providing a fair and consistent system for dealing with breaches of discipline or unsatisfactory job performance. The key purpose of any employer's disciplinary procedure should be to promote improvement in conduct and performance.

Disciplinary procedures are generally structured in stages along the following lines:

Stage 1: verbal (or oral) warning

This usually consists of a formal face-to-face review between you and your immediate supervisor concerning some minor breach of discipline, or unsatisfactory job performance. Although it is termed a 'verbal (or oral) warning', it is customary for the employer to keep a written record on the personnel file of the fact that the employee has been given a warning, and the reasons for it.

Stage 2: first written warning

A written warning will normally be issued as a result of a fairly serious offence, a collection of minor offences, or where there has been no improvement following a verbal warning.

There should be an interview with the employee (sometimes referred to as a disciplinary hearing), after which the employee will receive a letter (the written warning) containing details of the nature and outcome of the interview.

Stage 3: final written warning

Where the employee's conduct or performance fails to meet the standards set at stage 2, or in the event of a very serious breach of discipline, a final written warning would be issued. This, again, would occur after a formal disciplinary interview between the employee and (normally) a more senior manager.

Stage 4: dismissal

If, despite warnings, the employee's conduct or performance is still below the required standard, then the decision to dismiss may be taken.

Gross misconduct

The term 'gross misconduct' is commonly used to describe very serious breaches of discipline such as fighting, stealing, drunkenness, etc. Your employer should have written guidelines as to what type of conduct constitutes gross misconduct in your particular place of work. There is no legal 'list' of behaviour which would count as gross misconduct, as it will depend on the type of work you do, the working environment and the size of the company. Again, if you do not have access to such information, then you are entitled to ask.

CASE STUDY

Claypotts Construction Ltd had decided that instances when employees over-stayed lunch-breaks in pubs would be regarded as gross misconduct. Employees had been told verbally that such conduct would not be tolerated. Mr McCallum's original terms of employment, however, had stated that such offences would be dealt with by a written warning. One day Mr McCallum had lunch in a pub and over-stayed his break by an hour. He was subsequently dismissed for gross misconduct.

Q Was the employer within his rights to dismiss Mr McCallum for gross misconduct?

A The tribunal said that the employer was not entitled to dismiss for gross misconduct, because in this case the alteration to the rules had not been adequately drawn to the employee's attention. The change in policy had been introduced only verbally and without formal agreement. Consequently Mr McCallum's dismissal was unfair.

Based on the case *Claypotts Construction Ltd* v *McCallum*.

If you are guilty of gross misconduct, you are liable to be dismissed, even if there has been no previous instance of misconduct and you have received no previous disciplinary warnings. This is known as 'summary dismissal'. Furthermore, in cases of summary dismissal, the employer is entitled to dismiss you without notice, or pay in lieu of notice. (Note that this is the only situation in which an employer can legally dismiss an employee without notice).

Your employer must still, however, follow proper procedures, including investigation and consultation, even in cases of gross misconduct. One further point to note is that your employer does not require absolute proof that you are guilty of gross misconduct in order to fairly dismiss you. Provided your employer genuinely believes that you committed a serious offence, and provided this belief is based on reasonable grounds following on from a very thorough investigation, then dismissal may be fair (provided proper procedures have been followed). The concept of 'reasonable belief' here is quite different from the 'beyond reasonable doubt' approach taken by criminal courts.

It is a common myth that employers must always give an employee three warnings before dismissing. This, quite simply, is not true – the employer may enter the disciplinary procedure at any of the stages outlined above, including stage 4 (dismissal). If, for example, a first offence is very serious, there may be justification for a written warning as the first step in the procedure. It will depend on the nature and seriousness of the employee's conduct as to what type of disciplinary action may reasonably be taken.

Suspension from work

Sometimes where an employee has committed a fairly serious offence, the employer may suspend the person from work for a period of time, so that an investigation can be carried out.

Normally, if you are suspended from work in these circumstances, you must continue to be paid your full salary. Suspension without pay could well be illegal under the Wages Act 1986, unless there is a clause in your contract of employment stating that your employer is entitled to suspend without pay in disciplinary circumstances. Further information about illegal deductions from wages is given in Chapter 4, *Deductions from Wages – Legal and Illegal*.

It is normal practice for employers to give a reason for suspending an employee, and so you should ensure you are told clearly why you are being suspended, and any background information leading to the suspension.

Your right to fair treatment

At all stages of the disciplinary procedure, your employer should follow certain guidelines. This is important in legal terms (if you are subsequently dismissed), as well as from the point of view of fair and consistent treatment of people. Failure to adhere to these procedural formalities could mean that the employer would lose the case if an (ex)-employee subsequently claimed unfair dismissal.

The following 12 points – with case studies where appropriate – form a check-list of the manner in which your employer should proceed, if you are subject to disciplinary action. The employer should:

1 *Investigate (promptly) to try to establish the facts and explore background circumstances*, for example checking records, talking to witnesses. The employer must not prejudge what you have done or assume you are 'guilty'.

CASE STUDY

Mrs Maloney was employed by Nicholas Hotels as a ledger clerk in the accounts department. The company had decided to computerise its accounts department, with the result that Mrs Maloney was expected to input balances on the sales ledger into the computer, instead of working manually.

(CASE STUDY CONTINUED)
She was given one day's training on the new system and offered the opportunity to practise on a training terminal which the company provided.

Mrs Maloney had problems with the new system and one day she had an argument with her manager regarding some book-keeping work which she had been doing partly on computer and partly manually. Following this incident Mrs Maloney was threatened with a warning. Mrs Maloney was distressed by this and subsequently was signed off work for a week by her doctor, suffering from depression.

The company then decided that Mrs Maloney was unable to cope with the new computer system and, whilst she was off sick, sent her a letter terminating her employment.

Q Was this a fair dismissal?

A This is an excellent example of a catalogue of procedural flaws which made the dismissal unfair. The tribunal pointed out that:

- Mrs Maloney had never been given any warnings (she was only threatened with one, which, of course, is not the same thing);
- She had not been told that her employer was dissatisfied with her performance, thus she had been given no opportunity to improve;
- One day's tuition was inadequate for someone who had not previously worked with computers;
- Mrs Maloney was not interviewed prior to her dismissal, so she was not given the chance to discuss the problems or put forward any defence;
- The dismissal was handled in an arbitrary way.

Based on the case *Maloney v Nicholas Hotels Ltd.*

2 *Establish that your performance / conduct is worse than the required standard.* For example if the problem is poor attendance, your supervisor might seek advice from Personnel Department as to what is an acceptable or average level of absence within the company as a whole. It would be unfair to 'pick on' you if your conduct or performance is no worse than anybody else's.

3 *Arrange an interview with you.* You should be given reasonable notice of the time and place of the interview, given adequate information (in advance) as to what the interview is about and told that the interview is to be a disciplinary one. Such an interview may be called a 'disciplinary interview', a 'disciplinary hearing' or simply a 'disciplinary meeting'.

CASE STUDY

Mr Spink had been employed for about 12 years as a sales representative. His manager discovered that Mr Spink had failed to make scheduled visits to a large number of the company's customers, although his reports stated that the visits had been made. The manager subsequently investigated and put together details of calls which should have been made by Mr. Spink but had not taken place.

It was decided to call Mr Spink in for a disciplinary hearing. Prior to the hearing, Mr Spink was told that management had complaints about the way in which he was carrying out his job, and that the meeting would be a fact-finding one.

At the disciplinary hearing Mr Spink's manager went through all the calls which had not been made but had been reported, and asked for Mr Spink's comments. Mr Spink said he could not remember details and became confused. Later he fell silent. Ultimately, after a further disciplinary hearing, he was dismissed for gross misconduct.

Q Was Mr Spink treated in accordance with fair and correct procedure?

A This was an unfair dismissal. The company, without doubt, had very good reason to dismiss Mr Spink, but there was a key procedural flaw. The company had failed to inform Mr Spink of the nature and seriousness of the allegations against him. He should have been told in advance of the first disciplinary hearing that he was believed to have falsified his reports. Because he was denied this information, the disciplinary meeting did not constitute a fair hearing.

Based on the case *Spink v Express Foods Group Ltd.*

4   *Advise you that you have the right (if you wish) to be accompanied at the disciplinary interview by a colleague or trade union representative of your choice.* The information to be given to you under 3 and 4 may be provided either verbally or in writing.

CASE STUDY

Mr Goodchild, who worked for Rank Xerox, was accused of fiddling company expenses. The company's disciplinary procedure gave employees the right to have representation at disciplinary interviews, but the employer would not allow Mr Goodchild to be accompanied at the disciplinary interview by a colleague who was an official of a trade union which was not recognised by the company. They did, however, permit Mr Goodchild's solicitor to be present.

Mr Goodchild admitted the offence, but argued that it was justified on the grounds that he had spent the money on company business. The company

(CASE STUDY CONTINUED)
refused to accept this excuse and dismissed him.

Q Did the company breach procedure by failing to allow Mr. Goodchild to be accompanied at the disciplinary interview by the trade union official, bearing in mind that they did permit his solicitor to be present?

A Yes, the dismissal was unfair on those grounds. The employee's right is to be accompanied by a colleague of his choice.

Based on the case *Rank Xerox (UK) Ltd* v *Goodchild & Others*.

5   *Conduct the interview in private, and keep it confidential.*

6   *Give you a fair hearing.* During the interview, the employer should tell you clearly what the complaint is, by going through the facts and explaining why there is a problem. For example, if the problem relates to alleged poor time-keeping, the employer should be able to refer to specific dates and times when you supposedly came to work late.

CASE STUDY
Mr Louies was accused of being involved in the theft of material worth about £200 from his employer's stores. During the employer's investigation, written statements were taken from 12 employees. At Mr Louies' disciplinary hearing, he was told that there were two independent statements dealing with his alleged involvement in the theft, but he was not shown the statements.

At the appeal stage Mr Louies asked what the statements said, but was given only minimum information about them. He was not allowed to see the statements.

Q Was the company justified in refusing to give Mr Louies full information about what the witnesses' statements said?

A No, this refusal made Mr Louies's dismissal unfair. The tribunal ruled that where written statements were being relied upon to judge whether or not an employee was guilty of an offence, then the employee should be shown them, or at least be talked through them in depth.

Based on the case *Louies* v *Coventry Hood and Seating Co Ltd*.

You should be given every opportunity to talk openly about the problem – and to explain any factors which might be contributing to the problem, for example family difficulties may have contributed to poor timekeeping / attendance.

You must be given plenty of opportunity to state your side of the story fully, and the interview should be conducted in an objective and neutral manner. A fair hearing will always be fundamental to fair discipline.

7   *Specify the improvement required and discuss with you means of achieving the required improvements in performance/conduct.* This may include the offer of training, coaching or guidance, particularly if the problem relates to poor job performance.

8   *Specify a (reasonable) timescale within which you are required to improve.*

9   *Tell you clearly, in the event that performance/conduct does not improve, what further disciplinary action will be taken against you.*

CASE STUDY

Ms Lawrie was a researcher working for British Sulphur Corporation. She recently had been moved from doing pure research work to writing for the company journal. Although she was competent in most aspects of her job, her written work for the journal was sub-standard. She told her department head that she did not want to write any more articles for the journal, and shortly afterwards she was dismissed.

Q   Did the company act fairly in dismissing Ms Lawrie?

A   No, the dismissal was unfair on the grounds that Ms Lawrie had not been formally warned that failure to improve would mean dismissal. It was also relevant that she had been given insufficient instruction and an insufficient period of time to improve her journalistic skills.

Based on the case *British Sulphur Corporation* v *Lawrie*.

---

10   *Inform you of the outcome of the disciplinary interview.* You should be told what the disciplinary penalty is (e.g. written warning), the length of time any warning will be held on file, the likely consequences of further misconduct/failure to improve, and the reasons for the decision.

There is no legal minimum or maximum time limit for a disciplinary warning to be held on an employee's file. This is a matter for your company to decide and should be stated in the disciplinary procedure. You should ask, if you are not sure, how long a warning given to you will remain on your file. After the stipulated time period, the warning should, in general circumstances, be disregarded or removed from your file completely. Again this is not a legal requirement, hence it is advisable to check with your employer.

11   *Inform you that you have the right to appeal against the disciplinary decision* (see next Section for further information).

12   *Follow your company's disciplinary procedure exactly.*

If your employer fails to follow any of these guidelines during disciplinary action taken against you, you are perfectly entitled to object to the manner in which you are being treated. If your company recognises a trade union, you can gain useful advice and help from the trade union representative, and, if you wish, be represented by that person at disciplinary interviews. Otherwise you are quite entitled to insist on being treated in accordance with the guidelines given here.

UK law, however, provides no specific remedy for unfair disciplinary warnings. It is only if you are dismissed that procedural fairness becomes paramount. Your only possible legal remedy for unfair disciplinary warnings would be a breach of contract claim.

Appeals

The right to appeal against a disciplinary decision (e.g. a warning) is fundamental to fairness. You must therefore be told of your right to appeal and how you should proceed to make the appeal. You should also be informed of the time limit for lodging an appeal and given the name or designation of the person to whom you should appeal.

CASE STUDY

Mr Shearlaw was dismissed from British Aerospace for misconduct. Although a disciplinary hearing had taken place, Mr Shearlaw had not been told that the hearing was to be a disciplinary one, nor that dismissal could be the outcome. At the hearing itself he was not given the chance to explain his behaviour.

Mr Shearlaw appealed against the decision to dismiss him and a full appeal hearing took place, during which he was given full opportunity to be represented, state his case and have it properly considered The appeal was rejected, however, and the dismissal was implemented.

Q   Did the fact that a proper appeal took place make any difference to the earlier deficiencies in procedure?

A   Yes, the tribunal ruled that the appeal amounted to a complete and comprehensive re-hearing, thus curing the earlier defects in procedure.

Based on the case *Shearlaw* v *British Aerospace.*

The right of appeal should normally be to a more senior level of management, but in any event to a different manager from the one who took the disciplinary action against you. Failure to make you aware of your right to appeal would constitute a serious breach of procedure, which would, in all probability, render a subsequent dismissal unfair in law.

CASE STUDY

Mr Byrne, who was employed by BOC Ltd., was falsifying his overtime claims. His manager investigated the claims, consulted the personnel department to establish the correct procedure for handling the matter and ultimately took the decision to dismiss Mr Byrne.

When Mr Byrne appealed, the appeal was conducted by the same manager.

Q Was the appeal hearing fair, and if not, would this affect the outcome of Mr Byrne's unfair dismissal claim?

A The tribunal concluded that the appeal hearing was unfair because the manager who conducted it was the same person who had been involved in handling the matter to begin with. This made the dismissal unfair.

Based on the case *Byrne* v *BOC Ltd.*

Grievance procedures

Every employee is entitled to know how he or she can seek redress for an employment-related grievance. This information must be provided to you in writing, and is usually presented in the form of a grievance procedure.

The objective of a grievance procedure should be to settle problems or disputes fairly and as simply as possible. The main aim is to ensure that minor issues do not escalate into major disputes. Your company's procedure should be simple and rapid in operation. Some features of a good grievance procedure would be:

- The grievance should normally be discussed first between the employee and his immediate supervisor/manager. Often this results in the matter being resolved to everyone's satisfaction, so no further formal action is needed.
- If the grievance cannot be resolved with the immediate supervisor, then the employee should have the right to take the grievance to the next level of management. At this stage, the employee should be advised of the right to be accompanied during the discussion by a colleague or trade union representative (if he wishes).

- There should be a right of appeal to another higher level of management.
- Timescales should be defined for the grievance to be heard at each stage. The timescales should be short, but realistic, bearing in mind that the matter may involve senior managers who may have many other demands on their time.

Some companies' grievance procedures allow for the matter to be referred to arbitration in the final stage, for example to ACAS (Advisory, Conciliation and Arbitration Service).

If you have a grievance, or serious work-based problem, and you are not sure what to do, you should ask either your boss, or a trade union representative (if your employer recognises a trade union) to clarify the correct procedure.

Questions and Answers

Q My company has a set of rules regarding time-keeping and conduct. What would happen to me if I broke one of the rules?

A You would probably get a disciplinary warning from your employer. Depending on the seriousness of your actions, that might be a verbal warning, or a written warning. Ultimately, if you persist with the misconduct, you could be dismissed.

Q I have never been given a copy of my employer's disciplinary rules. Don't I have the right to see them?

A Yes, if your employer has 20 or more employees, he must make a copy of your company's disciplinary rules available to you. You should ask your boss or someone in personnel department to see a copy.

Q Last week my boss was angry with me when I failed to complete some work on time. He threatened me with a warning. What does this mean?

A A disciplinary warning may be given to you verbally (i.e. you are told you have done something wrong, and a record of it is kept on your personnel file) or in writing (you receive a letter explaining what you have done wrong). Either way, you should not be given a disciplinary warning without first being given the chance to talk through the problem and put forward your side of the story.

Warnings are usually held on an employee's file for a period of time, typically 12 months, and then removed from the record (provided there has been no further instance of misconduct). If an employee has been given a series of warnings for misconduct, then he may eventually be (fairly) dismissed.

Your boss should not have threatened you with a warning. Even if the failure to meet the deadline was your fault, you should have been given the chance to talk the matter through. If it happens again, you should insist on the opportunity to talk about the problem.

There is more detailed information within this Chapter on this rather complex subject.

Q I have already received a written warning for failing to comply with my employer's paperwork procedures. I wasn't too worried about it because I thought you couldn't be dismissed unless you had had three warnings. Am I right?

A No, this is simply not true. There is no law which compels an employer to give a minimum number of warnings before dismissing an employee. It all depends on the seriousness of the misconduct.

Q Years ago, I was given a written warning for something I had done wrong. Since then I have kept my nose clean, but I am concerned that this warning might still be on my record, and could affect my chances of promotion. How do I stand in law?

A There is no law which compels employers to remove old disciplinary warnings from personnel files. Your best bet therefore would be to express your concerns to your boss, and ask him to establish whether or not the warning is still held on file.

You could also read your company's disciplinary procedure to establish what it says regarding the removal of warnings from the record. If the procedure says that warnings should be removed from files after a set time period, then you would have the right to insist on the document's removal.

Finally, if your company's personnel records are computerised, then you have the right to ask to see a copy of the computerised information held about you under the Data Protection Act (see Chapter 9).

Q What does the term 'gross misconduct' mean?

A The term 'gross misconduct' is used to describe very serious breaches of discipline such as fighting, stealing, drunkenness, etc. Your employer should have written guidelines explaining what type of conduct constitutes gross misconduct in your particular workplace. There is no legal list of such misconduct.

Q Someone I know was dismissed for breaching his company's safety regulations. He didn't receive any notice pay, or warnings. Surely this is illegal?

A Employers are entitled to carry out what is known as 'summary dismissal' if an employee has committed some act of serious misconduct (known as gross misconduct). In the case of summary dismissal, no notice, or pay in lieu of notice needs to be given to the employee. Furthermore, summary dismissal may be carried out regardless of whether or not the employee has had previous warnings. So your friend's dismissal was not illegal as such.

It is worth noting, however, that even in cases such as these, the employer must still follow proper procedures, including investigation, and consulting with the employee to give him the opportunity to explain his actions, etc. Failure to follow procedure will render a dismissal unfair, even in cases of gross misconduct.

Q Can I be suspended from work without pay if I am guilty of misconduct?
A Normally no, unless your contract of employment specifically states that suspension without pay can be used as a penalty for misconduct.
If you are suspended without pay, and provided there is no such clause in your contract of employment, you could take a claim to an industrial tribunal on the basis that there has been an unlawful deduction from your wages.

Q Recently I was given a written warning by my boss for something which I considered quite trivial. Can I complain of unfair treatment?
A Yes, you can appeal internally against the decision to give you a written warning. Normally such an appeal would be to a manager more senior than your boss. Your contract of employment, or the company's grievance procedure, should state who you can appeal to and how you should go about it. If your company recognises a trade union, you can gain useful advice and help from the trade union representative, and, if you wish, be represented by that person.

There is no right in law to make a complaint to an industrial tribunal about unfair disciplinary warnings, so an internal appeal would be your only remedy.

Q I have had a few problems in my work since moving to a new department. A colleague has suggested raising a formal grievance. What would this involve?
A Normally the first step in a grievance procedure is to ask for an interview with your own supervisor or manager to discuss the problem formally, and be given the opportunity to air your views and concerns. If your company recognises a trade union, you could ask your trade union representative to help you.

You should also have been given written information about what you should do if you have an employment-related grievance. Check your written terms of employment, or alternatively ask your boss to see a copy of the company's grievance procedure.

The objective of a grievance procedure is to settle problems or disputes fairly and as simply as possible, and to prevent them from escalating into major issues.

11
Your Trade Union Rights

All employees have the right to belong to an independent trade union of their choice, or to refuse to belong to a trade union or staff association.

To join a particular trade union, you will, of course, need to satisfy the union's normal membership rules, which may, for example, involve restriction of membership to people in specific trades or professions.

Your employer must not put pressure on you to join a union, or not to join a union. Equally, your employer must not penalise you in any way for belonging to a union, or not belonging to a union (see later in this chapter under 'Action short of dismissal' for further information).

Right to take part in trade union activities

If you choose to belong to a particular trade union, you may wish to take part in its activities. Such activities may include attending union meetings, helping with union administration, and seeking advice from officials. Going on strike, however, does not count in this context as a 'union activity'!

CASE STUDY

Mr Lane and Mr Knowles were employed as asbestos strippers. Mr Lane was a member of the General Municipal and Boilermakers Union (GMB) and took an active part in trade union activities. Mr Knowles was not a member of the union. When a GMB meeting was held with a view to recruiting new members, there was evidence that the company believed that Mr Knowles had attended, even although neither Mr Lane nor Mr Knowles had in fact attended.

When the company undertook a redundancy exercise, both Mr Lane and Mr Knowles were dismissed along with 18 other employees. Shortly afterwards seven new workers were recruited. The two men submitted claims for unfair dismissal asserting that their dismissals were due to trade union activities.

Q Was there enough evidence for an industrial tribunal to conclude that the dismissals were due to trade union activities?

A The tribunal found first that there were indications that the company was clearly antagonistic to trade union activities. Secondly they accepted that there was a genuine redundancy situation, but noted that the company's need was to reduce the workforce by 13, not 20 (seven new employees had been recruited).

They concluded that the company had taken advantage of the situation to get rid of those involved in trade union activities. Consequently they decided that the principal reason for Mr Lane's and Mr Knowles's dismissals was their actual or intended membership and supposed participation in the activities of the GMB. Both dismissals were found to be unfair.

Based on the case *Controlled Demolition Group Ltd* v *Lane and Knowles*.

The law states that, where the union is an independent trade union recognised by your employer, you have the right to reasonable time off (without pay) for union activities. Furthermore, provided you take part in union activities at 'an appropriate time', then you must not be penalised. More specifically, your protection is as follows:

- Not to be dismissed for taking part in union activities;
- Not to have action short of dismissal taken against you to prevent or deter you from taking part in union activities (see 'Action short of dismissal' later in this chapter);
- Not to be chosen for redundancy because of your participation in union activities.

CASE STUDY

Mr Shaw wished to be nominated as a shop steward, but was not accepted for this role by his employer. He told management of his intention to call a meeting of union members. Management said nothing in reply. When the meeting was subsequently held, it led to an hour's stoppage of work.

Q Was Mr Shaw taking part in union activities at an appropriate time when he attended the meeting?

A The Court of Appeal in this case ruled that Mr Shaw did not take action at an appropriate time – there was no evidence that the employer had consented to the meeting being held.

Based on the case *Marley Tile Co Ltd* v *Shaw*.

An 'appropriate time' is therefore a time which is either outside your normal working hours (for example during your lunch break) or else a time within working hours which your employer has expressly agreed that you may take part in trade union activities.

Trade union subscriptions

It is customary for employers who recognise a union to have an arrangement under which trade union subscriptions are deducted from employees' wages at source, and paid over directly to the union. This arrangement is known as 'check-off'.

If you join a union, it is likely you will be asked by your employer to sign your agreement to a check-off arrangement. There may be a clause in your contract of employment stating that, if you join a union, you must agree to a check-off arrangement. In any event your employer is not entitled to deduct your union subscriptions from your wages without having obtained such express agreement in writing from you. You are also entitled to end your trade union subscription at any time on giving written notice to your employer (if you leave the union).

Under the Trade Union Reform and Employment Rights Act 1993 your employer must obtain renewed authorisation from you for deduction of union subscriptions every three years. You may, however, still withdraw authorisation of check-off at any time provided you give written notice.

Furthermore, if subscription rates rise, then your employer must give you written notification of this, stating the amount of the increase and the new level of subscription to be deducted from your wages. The notice given must be not less than one month, and must include a reminder that you have the right to withdraw your authorisation to the check-off arrangement at any time.

The closed shop – what it means today

Closed shop agreements (more correctly referred to as union membership agreements) are now unenforceable in law. A traditional closed shop agreement between employer and union imposed the condition that unless an employee was a member of a particular trade union, he or she could not be employed by the company.

It is now illegal for a company to refuse to employ, or to dismiss a person because he or she is, or is not, a member of a trade union, or refuses to join one. So in effect it is unlawful for an employer to try to operate a closed shop agreement.

CASE STUDY

Mr Ashfield was a member of a trade union. He proposed to leave the union unless it changed some of its policies. He was later dismissed on the pretext of dishonesty.

Q Could Mr Ashfield claim that he was dismissed on account of his proposing to leave the union?

A Yes, Mr Ashfield's dismissal was unfair.

Based on the case *Crosville Motor Services Ltd* v *Ashfield*.

Representation by your trade union

Whilst you may choose to belong to a trade union, your employer has no legal obligation to recognise the trade union, i.e. to allow the union to negotiate on behalf of employees. This is the case even where a substantial number of employees are members of the union, and wish union recognition. Even then trade union recognition by the employer is entirely voluntary.

Furthermore, where a union recognition agreement is in place, your employer can still choose to end it at any time by giving the appropriate notice to the union. This is the case regardless of the wishes of the workforce. This is known as 'de-recognition'.

Collective agreements

Collective agreements may be set up between employer and union to cover negotiations on some or all of the following:

● Pay
● Terms and conditions of employment

- Recruitment procedures
- Procedures for termination of employment (including redundancy procedures)
- Disciplinary and grievance procedures
- Job evaluation and grading
- Allocation of work and job duties of different groups of workers

Where a recognition agreement does exist between your employer and a trade union, it is likely that the key terms and conditions of your employment will be negotiated and agreed on your behalf by the union. This is known as collective bargaining.

For this to be valid in law, your contract of employment must contain a statement that your terms of employment are subject to variation in accordance with the terms of the union collective agreement. This is what is meant by incorporation of a collective agreement. It means that your terms and conditions of employment (e.g. hours of work) can be changed as a result of agreement between your employer and the union without your personal involvement.

This of course does not alter the fact that the contract of employment you have entered into is an individual contract between you and your employer. It just means that, if a collective agreement is in force in your workplace, you have effectively agreed to be bound by the terms settled between your employer and the union.

The interesting thing about this provision is that it can apply to all employees including those who are not members of the union, provided the majority of employees are members, and the non-members could choose to belong to the union if they wished.

Since the Trade Union Reform and Employment Rights Act 1993, all employees must be given written particulars of any collective agreements which directly affect their terms and conditions of employment.

Many employers are today moving away from collective agreements and returning to so-called 'personal contracts' and de-recognition of unions. Collective agreements in Britain are rarely legally binding between the employer and the union, and are therefore not enforceable in law. They are therefore held to be voluntary arrangements.

Some companies are nowadays offering financial inducement (e.g. a pay rise) to employees who agree to sign a new personal contract instead of being governed by a collective bargaining arrangement. This is because they wish to move away from contracts where pay rates are negotiated via collective bargaining, and instead operate personal contracts of employment with each employee. Such financial inducement in this situation is now perfectly legal. You may, of course, still choose to remain a member of the union because you retain that right even if your employer elects to de-recognise the union.

Appointment of safety representatives

Where your employer recognises an independent trade union, the union may appoint safety representatives to promote health and safety at work. If you have any concern regarding your health, safety or welfare at work, you may then complain to the safety representative who will have the authority to investigate potential hazards and raise any relevant issues with management on your behalf. In this situation safety representatives can represent all employees, and not just those who are trade union members.

Safety representatives may be appointed where there is no recognised trade union, but they do not have the legal status of those appointed by recognised trade unions.

Employees who are nominated as safety representatives have the right to reasonable time off work with pay to enable them to carry out their duties and undertake any necessary training. Please refer to Chapter 5 for more information about this.

Refusal of employment on the grounds of trade union membership or non-union membership

If you are seeking a new job, your prospective employer cannot legally oblige you to join a trade union, or insist that you should not be a member of a union. Thus it is illegal for an employer to refuse employment on grounds related to union membership. More specifically, it is illegal to refuse employment because the job applicant is unwilling to accept a requirement to join a union, not to join a union, or to leave a union.

The relevant legislation covers all employers and also employment agencies.

CASE STUDY

Ms Fitzpatrick was employed by British Rail. In her previous job, she had been very active in union matters, but had not informed her present employer of this when she was recruited. When British Rail discovered her record of union activities in her previous job, she was dismissed, ostensibly on the grounds of deceit in concealing her former union activities.

Q Was this dismissal fair under the circumstances?

A The tribunal refused to believe the reason for dismissal put forward by the employer. They found that the primary reason for Ms Fitzpatrick's dismissal was that her previous union activities had given her the reputation

(CASE STUDY CONTINUED)
of being a disruptive influence. Ms Fitzpatrick was thus dismissed because her employer believed that she proposed to take part in union activities. This meant that the dismissal was automatically unfair.

In this case study, if British Rail had declined to employ Ms Fitzpatrick on the grounds of her union activities in her previous job, then this would, similarly, have been illegal.

Based on the case *Fitzpatrick v British Railways Board*.

If you think you have been refused employment on grounds related to union membership, then you may complain of unlawful refusal of employment to an industrial tribunal. You must make your tribunal application within three months of the action which gave rise to your complaint.

Action short of dismissal

Action short of dismissal (on the grounds of trade union membership or non-membership) is not defined in law, but would include situations like discrimination in promotion, threats of dismissal or refusal to offer training. Such action will be illegal if it is taken for the purpose of:

● Putting pressure on you to join a union;
● Preventing or deterring you from being or becoming a member of a union;
● Preventing or deterring you from taking part in union activities at an appropriate time;
● Penalising you for doing any of the above;
● Forcing you to make payments in the event of your not joining, or leaving, a union.

All employees, regardless of length of service or number of hours worked, have the right not to have such action short of dismissal taken against them. You have the right to make a claim to an industrial tribunal within three months of the action complained of.

One actual case where a successful claim was made to an industrial tribunal concerned an employee of the Department of Trade. An unfairly adverse report was written about the employee in question because of his union activities, with the result that he was not considered for promotion. Since there was to be no other opportunity for promotion for another year, he was awarded an amount equivalent to the difference between his net current salary and the net salary he would have earned if he had been promoted.

Right not to be dismissed on trade union grounds

Your final, and perhaps most important, right in this area is the right not to be dismissed, or chosen for redundancy, because you are a member of an independent trade union, because you are not a member of a union, or because you refuse to join a union.

Any dismissal which is on such trade union grounds will be automatically unfair and a dismissed employee has the right to complain to an industrial tribunal. This right exists regardless of length of service, number of hours worked or the age of the individual. The application must be made within three months of the dismissal.

Where it is shown at tribunal that the reason for the dismissal is trade-union related, the compensation which is awarded is likely to be substantially higher than in other types of unfair dismissal case.

Your 'right' to strike – and the possible consequences

There is no such thing as a 'right' to strike in law. Going on strike, or taking other industrial action, is regarded in law as a serious breach of contract by the employee, which entitles the employer to dismiss summarily (i.e. immediate dismissal without notice).

A 'strike' is generally regarded as being a complete stoppage of work. 'Other industrial action' may mean action short of a strike such as a go-slow, an overtime ban or picketing, provided these activities are carried out for the purpose of applying pressure on the employer with regard to terms and conditions of employment.

A 'lock-out' on the other hand occurs (probably following on from industrial action) when an employer either closes the work-place, suspends work, or refuses to allow employees to work as a result of a dispute, where the action is taken in order to apply pressure on the employees to accept certain terms and conditions of employment.

If, therefore, you take part in a strike or other industrial action, you should be aware that your employer has the legal right to dismiss you, and there is nothing you can do about it. This is because industrial tribunals are barred from hearing a claim of unfair dismissal, if the reason for the dismissal was that the employee was on strike at the time of the dismissal. However, employers must take care when dismissing strikers to treat people consistently otherwise the tribunal bar will not apply.

If the employer dismisses some, but not all, employees who are taking part in an official strike, then this will enable those dismissed to have their claim for unfair dismissal heard at an industrial tribunal. Equally if a strike is taking place in your employer's premises, but you are not taking part in it (meaning that you are working normally), then your employer cannot (fairly) dismiss you.

It is important to pay regard to your position if you are off sick or on holiday during a strike. The legal position is that if you have been associated with a strike in any way, and if you are then off sick or on holiday during the strike itself, you may still be regarded as having taken part in the strike (and thus dismissed). This would occur unless you have specifically notified your employer that you are not taking part in the strike. In such circumstances, you would be well advised to notify your employer in writing that you are not taking part in the strike and do not support the strike.

CASE STUDY

Bill worked as a journalist for a newspaper, and was a member of the journalists' trade union. There had been some discontent amongst all the journalists over a period of time about pay, in particular overtime pay for weekend working. The union had held discussions with the employer, but no agreement had been reached.

Bill took a severe bout of flu and was signed off sick by his doctor. While he was off sick, a strike began at his place of work. Bill was unable to become actively involved in the strike, due to his illness. Subsequently the strikers were all dismissed, and so was Bill. Bill claimed that, because he had been off sick at the time of the strike, he could not be legitimately regarded as having taken part in it.

Q Did the company have grounds for dismissing Bill in these circumstances?

A Yes, because he was one of the group of employees associated with the strike. The fact that he was off sick during the actual strike was not a material factor.

Nevertheless the rule is that only those taking part in the strike are liable to be dismissed, and then all strikers must be dismissed, or none at all. If you are one of a group of employees participating in a strike, but you return to work before dismissal of the strikers takes place, then you cannot be legally dismissed. (If you are dismissed, you would have a high chance of success in a claim for unfair dismissal at an industrial tribunal).

A further rule is that, to avoid claims of unfair dismissal, the dismissals must take place during the strike, not before or after it.

Another aspect of going on strike is that there is no obligation on your employer to pay your salary whilst you are on strike.

CASE STUDY

Employees working for a fish merchant were on a shift from 7.00 a.m. to 4.00 p.m. with voluntary overtime in the evenings when it was required. They decided to register their disapproval of a change in conditions which their employer was proposing by refusing the next request to work overtime. They told management they were leaving work at 4.00 p.m. but would return to work the next day as usual. When they turned up the next morning, they were all dismissed.

Q Were the employees dismissed during the strike action?

A The tribunal concluded that the employees were no longer taking part in strike action at the time of their dismissals. Thus the employees were eligible to have their claims for unfair dismissal heard.

Based on the case *Glenrose (Fish Merchants) Ltd* v *Chapman & Others.*

So, before deciding to go on strike, you should think carefully of the financial consequences, since you are unlikely to be paid your salary during a strike, and you may well be dismissed from your job with no opportunity of recourse to an industrial tribunal.

Re-employment after strike action and dismissal

There is a legal period of three months after an official strike where the 'all or none' rule described in the previous section must continue to apply. This means that the employer cannot re-employ some, but not all, of the strikers during this period. If all are re-employed, then clearly there can be no claims of unfair dismissal. If, however, selected employees are offered re-employment, then those who are not made such an offer can make a claim to an industrial tribunal. Note that there is no obligation on the employer to offer re-employment to ex-employees all at the same time, as long as the offers are all made within three months of the dismissals. Because of this, dismissed employees have a period of six months (from the date of their dismissal) in which to make their claim to an industrial tribunal, rather than the usual three month period.

CASE STUDY

Mr Laffin was dismissed whilst on strike and after the dispute was over the employer wished to re-engage its workers. However there was not enough work for the original number of employees, and because Mr Laffin had a poor record with regard to time-keeping and other matters, he was not offered re-employment. The employer argued that Mr Laffin's prior conduct was the reason for not re-engaging him.

(CASE STUDY CONTINUED)

Q Could Mr Laffin bring a claim for unfair dismissal because he was not offered re-employment?

A The tribunal commented that Mr Laffin's conduct before the strike would not, of itself, have justified dismissal. Hence refusal to re-engage him on the grounds of his conduct was not justified. Thus Mr Laffin's claim for unfair dismissal was heard and was ruled unfair.

Based on the case *Laffin & Another v Fashion Industries (Hartlepool) Ltd.*

After three months have passed since the date of the dismissals, the employer can please himself as to whether he re-employs some, all or none of the strikers.

Re-engagement of workers who have been dismissed during strike action does not have to be on identical terms and conditions. Provided the changes to the terms and conditions are not substantial or unreasonable, an employer may offer dismissed strikers re-engagement on different terms and conditions.

The above provisions on dismissal and re-employment apply only in the event of an official strike i.e. one authorised by the union. If employees go on strike unofficially, then the employer is free to choose to dismiss any employee on strike, without the requirement to treat all strikers equally. The same provision applies to re-employment within three months. In other words, if you take part in an unofficial strike and are consequently dismissed, then you will have absolutely no right to claim unfair dismissal under any circumstances whatsoever.

Secret ballots

The law requires a trade union to hold a secret (postal) ballot when it wishes its members to agree to strike action. The ballot must always be held before the union organises the industrial action. More recent legislation requires unions to give the employer seven days notice of its intention to hold a ballot, and a further seven days notice if strike action is planned.

For the ballot to be conducted properly, and before industrial action can proceed, all employees who might take part in the industrial action must be given the opportunity to vote, and the result must show that the majority of those voting wish to take part in industrial action.

Without such a secret ballot, any industrial action will be illegal, unofficial, and almost certainly unsupported by the union.

You, as an individual, can in fact apply to a court for an order to prevent a union from inducing you (or other employees) to take part in a strike, if a properly conducted secret ballot has not first of all taken place.

What happens if you refuse to strike?

Employees who are union members are entitled to make up their own minds as to whether they should go on strike. This applies even where an official strike has been called by the union, and the majority of employees plan to take part. Unions are no longer allowed to discipline their members who refuse to take part in strike action. In effect, therefore, you have complete freedom of choice in this matter. Bearing in mind the potentially serious consequences of going on strike (i.e. you may lose your job), this freedom of choice is paramount.

Questions and Answers

Q I have recently become a member of the trade union which is officially recognised by my employer. Can I take time off work to take part in the activities of the union?

A Yes, within reason, although you do not have the right to be paid for any time off work taken for this purpose.

Q Having enquired about joining my firm's trade union, I was told that, if I join, I must agree to a 'check-off' arrangement. What is this?

A Check-off is an arrangement under which trade union subscriptions are deducted from employees' wages at source, and paid over directly to the union.

Q I am starting a new job soon. Most of the employees at the new company belong to a particular trade union. Must I join?

A No, you have complete freedom of choice in law as to whether you join, or do not join, the union. It is now illegal for a company to operate what is known as a closed shop agreement, i.e. an arrangement whereby all employees must belong to the union.

Q A large number of the people I work with are members of the same trade union. We would like our employer to recognise the union for the purpose of pay negotiations, but management are against it. Don't they have to recognise the union, if a certain percentage of employees are members?

A No, your employer has no legal obligation to recognise the trade union, i.e. to allow the union to negotiate on behalf of employees. This is the case even where a substantial number of employees are members of the union, and wish union recognition. Even then trade union recognition by the employer is entirely voluntary.

Q The company where I work operates a collective agreement with the trade union, and I have been told in writing that my terms and conditions of employment are subject to negotiations between management and the union. But I am personally not a member of the trade union, so how can it be right for my terms of employment to be subject to union negotiations?

A The fact that a collective agreement is in force in your workplace means you have effectively agreed (when you started work) to be bound by the terms settled between your employer and the union. This provision applies to all employees including those who are not members of the union.

Q I am currently seeking a new job and have three interviews lined up. In my present job I am a shop steward, and have been active in trade union issues all my working life. Could this count against me at interview?

A No, it is illegal for an employer to refuse employment on grounds related to union membership or union activities.

Q If I take part in a strike, can I be sacked?

A Yes, and, provided all strikers are sacked and none re-employed within three months, then you are not eligible to make a claim to an industrial tribunal for unfair dismissal.

Q The trade union of which I am a member has called an official strike. I personally do not agree with the decision to strike. Do I have to take part?

A No, employees are entitled to make up their own minds as to whether they should go on strike. This applies even where an official strike has been called by the union, and the majority of employees plans to take part. You cannot be penalised in any way for refusing to take part in the strike.

PART III: LEAVING EMPLOYMENT

12

Termination of Your Employment

A contract of employment may come to an end in a variety of different ways. For example, you may choose to resign from your job, and, provided you give your employer proper notice according to your contract, then you are entitled to do this at any time.

Alternatively your contract may be terminated by your employer for any one of a number of reasons. Details of fair and unfair dismissals are given in Chapter 13.

There are other ways in which a contract of employment can terminate, for example:

- Either you or your employer dies;
- You are employed to carry out a specific task, and the contract ends on the completion of this task (known as termination by performance);
- The contract ends by mutual agreement;
- The contract is 'frustrated' – i.e. it comes to an end because of some unforeseen event which results in you being unable to fulfil your duties,

161

e.g. imprisonment;

● Your company is wound up (i.e. ceases to trade) on account of insolvency;

● You are retired (more information about retirement is given later in this chapter);

● You are working on a fixed-term contract and it expires without being renewed.

The last three situations on the above list are dismissals in law, whereas the others do not constitute dismissals.

CASE STUDY

Mr Ryan worked for the same employer on a job-by-job basis for about five years. During this period he worked on 31 different jobs which varied in length from 1–11 weeks. Eventually there was no more work and, in order to claim a redundancy payment, Mr Ryan tried to claim that he had been dismissed on account of redundancy.

Q Did a dismissal take place in these circumstances?

A No, the tribunal concluded that the contract had been terminated by performance, meaning that no dismissal had taken place in law. Mr Ryan had genuinely been employed on a series of contracts for the duration of each job. Thus he was ineligible to claim a redundancy payment (or unfair dismissal).

Based on the case *Ryan* v *Shipboard Maintenance Ltd.*

Giving notice

The amount of notice required to terminate a contract of employment depends primarily on what has been agreed between you and your employer in the contract of employment. By law, however, both employer and employee are entitled to be given a minimum period of notice when the contract of employment is terminated. It is illegal to give notice which is less than the statutory minimum period. Details of statutory periods of notice are given in the next section 'Notice on resignation' and in the section titled 'Notice on dismissal'.

Longer periods of notice may, however, be agreed as a term of your contract. If your contract of employment spells out periods of notice which are longer than the statutory minimum periods, then the longer periods of notice will apply.

The amount of notice which you are required to give, and entitled to receive, has nothing to do with the timing of your pay, e.g. monthly or weekly. This is one of the common myths in employment law!

Notice on resignation

It is likely that your contract of employment will state what notice you should give if you wish to resign. If your contract of employment does not specify a notice period, then you are obliged in law to give only one week's notice. This provision comes into effect after one month's service, and is unaffected by your length of service. So, even if you had been employed for many years, you would be obliged to give only one week's notice unless of course your contract states a longer period of notice.

If you resign, your employer cannot legally refuse to accept your resignation (provided you have given the correct amount of notice). More importantly, once your employer has accepted your resignation, you are not entitled subsequently to change your mind. Once given, notice can only be taken back if both parties agree, which means that your employer is under no obligation to allow you to withdraw your notice. It is therefore prudent to be certain about any decision to resign, prior to handing in your notice!

CASE STUDY

Mr Ely had been employed as a spray painter for 13 years when he told his employer that he had accepted a job in Australia, thus he would be resigning in due course. About three months later the personnel manager told Mr Ely that a replacement was being recruited and proposed a leaving date of 21 December. When that date arrived, Mr Ely told his employer that he had changed his mind about going to Australia and no longer intended to leave. The personnel manager, however, stated that, as Mr Ely had already resigned, he was treating the contract as terminated as from that date. Mr Ely subsequently made a claim for unfair dismissal.

Q Did Mr Ely resign or was he dismissed?

A The tribunal decided first that Mr Ely had not in fact resigned because he had not given his employer a date when the contract would be terminated. He had merely notified his employer of his intention to resign at some future date. Consequently, because no resignation had taken place, logically there had been a dismissal in law. The tribunal found that Mr Ely had been dismissed on 21 December, the date from which the employer regarded the contract as terminated.

However, the tribunal was satisfied that the employer had acted genuinely in expecting Mr Ely to resign and ruled that, under all the circumstances, the dismissal was a fair one.

Note that this type of dismissal could well prove to be unfair, depending on the circumstances. For example if you genuinely tell your employer that you plan to resign in the near future and you are immediately dismissed for no good reason, then it is likely that an industrial tribunal would consider your employer's actions as unreasonable.

Based on the case *Ely v YKK Fasteners (UK) Ltd.*

There is no legal obligation for notice to be in writing, although your contract of employment may specify that notice must be given in writing. In this case you must follow the terms of your contract.

What happens if you resign without notice?

If you leave without giving proper notice, then technically you are in breach of contract. It is rare, however, for employers to sue ex-employees in these circumstances, although legally they could do so. What an employer can do, of course, is to state in any future reference that you left without giving notice. This could potentially damage your chances of obtaining another job.

Another remedy on the employer's part may be to write a clause into the contract of employment stating that an employee who leaves without giving proper notice, will forfeit any holiday pay due. Such a clause, properly written into the contract of employment, is perfectly legal. You should check your contract of employment to see whether there are special terms related to notice periods.

Notice on dismissal

Most employees, and apprentices, are entitled to notice based on their length of service as follows:

Length of Service	Amount of Notice
Less than 1 month's service	Nil
1 month – 2 years	1 week
2 – 3 years	2 weeks
3 – 4 years	3 weeks
etc.	
12 years or more	12 weeks (max.)

If you are dismissed from your job, or made redundant, then you are entitled to notice which is at least equivalent to the above. Again your employer may specify longer periods of notice in your contract of employment, in which case these longer periods take precedence.

There is one exception to the requirement for your employer to give you notice. This occurs where you are dismissed for gross misconduct (which means that you have breached your contract of employment in some fundamental way). Details of this are included in Chapter 13, *Summary Dismissal*.

There is also a restriction applying to your employer regarding withdrawal of notice. If you are dismissed, then your employer cannot later change his mind and tell you to stay. You may, of course, wish to stay on, and provided you both agree to this, then there is no problem. But your employer cannot in these circumstances force you to stay – you would be entitled to leave at the end of the notice period and still regard yourself as dismissed in law.

Lengthening or shortening the notice period

Notice can only be extended, or shortened, by mutual consent. If your employer accepts your notice, and subsequently tries to extend your notice period beyond the period stated in the contract of employment, then this, in law, is equivalent to an offer to re-employ you. This is probably academic – what is more immediately important is that you are under no obligation to work longer than your notice period provides for.

If your employer cuts short your period of notice, by insisting that you leave at an earlier date, then this technically converts the resignation into a dismissal in law. Such a dismissal would almost certainly be unfair if, for example, your employer just told you to leave immediately, and refused to pay you for your notice period. Where you have resigned, your employer cannot legally force you to leave on a date to which you have not agreed. There is, of course, nothing to stop you varying the notice period if both you and your employer agree to do so.

CASE STUDY

Mr Lewis resigned from his job at British Midland Airways, stating that he wished to leave on 28 January. He was told, however, that he was required to give three months notice, whereupon he asked if he could leave a month early. No agreement was reached. Later British Midland told Mr Lewis that, since they had found a replacement for him, he would have to go on 4 February.

Q Was this a resignation or a dismissal?

A This was clearly a dismissal, and an unfair one because Mr Lewis was forced to leave on a date to which he had not agreed, and prior to the expiry of the three months notice period.

Based on the case *British Midland Airways Ltd* v *Lewis*.

It is also possible for an employer to turn a resignation in to a constructive dismissal, as the following case study demonstrates.

CASE STUDY

Mr Ford, a sales manager, gave his employer, Milthorn Toleman, 3 months' notice. The employer promptly demoted him and changed the basis of his pay. He resigned immediately and claimed that he had been constructively dismissed on the basis that the employer had no contractual right to change his position or pay.

Q What decision did the industrial tribunal reach in this case?

A The tribunal decided that Mr Ford had been unfairly constructively dismissed.

Based on the case *Ford v Milthorn Toleman Ltd.*

Not all cases like this will amount to constructive dismissal, however. It depends on your contract of employment whether or not your employer has the right to alter your duties, the basis of your pay, or any other aspects of the terms and conditions of your employment. For full information about constructive dismissal, please refer to the next chapter.

So what can you do if you have been dismissed, and your employer has not given you the proper amount of notice? You would certainly have a claim for wrongful dismissal, which means dismissal in breach of contract. For full details on wrongful dismissal, please refer to Chapter 13.

Termination of a fixed-term contract

A fixed-term contract is, by definition, a contract with a fixed start-date and a fixed end-date. It is as if notice to terminate has been given when the contract is entered into. Where the contract is for more than 3 months the employer should give the statutory minimum period of notice (see page 164) prior to termination.

If, however, the contract is terminated early (by either party), then the normal notice provisions would apply in accordance with the terms of the contract itself and with the statutory minimum periods of notice. Some fixed-term contracts have no notice provisions, which means that termination before the expiry of the fixed term would amount to a breach of contract. Here, if you are dismissed early from a fixed-term contract (except in cases of gross misconduct) then you would be able to make a claim for payment for the whole of the outstanding period of the contract.

For more information about fixed-term contracts, please refer to Chapter 2.

Payment on termination of employment

When you leave your employment, you will be entitled to receive all your wages up to the date of the termination of the contract. There may also be outstanding holiday pay due to you – your entitlement to this will depend on the terms outlined in your contract related to holiday pay. Entitlement to pay in lieu of holidays not taken is not an automatic right.

If you are paid a periodic bonus as part of your overall remuneration, then you would normally be entitled to receive the portion of the bonus which you had already earned prior to your leaving date. However, your employer may have a case to argue that, in order to qualify for the bonus, you must be employed at the date on which the bonus is actually due for payment. If, therefore, you are planning to resign, you should time your departure date carefully in order to avoid losing out on any periodic bonus payment which would otherwise be due to you.

Other payments which might be due include statutory sick pay or statutory maternity pay. If you are entitled to these, then they must be paid to you.

If you have left your employment (through resignation or dismissal) and your employer has not paid you all the monies due to you under your contract of employment, then you may have a claim for illegal deduction from wages under the Wages Act. Please refer to Chapter 4, *Deductions from Wages – Legal and Illegal* for further information about this. A claim to an industrial tribunal under this heading is usually a fairly straightforward matter.

Sometimes employers pay an additional sum of money to employees who are dismissed, for example as compensation for job loss. This is known as an ex-gratia payment, and in some instances such sums may be paid tax-free. There is, of course, no obligation on employers to make ex-gratia payments.

Your employer should also give you your P45 form when you leave, which states the tax and national insurance contributions which have been made during your employment with that company. You will need this form to present to your next employer.

Pay in lieu of notice

Sometimes when an employee resigns, the employer prefers not to have the employee work out his notice period. Perhaps employers feel that the employee's heart is no longer in the job, or that there is no point in dragging things out. Here the employer may elect to offer you pay in lieu of notice, meaning that you are paid for the period of the notice, but are not required to work. You have no automatic right in law to be allowed to work during your notice period, provided you are paid your normal salary.

On a technical point, unless your contract of employment expressly states that your employer has the right to terminate your contract by giving pay in lieu of notice (instead of notice itself) then such pay in lieu will amount to a breach of contract. This may be academic, as many employees prefer, in the case of dismissal, to finish immediately and receive pay for the notice period.

Pay in lieu of notice should be sufficient to cover not only your normal wage or salary, but also the value of any fringe benefits (for the duration of the notice period) which form part of your contract of employment. This could include, for example, a company car, the company's contribution towards your pension fund and the value of free lunches.

The date of termination of your employment

It can be very important for you to be clear on the exact date on which your contract of employment has terminated. Normally it will be the date on which you stop work, but this may not necessarily be so, as, for example, in a case of 'garden leave' (explained in the next section).

The following is an explanation of the different situations which can occur, giving rise to different outcomes as regards calculation of the date of termination of a contract of employment:

1   Where you have worked throughout your notice period, then the date of termination is the the date on which notice expires and you stop work.
2   If you have received pay in lieu of notice, then it is probable that your contract terminated on the last day you worked.
3   Alternatively, your contract may continue to run during your notice period, even although you are not required to work (see next section, 'Concept of garden leave'.
4   If (in cases other than gross misconduct) your employer gives you less than the statutory minimum period of notice due to you (see 'Notice on dismissal' earlier in this chapter), then you are entitled to add the outstanding amount of statutory notice to the date on which you stopped work. This later date will be the legal date of termination of your contract.

CASE STUDY

Mr Barber began work for his employer on 7 August 1989 as a warehouse assistant. On 20 July 1991 he was given notice of termination of his employment on account of poor time-keeping and general job performance. The notice was to be effective immediately. Mr Barber made an application to an

(CASE STUDY CONTINUED)

industrial tribunal for unfair dismissal, and the tribunal had first to determine whether Mr Barber had sufficient service (two years) for his tribunal application to be eligible for hearing.

Q What was the legal date of the termination of Mr Barber's employment contract?

A The tribunal decided that Mr Barber should have been given notice, rather than dismissed immediately. Although Mr Barber's contractual period of notice was one month, the decision was that only the statutory notice period (rather than the contractual period of notice) could be added to the termination date. Since the statutory period of notice for an employee with between one and two years service is one week, the true date of the termination of Mr Barber's employment was 27 July. This meant that Mr Barber's service was still short of two years.

Based on the case *Valeo Distribution (UK) Ltd v Barber.*

5   If you are legally dismissed without notice by your employer (i.e. in a case of gross misconduct) the termination date is the day on which you are dismissed.

6   If on being dismissed, you appeal internally against the decision to dismiss you and the appeal fails, the date of termination will generally be the original date of the dismissal, and not the date on which the appeal was decided. The position could be different, however, if you continued to receive pay between the date of the 'dismissal' and the appeal hearing, in which case it is likely that your employment would be deemed to continue through to the date of your appeal hearing.

CASE STUDY

Sainsbury Ltd operated a contractual disciplinary procedure which gave all employees the right of appeal (to a director of the company) against dismissal or demotion. The procedure stated that 'pending the decision of an appeal to a director against dismissal, the employee will be suspended without pay, but if reinstated, will receive full back-pay for the period of suspension'.

Mr Savage, who had worked for Sainsbury's for just under two years, was instantly dismissed for gross misconduct in February. He exercised his right of appeal which was heard and rejected at the end of May. He wished to claim unfair dismissal. If the date in May was the effective date of his dismissal, Mr Savage had over two years service, but not otherwise.

(CASE STUDY CONTINUED)

Q What was the correct date of the termination of Mr Savage's employment?

A The appeal tribunal declared that in a case such as this, where an appeal was not successful, the dismissal would take effect on the original date, and not the date of the appeal hearing. This was despite the reference in the company's disciplinary procedure to suspension without pay.

Based on the case *Savage v J Sainsbury Ltd.*

7   Where you have been employed on a fixed-term contract, the termination date is the date of expiry of the contract which was agreed at the outset.

8   If you and your employer expressly agree a specific date of termination, then that date will apply.

Determining the precise date of termination can be very important for several reasons:

● Most claims to industrial tribunals, for example unfair dismissal, require you to have two years service. If your length of service is on the borderline of two years, it could be crucial to make sure of your precise date of termination.

CASE STUDY

Mr Godwin received a letter from his employer, SCCL, stating 'SCCL is not in a position to offer you any further employment, effective 23 October. The letter went on to explain his entitlement to 10 weeks' pay in lieu of notice.

Mr Godwin took the view that his employment terminated 10 weeks after the date of the letter. When he made a claim for unfair dismissal to an industrial tribunal, the date of termination was vital to the question of whether his claim had been lodged in time.

Q On what date did Mr Godwin's contract of employment officially end?

A The tribunal found that the letter was unclear and ambiguous as regards the date of termination of Mr Godwin's contract. As the employer was unable to provide any evidence to the contrary, they decided that Mr Godwin's interpretation of the letter was reasonable, and should be accepted for legal purposes.

Based on the case *Scottish Council for Civil Liberties v Godwin.*

- Similarly, most claims to industrial tribunals must be made within three months of the date of termination of your contract. If you are late, your application will normally not be heard.
- For purposes of claiming social security benefits such as unemployment benefit, you will be required to provide details of the correct date of termination of your employment. Failure to do so could delay payment of benefit.
- If under your contract of employment you are covered for life insurance, medical insurance and / or pension benefits, it may be very important for you to know when the cover runs out. No doubt you will wish to arrange private cover to start immediately.

It is therefore in your own interests to ensure that when your employment is about to terminate, you get a clear statement from your employer as to the precise date on which the contract of employment will end.

Two other cases demonstrate the sorts of problems which can occur with termination dates. In one case, an employee received a letter saying 'you are given 12 weeks notice of dismissal from this company with effect from 5 November. You will not be expected to work your notice but will receive monies in lieu of notice ...' Here the tribunal decided that the termination date occurred at the end of the 12-week notice period.

In the second case the employee was given a letter by his employers on 5 May saying they had 'no alternative but to terminate your employment immediately. A cheque covering your salary for the full month of May, plus one month in lieu of notice, is enclosed...' In this case the legal decision was that this was a summary dismissal taking immediate effect from 5 May. Payment of salary for May and June was made as compensation for immediate dismissal, and not by way of continuation of employment.

Concept of 'garden leave'
Situation 3 in the previous section, where you continue to be employed during the notice period, but are not required to come to work, is affectionately known as 'garden leave'. Presumably the assumption is that the employee on notice spends his or her time digging the garden!

The key point about garden leave is that you are still employed, and therefore subject to all the normal terms of your contract of employment. The only difference is that you are at home instead of going in to work.

This means that you cannot legally take up another job which would occupy you during the same hours as your existing job, since you are still technically employed in it. It also means that you must in theory be available for your employer to call on your services.

Garden leave clauses are often included in the contracts of employees who, through their work, have access to highly sensitive or confidential information. It is clearly in the employer's interests to prevent such employees from going immediately to join a competitor company. Generally, provided full pay is made throughout the notice period, garden leave clauses are quite legal in employment. In this situation, if you were to commence employment with a new employer during your period of notice, your old employer would be quite within his rights to take legal action to prevent you doing so.

Continuous employment / length of service

Your period of continuous employment with your employer forms the basic qualification for most employment rights. For example you normally need two years continuous service to have the right to claim unfair dismissal. Each right has its own qualifying period and some rights increase with length of service, for example redundancy pay.

Continuous employment normally means working for the same employer without a break, but there are some types of (temporary) break in employment which do not result in a break in continuity of service.

If there is a dispute about length of service, a tribunal will examine the employee's history week by week. A week will count towards a period of continuous employment if:

- You are incapable of work due to sickness or injury;
- You are away from work on holiday;
- You are laid off temporarily (see Chapter 14, *Short-Time Working and Lay-Off*);
- You are on maternity leave;
- You are away from work in circumstances which are customary in your industry. An example of this would be an offshore worker employed on a four week rota cycle, with two weeks spent working offshore, followed by two weeks leave. Another example could be a seasonal worker employed during most of the year, but laid off by arrangement for a short temporary period during the off-season;
- You are dismissed and subsequently, as a result of a successful unfair dismissal claim, are reinstated in your job. Here all the intervening weeks count towards continuous service.

CASE STUDY

Ms Mackay worked on a seasonal basis for a hotel in the north of Scotland. In October when the summer season ended, she was laid off along with other staff. Unlike most of the others, however, she was not given her P45 and she was asked to keep herself available for relief work at functions. In January she returned to work full-time when the hotel barman left.

Q Was Ms Mackay's continuity of employment preserved between October and January?

A This was an example of a case where continuity of employment was preserved. The tribunal held that there was sufficient evidence of an arrangement in October that Ms Mackay was continuing in employment.

Based on the case *Tongue Hotel Co Ltd* v *Mackay*.

CASE STUDY

Mr Pearson had been employed by Kent County Council for almost 30 years and had risen to the post of head of department. When he began to suffer from anxiety, he was advised by his doctor to find less strenuous employment and so he applied for early retirement from the Council on health grounds. His manager suggested that he return to the department in a non-managerial capacity, and Mr Pearson agreed to this.

In order to be able to draw his pension Mr Pearson had to terminate his employment, and he agreed with his manager to a 10-day break between termination and the commencement of the new job. Just over four years later Mr Pearson was made redundant. He received redundancy pay based on four years' continuous service, rather than on his total service.

Q Should Mr Pearson's redundancy pay have taken into account his service prior to the short break in his employment?

A The tribunal judged that Mr Pearson's break in employment was not due to incapability for work due to sickness, nor did it constitute an arrangement by which his employment could be regarded as continuing. Rather the gap was due to the agreement between Mr Pearson and his manager to allow him to claim his pension. Thus the employer acted correctly in allowing him redundancy pay based on only four years' service.

Based on the case *Pearson* v *Kent County Council*.

Some weeks during your period of employment will not count towards your total length of service, but will not actually break continuity. Such situations include:

- Where you take part in a strike (provided you are not dismissed);
- Where you are absent on service with the armed forces;

● Where you are employed abroad for a temporary period.

In the above cases, if you wish to calculate your total length of service, you must subtract such periods from the total time you have been employed with the company.

Change in employer

Normally, if you leave one job and go to another, this breaks your continuity of service. In some circumstances, however, service with a previous employer will count towards your service with your current employer. The most common circumstances in which such a situation arises are where:

● A business is transferred to another employer, e.g. is bought out, taken over or merged. This is known as a transfer of undertaking. Here your continuity of service is preserved, in some cases even where you have been paid a redundancy payment from your original employer before being taken on by the new employer (provided there is no gap between the two employments).

A business transfer can also occur where your employer contracts out part of his business to another firm – once again you would have continuity of service if you transfer over to the new employer. The most common situation where this occurs is where local councils put services out to competitive tendering, and an outside business wins the contract.

Following on from various recent court decisions, there can also be a transfer of undertaking where one company takes over a contract which was previously carried out by another company. An example of this would be where company A wins a contract with company X to carry out catering and cleaning functions on company X's premises for a fixed period. At the end of the fixed period when the contract is re-tendered, company A loses the contract to company B. Company B then takes over from company A and carries out the same business as before for company X, (with no time-gap between), taking on all or some of company A's employees. Such instances have, in recent times, been deemed to be transfers of undertakings, thus giving employees who transfer to the new company continuity of employment.

Not every contracting-out situation will necessarily be a transfer of undertaking, however. The key criteria is whether the activities undertaken before and after the transfer from the old to the new company are the same.

● Your employer dies and personal representatives or trustees of the firm keep you on;

● You move from one employer to another which is associated with your original employer. To be 'associated' in this context means either that one company has control over the other, or that both companies come under the control of a third company.

Your right to a written statement of reasons for dismissal

Most employees who are dismissed are entitled to be given a written statement giving the reason for their dismissal. You do, however, require two years service to qualify for this right. Technically you must ask for the statement, before your employer is obliged to give it to you. Provided you do ask for a statement, then your employer must comply with your request within 14 days. Many employers will automatically provide such a statement upon dismissal regardless of the person's length of service, but if not, then you should certainly ask for one.

References

There is no legal obligation except in limited circumstances for an employer to provide references for ex-employees. You may request a reference, and in practice most employers will oblige, as they too will frequently be in a position where they need to request references from other employers.

You have no automatic right to see what is written in a reference about you, although some employers may choose to permit you to see the reference.

Where a reference is given, the employer giving it has a duty to take care to ensure it is accurate. In certain circumstances, you could sue an ex-employer if a reference makes a false statement about you which is defamatory and where you consequently suffer financial loss, loss of a new employment opportunity or damage to your reputation.

This situation contrasts with normal claims for defamation where there is a defence of 'qualified privilege'. This defence is available where the person making a statement has an interest or duty – legal, social or moral – to make the statement, and the recipient has a corresponding interest or duty to receive it. The defence protects individuals from liability for untrue statements provided they 'honestly believed' in the truth of what they stated. Once that has been established, a person only becomes liable for an untrue statement if it can be proved that he was motivated by malice (i.e. intended to cause damage to another person's character or reputation).

The situation with references, however, is one where you are protected despite the defence of qualified privilege. Once you have established that your ex-employer has been negligent in preparing a reference, you only have to prove that you have suffered a loss, and not that there was malicious intent behind the statements made.

CASE STUDY

Mr Spring applied for a position as insurance sales manager with an insurance company, having been dismissed from his previous job with Guardian Assurance. His prospective new employer sought a reference from Guardian Assurance regarding his character and experience, and having received it, refused to take him on. The reference stated that Mr Spring was dishonest, and that he had tried to sell a client an unsuitable insurance policy for the sole purpose of maximising his own commission. Mr Spring went to court on account of the reference.

Q Could Mr Spring succeed in sueing his ex-employer for defamation or negligent misstatement?

A The High Court found firstly that Mr Spring had not been acting dishonestly when he recommended the insurance policy to the client, although he had been incompetent. They also found, however, that Guardian Assurance believed what they had written about him, and had therefore not acted maliciously. The case then centred around whether the employer owed Mr Spring a 'duty of care' over the accuracy of the reference, and whether they were liable in negligence because they had failed to exercise such care.

This case was eventually decided by the House of Lords in 1994 and the judgment was that employers are under a duty to exercise reasonable skill and care in the preparation of job references. If an employee suffers financial loss as a result of an employer's failure to take care, then he or she can sue for damages on account of the employer's negligence. Mr Spring won his case.

Based on the case *Spring* v *Guardian Assurance plc.*

Retirement

The date on which you must retire from your employment should ideally be clearly stated in your terms and conditions of employment (although this is not a legal requirement). Your employer's pension arrangements may also indicate the age at which early retirement may be taken on medical or other grounds.

Provided your employer's retirement age is the same for men as for women, then any age may be nominated as the company's normal retirement age (for information about discrimination in retirement, see Chapter 6).

If your employer has no normal retirement age and your contract of employment is silent on the subject, then you have the right not to be dismissed on account of retirement prior to age 65. Prior to your retirement, your employer must give you your normal notice according to your contract of employment.

If in doubt about your contractual retirement age, then you should ask your employer for clarification.

Early retirement

Early retirement is not a dismissal in law unless it is clearly involuntary, neither is it a redundancy. If, therefore, you request early retirement from your job, perhaps because of ill-health, and your employer agrees to your request, your employment will terminate by mutual agreement. Normally you would not be entitled to redundancy pay in such circumstances (unless your early retirement is caused by a genuine redundancy situation).

This contrasts with a situation of voluntary redundancy which the law regards as dismissal, provided of course it is in response to a genuine redundancy situation. (Refer to Chapter 14 for further details).

CASE STUDY

The University of Liverpool was forced in 1985 to make a substantial reduction in its staff numbers. They circulated letters inviting employees to take early retirement and all applications were subject to the employer's final approval.

Mr Birch applied for, and was granted, early retirement. After he left, however, he went on to claim a redundancy payment.

Q Was Mr Birch dismissed, (in which case he would be eligible for a redundancy payment), or was his employment terminated by mutual agreement?

A The Court of Appeal found that this was not a dismissal but a termination by mutual agreement.

Based on the case *Birch & Another* v *University of Liverpool.*

Insolvency

If the company you work for becomes insolvent (meaning that it can no longer pay its debts), this does not necessarily mean that your contract of employment will terminate.

If your company goes into administrative receivership, (i.e. someone is appointed by a court to manage the affairs of the company after it has become insolvent), the receiver will be held to be the company's agent until and unless the company goes into liquidation (ceases trading). This also applies where an administrator is appointed under the Insolvency Act 1986. The purpose of administration is usually to allow administrators to carry on the business with a view to bringing the company back into profit, or else to allow them to find a buyer for the business.

If your company is in receivership and you decide to leave your employment before being given any notice of dismissal, then this will be regarded as a normal resignation and you will lose any right to claim a redundancy payment.

Whilst the receiver is deemed to be the company's agent until the company goes into liquidation, he becomes responsible for all the contracts of employment of the company's employees. This only comes into practice, however, after a period of 14 days has passed following on from the appointment of the receiver. In effect, therefore, the receiver has the first 14 days to decide whether or not the company should carry on trading so that it can be sold later as a going concern.

If you are dismissed before your contract is adopted, i.e. within the 14 day period, any claim for payment of wages, notice pay, redundancy pay or unfair dismissal will have to be made against your ex-employer, and not the receiver.

If, on the other hand, you are kept on by the receiver beyond the 14 day period, then you are deemed to have your contract of employment adopted by the receiver. This means that the receiver becomes responsible for your salary and certain other payments due to you from that date onwards.

However, because of an amendment to the Insolvency Act introduced in March 1994, the liabilities which administrators and receivers become responsible for on adoption of contracts of employment are restricted. They become responsible only for wages or salary, pension contributions, and holiday and sickness payments which arise after the adoption of the contract, i.e. in respect of your service after the date of the adoption of the contract. This means that any liability which has arisen before the adoption of the contract, for example arrears of holiday pay, redundancy pay and compensation for unfair dismissal, is the responsiblity of the insolvent company and not the receiver.

Such payments are normally treated as unsecured claims against the insolvent company, which means that you will have much less chance of actually getting your money. If you have lost out in this way, you can make a claim to the Redundancy Payments Office of the Department of Employment for certain payments – please refer to the next Section for more information.

Thirdly, if you are kept on, and the business is subsequently transferred to a new owner, then the new business will automatically become responsible for your contract of employment. In these circumstances, you cannot normally be (fairly) dismissed.

Although insolvency of itself will not terminate your contract of employment, if a liquidator is appointed, this will automatically terminate your contract because the company will be wound up (i.e. cease operating). In these circumstances your dismissal is due to redundancy. If the liquidator subsequently retains your services, then you will be deemed to have entered into a new contract of employment with the liquidator.

Payment of wages and other rights in insolvency

If you are dismissed as a result of receivership or liquidation, then you will be entitled in law to all your usual rights, e.g. proper notice, redundancy pay, etc.

Employees who are dismissed on account of insolvency are treated as preferential creditors, meaning that your claim would take precedence ahead of other creditors in respect of the following:

- Arrears of wages or salary in respect of the last four months;
- Holiday pay and sick pay;
- Any payment due as a result of medical suspension;
- Any guarantee payments;
- Time off payments (i.e. payment for time off for trade union duties, for ante-natal care or to look for work following redundancy);
- Any remuneration due under a protective award upon redundancy.

If the insolvent company cannot meet all the claims in full, the receiver or liquidator will settle each preferred claim by collecting the proceeds and distributing them in equal proportions. However claims for unpaid wages have priority over other creditors only up to £800 (total) per employee. If your claim is in excess of this figure, the outstanding balance will rank equally with other ordinary creditors of the company, meaning that there may not be enough money to go round.

In this case, where the company's assets are not enough to meet the claims of unsecured creditors, the Government offers a limited guarantee. You can apply to the Redundancy Payments Office of the Department of Employment for certain payments as follows:

- Arrears of pay for up to 8 weeks (including statutory sick pay, guarantee payments, remuneration for suspension on medical grounds, time off payments and remuneration under a protective award). The maximum you can receive under this heading is £1,640;
- Holiday pay due for a period not exceeding six weeks (maximum £1,230);
- Pay in lieu of (statutory) notice up to a maximum of £2,460;
- Basic compensation for unfair dismissal (maximum £6,150);
- Payment of unpaid contributions to occupational pension schemes;
- Reimbursement of fees, etc. paid by apprentices.

These payments will be paid to you provided you can establish that your employer was liable to pay you the sums in question; that your employer is in fact insolvent; that your employment has been terminated; and that the payments in question remain unpaid in whole or in part.

If you believe that you have been refused a payment to which you are entitled, you can complain to an industrial tribunal. The claim must be brought within three months of the Department of Employment's decision not to pay you the amounts in question.

Questions and Answers

Q My contract of employment states that, if the company terminates my employment, they will give me notice in accordance with my statutory rights. What does this mean?

A The law lays down minimum notice periods which employers must give you if you are dismissed from your job. Full details are given in this chapter, but basically you are entitled to receive one week's notice for each complete year of service, up to a maximum of 12 weeks.

Q My contract states that if I resign, I must give three months notice. Must I adhere to this?

A If you leave without giving proper notice, then technically you are in breach of contract. In practice it is unlikely that your employer would take any action against you, although you could be damaging your chances of getting a good reference from your employer.

There is nothing to stop you asking your employer to agree to a shorter period of notice if and when you do decide to resign. A mutual agreement to a shorter period of notice would be preferable to a breach of contract!

Q I resigned from my job two weeks ago and gave my employer one month's notice in accordance with my contract. Now I am regretting it and would like to change my mind. Can I withdraw my resignation?

A You do not have the automatic right to withdraw your resignation. Naturally you can ask your employer to agree to the withdrawal of your resignation, but he has the right to either agree or refuse as he wishes. Good luck!

Q Most people who resign in my company are told to leave immediately. Is this legal?

A Yes, normally, provided they are paid for the period of their notice.

Q I am planning to leave my job in September or October of this year. I have not arranged any holidays this year as I would prefer to be paid for them when I leave. What are my rights in this respect?

A You should read your contract of employment/terms and conditions carefully, as entitlement to pay in lieu of holidays not taken is not an automatic legal right.

If nothing is stated in your terms of employment regarding payment in lieu of holidays on termination, then you should ask your manager, or try to find out what has happened in the past when other employees have left. Most employers do, in practice pay for holidays not taken, but there is no guarantee.

Q I was made redundant from my last job and given pay in lieu of notice. I am unclear as to the date on which my employment actually ended – would it have been the date I actually left, or the date on which the notice period would have expired?

A This can often be a difficult issue to fathom out. You should refer to any notice of termination you received from your employer to see whether it clarifies the date of termination of your contract. Usually, in cases of pay in lieu of notice, the date of termination is the date you actually stopped work, but this is not always the case. Please read the section in this chapter on 'Date of termination of your employment' for a fuller explanation.

Q Is my employer obliged to provide me with a reference?

A No, there is no legal obligation on employers to provide references, although most do so.

Q The company I work for does not seem to have a set retirement age – employees retire at various ages. How long can I continue to work in law?

A If your employer has no normal retirement age and your contract of employment is silent on the subject, then you have the right not to have your contract terminated until age 65. This applies equally to men and women. After that age, you could have your employment legally terminated at any time because people aged 65 or over are not eligible to claim unfair dismissal. You would, however, still be entitled to your normal period of notice.

Q I would like to retire early under the provisions of my employer's company pension scheme. If I do so, can I claim redundancy pay?

A Early retirement is not a dismissal unless it is clearly involuntary. If, therefore, you retire early from your job, your employment will terminate by mutual agreement. Hence you would not be entitled to re-dundancy pay.

Q If my company goes into liquidation, what chances would I have of being paid salary and other monies due to me?

A If you are dismissed as a result of receivership or liquidation, then you will be entitled in law to all your usual rights, e.g. proper notice, redundancy pay, etc. Employees who are dismissed on account of insol-vency are treated as preferential creditors, meaning that your claim would take precedence ahead of other creditors in respect of wages, holiday pay, sick pay and certain other payments.

If the company's assets are not enough to meet your claim, you can apply to the Redundancy Payments Office of the Department of Employment for certain payments. Fuller details are given in this Chapter.

13

Dismissal – Fair and Unfair

What is dismissal?

A dismissal can occur in law in any of the following circumstances:

- Where your employer terminates your contract of employment either with or without notice;
- Where a fixed-term contract expires without being renewed;
- Where your employer stops trading, perhaps because of insolvency;
- Where you are not permitted to return to work after maternity leave, where you have the legal right to do so;
- Where you resign as a direct result of a serious breach of contract on the part of your employer – this is 'constructive dismissal' (dealt with more fully later in this chapter).

Some of the above types of dismissal, in particular the last two, will usually be unfair, others types may be fair, depending on the circumstances.

Dismissal or resignation?

Sometimes employers may say things like 'there's no future for you in this company', or 'you might as well pack it in'. Such statements, especially if uttered in the heat of the moment, will probably not amount to dismissal in law. To be sure that you have been dismissed, you should ask your employer exactly what is meant by any statement of this nature, and then ask for details of the dismissal to be put in writing. If you just walk out, then there is the risk that you will be taken to have resigned (meaning that you would have no claim later for unfair dismissal).

Equally you should avoid saying things to your employer like 'I'm fed up, this job's no use to me' or 'I'm not prepared to go on working in this place' – in case your employer interprets this as your resignation. Bear in mind that there is no law which requires notice to be given in writing either way, so there is room for misunderstanding. There are many unfortunate examples of employees being taken by complete surprise upon receiving their P45, following on from an argument with their employer where they were just letting off a bit of steam!

CASE STUDY

Elaine worked in the head office of a large insurance company as supervisor of the secretarial resources department. She did not get along too well with Steve, her manager, and had, in the past, had several arguments with him regarding work which he assigned to the secretarial staff without involving her, or even informing her.

One day when Elaine returned to work after a couple of days holiday, she discovered that Steve had given some of her work to a junior employee in the department. Elaine felt very angry about this and marched straight up to Steve's office. In the ensuing argument, Elaine said: 'If that is how things are, I might as well leave'.

Shortly afterwards, it came to light that Steve had interpreted Elaine's words as a resignation and arrangements had been made for her employment to terminate at the end of the following month.

Q Did this situation amount to a resignation, or a dismissal?

A It is highly likely that, if Elaine made a claim to an industrial tribunal for unfair dismissal, the tribunal would construe the situation as a dismissal, rather than a resignation.

Industrial tribunals often have problems with cases like this – trying to establish whether a dismissal took place, or whether in fact the employee resigned. It's not worth the trouble!

'Resign or be fired'

If you are persuaded or pressurised into resigning on the basis that you will be dismissed if you refuse, then in law this is the same as being dismissed.

This is the case even where the invitation to resign is made without any aggression or threat. A typical example of this might be where an employer says to an employee 'if you resign by the end of the month, we will pay you three months salary and give you a good reference. If you do not resign, then you may be dismissed, in which case we will give you only the minimum notice and no reference.' This is clearly a dismissal in law whether or not the employee resigns.

The reasoning behind this is that you are not being given a choice of whether or not to remain in employment – either way you will be out of a job. The only element of choice lies in the manner in which the contract comes to an end. The law, therefore, regards such situations as dismissals.

Where, however, it is agreed that the employer will pay an ex-gratia sum of money, what seems on the surface to be an enforced resignation could possibly turn into a voluntary resignation, or termination by mutual agreement (see next section).

Termination by mutual agreement

It is perfectly feasible for an employer and employee to agree mutually to terminate their contract of employment with or without notice, with or without any payment. This may occur, for example, where both parties realise that it is no longer in anybody's interests for the employment contract to continue.

In such circumstances, provided the agreement to terminate is genuine, mutual, and not enforced, there is in law no resignation, and no dismissal. Neither party therefore would be entitled to any compensation via an industrial tribunal.

Despite the above, your employer cannot prevent you from taking a case of unfair dismissal to an industrial tribunal (provided you have the required length of service). What happens then if your employer asks you to sign a document containing a clause along the lines of 'I agree, upon termination of my employment, not to make any claim to an industrial tribunal for unfair dismissal'? You need not worry about signing such a clause, because it is, in any event, unenforceable in law whether or not it is signed. No matter how much money your employer has paid you, he cannot in this way legally prevent you from exercising your right to take a case of unfair dismissal to an industrial tribunal.

Your employer may, however, seek to draw up a proper legal agreement detailing the terms of the termination of your employment. This can be done in two ways:

- If you are in dispute with your employer over the terms of your termination, an ACAS Conciliation Officer may be brought in and a special form, known as a COT 3 completed and signed by both parties.
- Where there is no dispute as such, an independent qualified lawyer may be brought in to give you advice as to the terms of the proposed termination agreement, including the fact that the agreement will effectively prevent you from taking proceedings before an industrial tribunal. Thereafter the agreement must be put in writing and signed by both parties. The lawyer involved in such termination agreements must be independent in the sense that he is not a lawyer who acts for your employer, or an associated employer.

In both these two cases, the effect will be that you have entered into a binding legal agreement not to pursue a claim through an industrial tribunal.

Eligibility to claim unfair dismissal

Most employees with two or more years continuous service may complain to an industrial tribunal if they believe they have been dismissed unfairly. This provision now also applies to part-time workers. The complaint must normally be instituted within three months of the date of termination of the contract of employment.

In certain circumstances employees without two years service may complain of unfair dismissal. Such instances are highlighted later in this chapter under 'Automatically unfair dismissals'.

Certain categories are excluded from eligibility to claim unfair dismissal, namely:

- Certain crown servants;
- Share fishermen;
- The police;
- Employees over the company's normal retirement age, or if no normal retirement age exists, then over age 65;
- People who normally work outside Great Britain.

CASE STUDY

Mr Wood worked exclusively on a UK-registered ship based in Puerto Rico. He had been employed, and was paid by, his employer's head office in Southampton. His contract of employment stated that each voyage terminated in Great Britain. In practice, however, the ship on which Mr Wood worked never entered UK waters.

When Mr Wood was dismissed, he claimed unfair dismissal.

(CASE STUDY CONTINUED)

Q Was Mr Wood eligible to claim unfair dismissal?

A The Court decided that Mr Wood's employment was 'wholly outside Great Britain' on the basis that the work on board the ship was performed outside Great Britain — even although the employment was based in Britain. Thus, Mr Wood was not eligible to claim unfair dismissal.

Based on the case *Wood* v *Cunard Line Ltd.*

Note that members of the armed forces, national health service employees and mariners (working in UK waters) do have unfair dismissal rights in the normal way.

Potentially fair reasons for dismissal

For a company to fairly dismiss an employee, two conditions must be met:

- There must be a valid reason for the dismissal.
- The employer must have acted reasonably in carrying out the dismissal, and must have followed a fair procedure prior to dismissal.

Potentially fair reasons for dismissal fall under five categories:

- Capability
- Conduct
- Redundancy
- Legal restriction
- Some other substantial reason

Capability

Lack of capability can occur as a result of lack of qualifications, lack of knowledge or skill, aptitude or ill-health.

Cases of lack of qualification are relatively unusual, since most employers recruit people with the qualifications required to perform the job. Cases may arise, however, where a person is recruited on the understanding that he will acquire a particular qualification, and then fails to do so.

Lack of knowledge or skill to do the job usually manifests itself in poor job performance. Poor performance may arise when an employee simply does not have the ability to achieve the required standard of work, however hard he tries. Such cases of lack of capability are not usually the employee's fault, and a good employer will always give support to such an employee in the first instance to help him to develop to the required standard of competence. This may be done through the provision of training, coaching or informal supervisory guidance.

CASE STUDY

Mr Campbell worked as a bagpipe maker, but was given the opportunity to act as relief manager at one of his employer's tourist shops. He received four weeks' training, but was given no instruction in the use of weekly balance sheets.

Initially Mr Campbell's performance was satisfactory, but, following a downturn in trade, he was dismissed for ordering too much stock and failing to fill in weekly cash sheets correctly.

Q Was this a fair dismissal on the grounds of capability?

A No, the dismissal was found to be unfair, on the basis that the training given to Mr Wood had been inadequate.

Based on the case *Duncan MacRae Ltd* v *Campbell*.

Some steps which your employer should take if you are not coping with the demands of your job are:

- Explain the standards of work required of you fully and clearly and ensure they are reasonable;
- Tell you clearly and specifically in what way you are failing to meet the required standard;
- Listen to your side of the story, in case there are any factors outside your control which are adversely affecting your job performance (for example lack of cooperation from another employee);
- Explain clearly the consequences of your continued failure to meet the required standards (e.g. eventually you may be dismissed);
- Establish whether further training or guidance is required from your point of view, and if so, provide it;
- Set reasonable time limits for you to come up to the required standard (and then stick to these time limits);
- Consider the possibility of offering you alternative employment. Note, however, that the employer is not obliged to offer you your old job back in the case of a promotion which has not worked out, nor to create a special job for you.

One case demonstrating this last point occurred when a maintenance fitter was dismissed when heart trouble meant he could no longer work shifts. The subsequent dismissal was held to be unfair because the employer had not investigated the possibility of another job being available. The employer was not required to create a special job for the employee, but did have a duty to investigate the possibility of alternative work.

It is of course permissible for employers to change the method of doing a job (e.g. computerisation) or to alter the standards required of a particular job, or even to set standards which are higher than another company in the same industry, provided the standards required of employees are generally reasonable.

CASE STUDY

Mr Maidment was a teacher employed by Kent County Council. The school's headmistress raised complaints about Mr Maidment's competence, and subsequently he was dismissed by a disciplinary sub-committee. He was given no reason for his dismissal and so made a claim to an industrial tribunal for unfair dismissal.

At the tribunal hearing the employer produced no evidence from the members of the disciplinary sub-committee who had taken the decision to dismiss Mr Maidment.

Q Was there sufficient reason to dismiss Mr Maidment?

A The tribunal held that the employer had failed to prove the reason for dismissal, therefore by deduction it was unfair.

Based on the case *Kent County Council* v *Maidment*.

Cases of ill health also fall under the category of capability. Obviously if you are ill, suffering from a disability or physical condition which affects your work, or absent from work due to sickness or injury, then you are 'incapable' of performing your duties. Physical conditions affecting work could include, for example, colour blindness in a person working in a photo processing laboratory.

Even if your illness is genuine, it is ultimately possible for your employer to fairly dismiss you, provided proper procedures are followed prior to the dismissal. In this event the employer would normally seek expert medical advice either from a company doctor or from your own GP (but only with your permission – see Chapter 8, *Access to Medical Reports*).

CASE STUDY

Mr Lynock joined Cereal Packaging as a skilled operator in February 1980. He had a poor attendance record, caused principally by genuine ill-health.

(CASE STUDY CONTINUED)

Over a period of time he received an oral warning, a written warning and a final written warning, then in February 1986, the company decided to dismiss him.

Mr Lynock appealed against the decision to dismiss him (using the company's internal appeal system) and the appeal succeeded – the penalty of dismissal was removed and instead he received another final written warning which was to remain on his file indefinitely.

Thereafter Mr Lynock's attendance record improved. Between July 1986 and July 1987, he was off sick for just under five weeks, but this was still worse than the average of the workforce. No further warnings were given during this period. In July 1987, however, Mr Lynock was dismissed, even although he had not exhausted his entitlement to sick pay under the company's sick pay scheme.

Q Was this dismissal fair?

A The industrial tribunal ruled that the dismissal was fair. They found that the reason for the dismissal was related to Mr. Lynock's capability to do the job and that, despite the undisputed genuineness of his illnesses, the company had acted fairly and followed its procedures. The fact that he had not exhausted his sick pay entitlement was not a key factor.

Based on the case *Lynock* v *Cereal Packaging Ltd.*

The next case study is very similar to the one above, but with a different outcome:

CASE STUDY

Mrs Scott began working for the Scottish Office in 1982. By the beginning of 1984, there was concern regarding her attendance and she was told that her attendance record would have to improve if her appointment was to be confirmed. In June 1984, Mrs Scott suffered a neck injury which resulted in an operation, and further complications over the next three years. In August 1985, she was told again that her attendance would have to improve.

In December 1986, the personnel manager sought medical advice. A doctor provided a report in which he stated that he was not optimistic about the likelihood of Mrs Scott rendering regular and effective service in the future. However he did not interview or examine Mrs Scott.

Looking at her absence record, the Personnel Manager established that over the five years of her employment, Mrs Scott had been absent for 91 days, 163 days, 142 days, 271 days and 1 day respectively!

In March 1987, Mrs Scott was called to an interview with the personnel manager, and dismissed.

(CASE STUDY CONTINUED)

Q Was this dismissal fair?

A This dismissal was found to be unfair on procedural grounds. The reason for the dismissal was undisputed, but there were three procedural flaws which made the dismissal unfair. These were:

- There had been no personal consultation with Mrs Scott — no proper warnings had been given, and she had not been made aware that her poor attendance might lead to dismissal;
- The so-called medical report had been inadequate;
- The employer had failed to take into account the marked up-turn in Mrs Scott's attendance during her last year, indicating that there had been considerable recovery.

Based on the case *Scott* v *Secretary of State for Scotland.*

Where mental qualities clearly have an adverse affect on job performance or efficiency at work, or relations with customers, dismissal would normally be regarded in law as being on account of capability. This aspect of capability could cover, for example, an employee with a negative attitude which affected job performance.

CASE STUDY

Mr Jacomb, a contracts manager with a firm of shopfitters, was regarded as technically competent and experienced, and it was recognised that he had detailed knowledge of his job. He was also conscientious in his work and very loyal.

Despite this, Mr Jacomb was uncooperative and unbending in his attitude, as a result of which his relationships with clients were poor. This was so bad that several contractors refused to have him on their sites. Ultimately he was dismissed.

Q Could this be a fair dismissal under the heading of capability?

A Yes, it could be, and in this case it was. The tribunal judged that Mr Jacomb lacked the necessary aptitude and mental quality for the job of contracts manager and his dismissal was fair.

Based on the case *A J Dunning & Sons (Shopfitters) Ltd* v *Jacomb.*

Conduct

There is no legal definition as to what constitutes unsatisfactory conduct at work. It is up to each employer to define the rules and to lay down guidelines for conduct and behaviour for all employees.

Most cases of misconduct would be dealt with under the company's standard disciplinary procedure, with appropriate warnings being given, leading eventually to dismissal.

Some examples of misconduct might be:

- Poor time-keeping
- Unauthorised absence from work
- Over-staying leave
- Misuse of company resources
- Breach of confidentiality
- Minor breaches of safety regulations
- Being under the influence of drink at work
- Smoking in non-smoking areas
- Refusal to carry out lawful and reasonable instructions

Whatever kind of misconduct an employee is guilty of, the employer is still obliged to follow fair procedures prior to dismissal, otherwise the dismissal will be unfair.

CASE STUDY

Mr Mintoft, an experienced sales manager, worked for a garage. His employer had paperwork procedures detailing repairs to their second-hand cars, which were important for the issuing of warranties.

Mr Mintoft persistently refused to comply with the procedures, despite receiving written instructions from his employer requiring him to follow them. He received various warnings.

Finally Mr Mintoft was abusive to his branch manager and stated in clear terms that he was not prepared to work to the paperwork system. He was dismissed.

Q Was Mr Mintoft dismissed fairly or unfairly?

A This was a fair dismissal – the company's instructions were clear and reasonable and Mr Mintoft had made it plain he was not going to operate the procedures.

Based on the case *Mintoft* v *Armstrong Massey Ltd.*

Contrast this with the following case study:

CASE STUDY

Mr Davies was an HGV driver. One day he was told to collect a trailer from Sheffield and take it to Grimsby. After collecting the trailer a fault developed and it became obvious that he could not get to Grimsby that day without breaking hours regulations.

Mr Davies telephoned his employer and explained that he did not have any money or clothes for an overnight stay, and that he therefore intended to return to the depot. His employer was extremely angry at this and dismissed him.

Q Was Mr Davies dismissed fairly or unfairly?

A This dismissal was unfair. The tribunal accepted that the employer was entitled contractually to instruct Mr Davies to start out for Grimsby and stay overnight, but concluded that to ask him to do so when he had no money or change of clothes was an unreasonable instruction.

Based on the case *Davies* v *Richards Transport.*

For more detailed information on disciplinary rules and procedures leading to dismissal, please refer to Chapter 10.

Redundancy

In law redundancy constitutes dismissal, whatever the circumstances. A true redundancy occurs where the employer needs to reduce the workforce in one of the following circumstances:

- Where the employer has ceased trading;
- Where the employer has closed down a particular business premises (whether he has moved to other premises, or closed down completely);
- Where fewer employees are required to do the kind of work you are employed to do.

The most important aspect of redundancy is that it is jobs which become redundant, not people. If the employer immediately engages a replacement for the 'redundant' employee, then this is not a redundancy at all. Your rights in a redundancy situation are explained fully in Chapter 14.

Legal restriction

Legal restriction occurs where it becomes unlawful for the employer to continue to employ a particular person. Examples of this include situations where someone employed as a driver loses his driving licence, where a foreign employee's work permit runs out, or where continuation of employment would contravene health regulations. Employers must, however, be able to show that the continued employment of the individual would, as a matter of fact, contravene the law.

There would also be an obligation in these circumstances for the employer to make a reasonable attempt to find suitable alternative work for the employee (except, of course, in the case of a foreign employee's work permit running out).

CASE STUDY

Mr Mathieson, a salesman, was disqualified from driving. He wanted to arrange to engage a private chauffeur to drive him during the disqualification period, and was willing to pay the cost of this, plus the additional insurance premiums on his company car. Despite this, his employer dismissed him.

Q Did the employer act reasonably in dismissing Mr Mathieson in these circumstances?

A The dismissal was unfair for two reasons. The tribunal found firstly that Mr Mathieson's contract did not oblige him to drive, and therefore the 'legal restriction' argument did not apply. Secondly they found that the dismissal was unfair on the grounds of the employer's unreasonableness in refusing to consider the alternative arrangements adopted by Mr Mathieson.

Based on the case *Mathieson v W J Noble & Son Ltd*.

Some other substantial reason (SOSR)

'Some other substantial reason' as a reason for dismissal provides employers with a way of fairly dismissing employees for reasons that do not fall within the other four categories. The reason, however, must be substantial, and not trivial. Some examples of cases which tribunals have heard under the heading of 'some other substantial reason' are:

Reorganisation of a business

Provided there is a sound business reason for a reorganisation, and provided the employer has followed a fair procedure, dismissal on account of refusal to agree to new terms and conditions may be shown to be fair.

CASE STUDY

Ms Damerel was employed as a school caretaker, working a 39-hour week of which 25 hours were cleaning duties and 14 caretaking. Following a successful in-house tender for the provision of cleaning services, she was

(CASE STUDY CONTINUED)
required to spend 34 hours a week cleaning and only five caretaking. The change, which did not affect her pay, was as a result of the removal of the post of cleaning assistant. Ms Damerel refused to accept the new duties and was dismissed.

Q Was this a fair dismissal?

A The Council had undertaken a business reorganisation and the change in Ms Damerel's duties was reasonable, particularly since she would have suffered no loss in pay. The tribunal found that if the Council had not undertaken some reorganisation, it would have been unable to put in a competitive in-house bid for the contract.

Based on the case *Damerel* v *Devon County Council.*

Dismissal of a replacement for a woman who has been on maternity leave
Provided the replacement employee was properly informed at the beginning of employment that it would terminate when the permanent job holder returned to work, then such a dismissal would normally be fair.

Pressure from third parties
If a company is coming under pressure from one of its clients to 'get rid of' a particular person, then dismissal of the person may be fair depending on all the circumstances of the case.

Note, however, that pressure placed on the employer as a result of threats of industrial action is a different matter altogether. Employers cannot legally use threats of industrial action or shop-floor pressure as a reason for dismissal. If they do, the dismissal is likely to be unfair.

CASE STUDY
Mr Hogarth worked as a charge-hand rigger for Rigblast Energy Services, a contracting company in the offshore oil industry. Rigblast's contract with its client gave the client the right to require Rigblast to remove from the off-shore platform any employee whom the client considered unsuitable. This type of clause is normal in the North Sea oil industry.

Mr Hogarth had been off work for a period of three months following an injury at work. When he was ready to return, Rigblast's client refused to have Mr Hogarth back and gave no reason for their refusal. Rigblast had no other work to offer Mr Hogarth, and so consulted ACAS regarding dismissal. They also asked the client to reconsider, but failed in their bid to persuade the client to take Mr Hogarth back. Mr Hogarth was thus dismissed.

(CASE STUDY CONTINUED)

Q Was this dismissal fair?

A The tribunal found firstly that the reason for the dismissal was potentially fair. However, in examining whether the company had acted
reasonably in dismissing Mr Hogarth, they concluded that they had not.

The two key reasons for this decision were that, in the tribunal's judge-
ment, Mr Hogarth should have been told via his contract of employment
that he could be dismissed at the request of a client. Secondly the tribunal
said that Rigblast should have done more to ascertain the client's reasons for
wanting Mr Hogarth removed – in particular they should have requested
written notification from the client to enable them to explain the reasons for
dismissal to Mr Hogarth.

Based on the case *Rigblast Energy Services Ltd* v *Hogarth*.

Potential breach of trust

If the spouse, or other close relative, of an employee works for a competitor,
dismissal for a potential breach of trust may be substantial, provided there is
a real risk. This could be fair, even if no breach of trust (for example leaking
of confidential information) had actually occurred. It is the risk factor which
makes such a dismissal potentially fair.

CASE STUDY

Miss Simmons was a telephonist / filing clerk working in a position where
she had access to confidential information. She lived with a colleague who
was a senior sales manager with the company. Her partner subsequently
moved to work for a competitor of her employer. Miss Simmons was dismissed.

Q Did the company have reasonable grounds for dismissing Miss
Simmons?

A The finding was that Miss Simmons was fairly dismissed. There was a
genuine risk involving two employees with a close personal relationship each with access to confidential information and working for competing
companies.

Based on the case *Simmons* v *S D Graphics Ltd*.

Refusal to sign a restrictive covenant

Provided the restrictive covenant is reasonable in its scope, then an employee's refusal to agree to it may constitute a substantial reason for

dismissal. See Chapter 2 (last section) for further information on restrictive covenants.

CASE STUDY

R S Components Ltd, manufacturers of electrical components, found that their employees were leaving and setting up in competition against them. They were also soliciting former customers. Naturally this was very damaging to the company's business.

Consequently the company imposed a restrictive covenant on all their sales staff which would prevent them from soliciting customers for up to 12 months after leaving employment.

Mr Irwin, an employee of R S Components, refused to agree to the terms of the restrictive covenant and was dismissed.

Q Was this dismissal reasonable?

A Yes, this type of dismissal is valid in law.

Based on the case *R S Components Ltd* v *Irwin*.

Personality clash
A dismissal due to difficult working relationships may be fair, provided the employer has investigated thoroughly, and first made every effort to solve the problem in some other way.

Expiry of a fixed-term contract
A dismissal which occurs on the expiry of a fixed-term contract would normally be fair under the 'some other substantial reason' heading.

Has your employer followed a fair procedure?

The fairness of any dismissal will depend on whether the employer has followed proper procedures, and has acted reasonably in dismissing the employee for the particular reason given.

The question as to whether the employer acted reasonably (which has never been, and probably cannot ever be precisely defined in a legal sense!) includes the treatment of the employee in the lead-up to the dismissal. For example, in a case of misconduct, a tribunal would wish to establish whether the employee was given proper warnings, and in a case of incapability whether he was offered training to increase job skill.

Most successful unfair dismissal claims these days arise as a result of the employer having failed to observe reasonable procedures, rather than because the employer had no good reason to dismiss. Even in cases where the reason for the dismissal is absolutely clear and very strong, a dismissal will usually be unfair if there is any procedural shortfall.

Summary dismissal

Summary dismissal is dismissal without notice, or pay in lieu of notice, in circumstances where the employee has committed an act of gross misconduct. It is irrelevant whether or not the employee has had previous warnings. Note that this is the only circumstance where the employer is legally able to dismiss without notice.

What is gross misconduct?

Gross misconduct is misconduct of such a serious nature that dismissal is justified, even if no previous warnings have been given. Gross misconduct effectively destroys the contract between the employer and the employee and renders any further working relationship and trust impossible.

Examples of gross misconduct might include (but are not restricted to):

- Fighting or physical assault
- Stealing from, or defrauding the company
- Deliberate damage to company property or equipment
- Falsification of records
- Gross negligence in carrying out duties
- Drunkenness on company premises
- Serious breach of safety regulations
- Insubordination or unreasonable refusal to obey a legitimate order
- Deliberate breach of confidentiality
- Sexual or racial harassment

Whether a particular type of behaviour would constitute gross misconduct in a particular company would depend on the working environment and circumstances. For example, in an environment where employees operate potentially dangerous machinery, being under the influence of drink whilst at work would certainly amount to gross misconduct. On the other hand, in an office environment the day before Christmas, a different interpretation might be put on such an occurrence!

CASE STUDY

Mr Connor worked for George Wimpey Ltd as a scaffolder offshore. His contract of employment stated clearly that reporting for work at the airport under the influence of alcohol was an offence which could lead to dismissal. Mr Connor was dismissed for being drunk in the course of his return to work

(CASE STUDY CONTINUED)
after a period of onshore leave.

Q Did the employer act reasonably in dismissing Mr Connor?

A Yes, under the circumstances because safety on offshore platforms and during transport to them is paramount. Mr Connor had been found to be so much under the influence of alcohol as to be considered unsafe to let on board the transport plane to the oil platform.

Based on the case *Connor v George Wimpey ME & C Ltd.*

Your employer should provide a list of what constitutes gross misconduct in your company. This would normally be written into the disciplinary procedure.

Importance of procedure
In cases of gross misconduct/summary dismissal, the employer is still under an obligation to follow a correct procedure prior to dismissal, including the requirement to conduct an interview with the employee, establish the full facts, give the employee a fair hearing and act reasonably in all the circumstances. Many potentially fair dismissals are rendered unfair because of procedural faults on the part of the employer.

Dismissal in connection with a criminal offence

If an employee commits a criminal offence within employment, e.g. stealing from the company, then this will certainly constitute gross misconduct.

Complications can arise, however, where an employer suspects that an employee is guilty of some crime or gross misconduct, but cannot prove it. Here the test of fairness is based on three factors:

- Does the employer genuinely believe that the employee committed the offence?
- Does the employer have reasonable grounds for this belief?
- Has the employer conducted a very thorough investigation (note — relying on a police investigation is not sufficient in this context)?

Provided the answer to all three questions is clearly 'yes', then the employer may fairly dismiss the employee (provided proper procedures are followed), even where there is no proof. Even if the employee is subsequently acquitted by a criminal court, this will not affect the fairness or otherwise of the dismissal.

CASE STUDY

Mr Mitchell was dismissed two days after a break-in at his employer's premises. The premises had been vandalised and £30 stolen. Prior to his dismissal Mr Mitchell had had several disciplinary warnings for conduct offences.

After the break-in, the police told the employer that Mr Mitchell was in police custody in relation to similar incidents on the same night. They indicated that Mr Mitchell was implicated in the employer's break-in because of similarities with the other incidents, including similar footprints. Mr Mitchell was due to appear in court on the following Monday.

On the Monday, Mr Mitchell was charged, but later in the day he telephoned his employer and claimed he was innocent of the break-in at the company premises. His manager said he did not believe him and dismissed him over the telephone.

Q Did the employer's action satisfy the tests of fairness for cases such as this?

A No, the dismissal was unfair. The tribunal found that the employer had failed to carry out a satisfactory investigation of its own. In particular the employer had failed to interview Mr Mitchell personally, thus denying him the opportunity to state his case.

Based on the case *Gael Force Marine Equipment Ltd* v *Mitchell.*

To understand the thinking behind such cases, you have to consider the function of an industrial tribunal in an unfair dismissal case. The purpose of the tribunal is to judge whether or not the employer acted reasonably in all the circumstances at the time of the dismissal, not whether the employee is innocent or guilty. It is, the employer who is 'on trial', and not the employee.

In judging the employer's actions, the tribunal will take into account only factors known to the employer at the time the decision to dismiss was taken (so subsequent events cannot be considered). This is quite logical when you think about it.

Furthermore, tribunals do not require absolute proof of events. This is a completely different approach from a criminal court where guilt must be established 'beyond reasonable doubt'. The tribunal will listen to the evidence from both the employer and the ex-employee, and make up their own minds as to the fairness or otherwise of the employer's actions.

One famous case concerned four employees in an off-licence where it was discovered that thefts of cash and vouchers had occurred. The police concluded, after investigation, that it had been an 'inside job' (there were no signs of a break-in). The employer conducted his own thorough investigation and established genuine grounds for believing that one or more of the four employees could have committed the thefts. But there was no tangible evidence as to which of the employees was guilty. The employer dismissed all four, and a subsequent claim for unfair dismissal by one of them failed. The tribunal found that the company had, under all the circumstances, acted reasonably.

Criminal offences committed outside work may also be complicated in the context of fair dismissal.

Here there are three key questions to be answered:

- Does the offence make the employee unsuitable for the type of work he is employed to do?
- Is the nature of the offence such that the employer's name could be brought into ill-repute (e.g. through adverse press publicity)?
- Does the offence render the employee genuinely unacceptable to other employees?

   If the answer to any of the above questions is clearly 'yes', then dismissal may be fair, provided proper procedures are followed.

An example of an offence making an employee unsuitable for a particular type of job might be where a sales assistant in a store is convicted of shop-lifting from another store nearby. Shop-lifting on the part of a typist employed in an office might possibly not be regarded in the same light.

CASE STUDY

Ms Bardin was a part-time cleaner working for Lloyds Bank. She was dismissed after she pleaded guilty to three charges of obtaining money by deception, even although the offence had nothing to do with her employment.

Q Did the bank act reasonably in dismissing Ms Bardin for such an offence outside work?

A Yes, her dismissal was found to be fair. The tribunal found that the link between the type of offence and the employee's type of work was adequate to justify dismissal.

Based on the facts of the case *Lloyds Bank plc* v *Bardin*.

It is clear, therefore, that an employee who has committed some criminal offence outside work cannot be automatically (fairly) dismissed. Equally a dismissal solely on the grounds that an employee is remanded in custody is likely to be unfair.

What is constructive dismissal?

Constructive dismissal occurs in the following circumstances:

● Where the employer takes some action which fundamentally breaches your contract of employment;

and

● You resign (with or without notice) immediately as a direct result of this breach.

Your employer's action must constitute a breach which is significant enough to go the very root of the contract, and typically would involve some major change to one of the key terms of your employment, introduced without your agreement. The effect is that you feel the situation is intolerable to the extent that there is no alternative but to resign.

In this type of case an industrial tribunal will expect you to demonstrate that your resignation could reasonably be viewed as a dismissal.

CASE STUDY

Ms Jordan was working as an assistant manager in the newspaper industry, earning salary and commission. Her employer asked her to agree to a reduction in the size of the geographical area from which she earned commission. Ms Jordan refused, but her employer eventually imposed the change anyway. Ms Jordan concluded that, as this action would result in her losing commission, it was a fundamental breach of contract. She resigned and claimed unfair constructive dismissal.

Q What would a tribunal decide in a case such as this?

A The tribunal noted that the employer was not contractually obliged to assign Ms Jordan to a specific sales area, and was entitled to reduce the size of the area from which she earned commission.

They concluded, however, that the company acted unfairly in not reaching an agreement with Ms Jordan that her commission would not be reduced. The substantial loss of income amounted to a fundamental breach of contract, and the subsequent constructive dismissal was unfair.

Based on the case *Star Newspapers Ltd* v *Jordan*.

Note that a breach of contract does not of itself terminate a contract. To claim constructive dismissal, you must actually resign from your employment. Your resignation does not have to be expressed in any formal way, but it is important that you do not continue to work for your employer — it must be clear that the contract is at an end.

The subject of breach of contract has been examined in depth in Chapter 3, but for convenience a list of examples of possible breach of contract is given below:

- Reduction in pay;
- Major change to hours of work;
- Major change to job duties or reduction in responsibilities;
- Demotion to a lower graded job;
- Withdrawing a company car or other key 'perk' to which the employee is contractually entitled;
- Failure to give reasonable support to an employee who is the victim of harassment;
- Falsely and deliberately accusing the employee of dishonesty;
- Any act which breaches the implied duty of trust and confidence.

CASE STUDY

Mrs Austin had worked for her employer for 23 years, latterly as a quality control inspector. For 19 years she had worked a two-shift system, working days only. The company rules contained a provision that the company could re-arrange employees' working hours to meet the requirements of the business.

The company decided that standards and quality would be improved if the inspectors were to work a three-shift system, including night-shifts. Mrs Austin could not work the night shift for health and family reasons.

Two offers of alternative employment were made to Mrs Austin, both involving loss of pay and one also involving loss of status. She refused both offers. Eventually she was told she would have to work the new shift system. Later the company wrote to her indicating that because she had refused both offers of alternative employment, her employment was deemed to be at an end. She claimed unfair dismissal.

Q Was this a resignation or a dismissal, and if it was a dismissal, was it fair or unfair?

A At the tribunal hearing, the employer argued that Mrs Austin had resigned whereas Mrs Austin alleged that she had been constructively dismissed.

The tribunal held that Mrs Austin had been dismissed (she had not resigned) for 'some other substantial reason', i.e a business reorganisation, and decided that the company had not acted reasonably. Despite the company rule on re-arranging hours of work the employer did not have the right to unilaterally change shift patterns and impose a change from day to night

(CASE STUDY CONTINUED)
shift on Mrs Austin against her will, considering her particular personal circumstances.

Based on the case *Kenwood Ltd* v *Austin*.

Remember that not every breach of contract will be fundamental enough to justify a claim of constructive dismissal. Each case will depend on the circumstances surrounding it.

It is also possible for an ordinary resignation to turn into a case of constructive dismissal. One case concerned an employee who resigned giving three months' notice, upon which his employer promptly demoted him and changed the basis of his pay. He then resigned immediately, claimed constructive dismissal and won his case at tribunal.

It is possible for a constructive dismissal to be fair, although this is relatively unusual. Because constructive dismissal hinges around an employer's breach of contract, unfairness is often a *fait accompli*.

The most likely circumstance giving rise to fair constructive dismissal would be where changes to terms and conditions result from a genuine business reorganisation. If the employer can show that there were sound business reasons for the changes, and if a reasonable approach had been taken prior to imposing any changes to employees' terms, then a resultant constructive dismissal may be fair. This situation is discussed more fully in Chapter 3.

Dismissal during a strike

If you choose to take part in a strike or other industrial action, your employer has the legal right to dismiss you, and you will have no remedy in law. Industrial tribunals are barred from hearing claims of unfair dismissal, if the reason for the dismissal was that the employee was on strike at the time of the dismissal.

The only exceptions to this are where the employer dismisses some, but not all, employees who are on strike, or dismisses employees who are not taking part in the strike.

Further information on this is to be found in Chapter 11, *Your Right to Strike – and the Possible Consequences*.

Automatically unfair dismissals

Certain types of dismissal are automatically unfair in law:
1 Dismissal on account of a business transfer.
2 Dismissal on the grounds of pregnancy or maternity leave.
3 Dismissal due to trade union membership or activities, or non-membership of a trade union.
4 Dismissal due to health and safety activities.
5 Dismissal for asserting a statutory right.
6 Dismissal of a protected or opted-out shop worker for refusing to work on a Sunday (see Chapter 6).
7 Dismissal on the grounds of sex or race (see Chapter 6).
8 Dismissal relating to a spent conviction under the Rehabilitation of Offenders Act (see Chapter 6).
9 Where the reason for the dismissal is not one of the five potentially fair reasons for dismissal.

The first five items are examined below.

Dismissal on account of a transfer of a business
If the business you work for is transferred to a new owner, you automatically become the employee of the new owner. In law it is as if your contract of employment had originally been made with the new owner. The only item which the new owner need not take on is your old employer's pension scheme.

The Transfer of Undertakings Regulations 1981 protect your employment in the event that the business you work for is taken over, merged with another business or bought out. Recently the regulations have also been applied to situations where an employer contracts out part of his business to another firm. The most common situation where this occurs is where local councils put services out to competitive tendering, and an outside business wins the contract.

There may also be a transfer of undertaking in a situation where one company takes over a contract which was previously carried out by another company. An example of this is given on page 174.

Not every contracting-out situation will necessarily be a transfer of undertaking, however. The key criteria is whether the activities undertaken before and after the transfer from the old to the new company are the same.

If you are dismissed by either your original or your new employer on account of a transfer, then the dismissal will be automatically unfair. The only exception to this is where it can be shown by your employer that your dismissal was for an 'economic, technical or organisational reason entailing changes in the workforce'. Even in these circumstances the employer still has an obligation to act reasonably, as in all other dismissals.

Of course a transfer or take-over creates a situation which is particularly likely to give rise to changes to terms and conditions of employment. But because your contract of employment is transferred along with the business, all your terms and conditions remain unchanged. Any subsequent attempt by your new employer to alter your terms will be liable to constitute a breach of contract, possibly entitling you to claim constructive dismissal. Please refer to Chapter 3 for full details of breach of contract and to the section on constructive dismissal earlier in this chapter.

Dismissal on the grounds of pregnancy

It is automatically unfair to dismiss a woman because of pregnancy, or for any reason connected with pregnancy. Dismissal on account of pregnancy is also likely to amount to sex discrimination in law. Indeed any dismissal on account of a person's sex is unlawful. All pregnant women are protected by these provisions, regardless of length of service or number of hours worked.

If an employee's pregnancy makes it impossible for her to do her job adequately or safely, the employer must make every reasonable attempt to alter her working conditions or offer her suitable alternative employment for the temporary period of her pregnancy. Even in this situation, a dismissal will be unfair. The only other possible remedy for the employer in these circumstances is to suspend the employee, with pay, until the time she is due to begin maternity leave.

Furthermore, if an employee is entitled in law to return to work after maternity leave, and her employer does not permit her to do so, then normally this will constitute an unfair dismissal. There is no minimum service qualification for the right to take maternity leave and return to work. Please refer to Chapter 7, *The Right to Return to Work*, for full details.

Where an employee's job no longer exists due to a redundancy situation, she is entitled to be offered a suitable alternative job if one is available. If no alternative job is available, then the dismissal would be treated as a genuine redundancy.

Dismissal due to trade union membership or non-membership

All employees have the right not to be dismissed, or chosen for redundancy, because they are members of an independent trade union, because they are not members of a union, or because they refuse to join a union.

Any dismissal which is on the basis of trade union membership or activities will be automatically unfair. An employee dismissed on this basis has the right to complain to an industrial tribunal regardless of length of service, number of hours worked or age at the time of dismissal. This is an exception to the usual rule that employees over the age of 65 may not bring a claim before an industrial tribunal for unfair dismissal.

Even if a trade union puts pressure on a company to dismiss a particular employee (for example by threatening to call a strike), this will have no bearing on the fairness or otherwise of the dismissal. In law you are free to choose whether or not to belong to a union, and whether or not to take part in its activities in your own time. Further information is contained in Chapter 11, *The Right not to be Dismissed on Trade Union Grounds*.

Dismissal due to health and safety activities

The Trade Union Reform and Employment Rights Act 1993 brought in new provisions which give protection to all employees who are dismissed on account of health and safety activities. Such dismissals are automatically unfair.

As in the case of trade union-related dismissals, there is no qualifying period of service, qualifying hours per week or age limit for employees wishing to complain. Full details are to be found in Chapter 6, *Discrimination on Account of Health and Safety Activities*.

Dismissal for asserting a statutory right

The same 1993 law introduced a new concept in unfair dismissal, giving considerable additional protection to employees in all walks of life against unfair treatment. Employees have a right not to be dismissed for 'asserting a statutory right'.

Asserting a statutory right could mean making a complaint to your employer that one of your legal employment rights has been breached in some way. It could also mean taking a case to an industrial tribunal as a result of an infringement of one of your employment rights. If you are then dismissed because you have made such a complaint, you would have a very sound case for a claim of unfair dismissal.

The rights covered in this legislation are:

- Not to have illegal deductions made from your wages (see Chapter 4, *Deductions from Wages — Legal and Illegal*);
- Not to be prevented or deterred from joining a union, penalised for joining a union, or compelled to join a union (see Chapter 11);
- To be given reasonable time off for trade union duties or activities (see Chapter 5);
- Your right to minimum notice (see Chapter 12, *Notice on Dismissal*).

As long as you make it reasonably clear to your employer that you believe one of your rights has been infringed, which right you are referring to, and provided you do so in good faith, then you cannot be fairly dismissed. If you are dismissed, you may make a complaint to an industrial tribunal. This right applies regardless of your length of service.

Wrongful dismissal

Wrongful dismissal is not the same as unfair dismissal. Wrongful dismissal means any dismissal which is technically in breach of contract. Hearings for wrongful dismissal do not take into account the reasonableness or otherwise of an employer's actions. This contrasts with unfair dismissal which gives much emphasis to the manner in which the dismissal was carried out and whether or not the employer followed a fair procedure prior to dismissal.

The most common type of wrongful dismissal is where an employee is dismissed without being given proper notice under the contract of employment.

So, if for example, your contract entitles you to receive three months' notice on dismissal, and you are dismissed with only four weeks' notice, then this will be a wrongful dismissal.

CASE STUDY

Sheila had worked for Bishop Transport for 14 years and was approaching age 60 which was the company's normal retirement age for men and women. Her original contract of employment stated that if her employment was terminated for any reason, she would be entitled to one month's notice. She was also required to give one month's notice if she resigned.

Bishop Transport, on checking Sheila's file and establishing that she was within a few weeks' of her sixtieth birthday, issued her with official notice of termination of her employment, due to retirement. She was given one month's notice.

Q Did the employer's action constitute wrongful dismissal in this case?

A Yes, Sheila was entitled legally to a minimum period of notice based on her length of service, which in this case would be 12 weeks. (See Chapter 12, *Giving Notice*, for full details of statutory notice periods). This statutory term takes precedence over the notice provision detailed in the contract of employment. The fact that Sheila's dismissal was on account of retirement had no effect on the outcome of the situation.

One exception to the usual rules about notice of dismissal is the situation where an employee is guilty of gross misconduct. This can entitle the employer to implement summary dismissal, which means dismissal without notice, or pay in lieu of notice. This was discussed earlier in this chapter.

The termination of a fixed-term contract before it is due to expire could be wrongful dismissal, if there is no provision for notice contained within the contract.

Thirdly, if you are dismissed in breach of your employer's contractual disciplinary procedure, then this too could amount to a wrongful dismissal. This could occur, for instance, if you are dismissed summarily where you are not guilty of any gross misconduct.

Another situation in which wrongful dismissal could possibly occur could be where you are dismissed with pay in lieu of notice instead of being allowed to work your notice, and your contract of employment does not contain a clause entitling your employer to end your contract in this way. This would not apply to situations of gross misconduct where your employer would, as mentioned above, be entitled in any event to end your contract without either notice or pay in lieu of notice.

One interesting point to note about wrongful dismissal is that if a contract is wrongfully terminated, then any post-termination clause contained within the contract, for example a restrictive covenant, would be unenforceable. In other words, if your employer wrongfully terminates your contract, then he cannot legally oblige you to adhere to any of its terms which continue to apply after the termination. Please refer to Chapter 2 for full information about restrictive covenants.

Claims for wrongful dismissal may be made either to an industrial tribunal, or to the ordinary courts. Industrial tribunals are authorised to hear claims of wrongful dismissal, provided the claim is made within three months of the effective date of termination of employment. A limit of £25,000 applies on awards which a tribunal can make for wrongful dismissal. Most awards for wrongful dismissal are, however, nowhere near this figure.

If you elect to take a claim for wrongful dismissal to a county court or High Court, you have a much longer time limit to apply – six years – long enough even for the tardiest individual to take action!

Unlike claims for unfair dismissal where there is normally a minimum service requirement of two years, there is no minimum service requirement for a claim for wrongful dismissal. So, if you are dismissed in breach of your contract of employment, but do not have enough service to claim unfair dismissal, you may, depending on the circumstances, be able to take up a claim for wrongful dismissal.

If you are unfortunate enough to find yourself in a situation where you have not only been dismissed, but you have grounds to believe that the dismissal is both wrongful and unfair, then generally there will be little point in pursuing both remedies.

Usually you will be better off electing to pursue a claim for unfair dismissal since compensation will probably be higher and costs are likely to be substantially less.

Damages for breach of contract have one key purpose – to put the person back in the situation which they would have been in, had the employer not breached the contract of employment. In a case of wrongful dismissal, this means compensation will be calculated as equivalent to the remuneration package (pay plus fringe benefits) which you would have been entitled to, had the contract been correctly terminated. Damages are calculated net of tax, national insurance, and any unemployment or social security benefit received.

In cases of wrongful dismissal, there is no compensation for injured feelings or distress arising from the dismissal.

Although levels of compensation for wrongful dismissal are usually lower than for unfair dismissal, it may in certain circumstances be more financially worthwhile to go for wrongful dismissal than unfair dismissal. Such circumstances include:

- Where you are not eligible to claim unfair dismissal – for example if you do not have two years' continuous service, or if you are over retirement age.
- Where you suspect that your dismissal may be regarded by an industrial tribunal as fair – and a claim for unfair dismissal would therefore not succeed.
- Where you have reason to believe that compensation for unfair dismissal would be reduced as a result of your own contributory conduct. There can be no deduction for contributory conduct in a successful claim for wrongful dismissal.
- If you are a highly paid employee on a fixed-term contract with no provision for early termination, or one with a long contractual notice period (say six months). Here damages for wrongful dismissal may amount to a greater sum than unfair dismissal compensation. Each case would depend on its own circumstances.
- Where you are too late to present a case for unfair dismissal (normal time limit is three months), you will probably still be able to put in a claim for wrongful dismissal. The basic limitation period for an action in a county court or High Court for breach of contract is six years.

Questions and Answers

Q My boss has openly said he wants to recruit someone younger and more qualified into my job. He suggested that, if I left before the end of the year, I would receive an ex-gratia payment from the company based on my five years service, but I felt I was being pressurised into leaving. Now my boss has said I must go by the month end and has asked me to sign a statement agreeing that, in exchange for the ex-gratia payment, I will not pursue a claim for unfair dismissal after I leave. What rights and options do I have under these circumstances?

A Firstly, no-one can force you to resign — if you are presssurised into resigning, then in law you have actually been dismissed. The principle behind this is that you have not been given the choice to remain in employment, hence a dismissal has taken place.

Secondly, the statement your employer has asked you to sign is not worth the paper it is written on, whether or not you sign it. If you have two years (or more) service, and you have been dismissed, your employer cannot remove your right to claim unfair dismissal by 'buying you out'.

Please read the sections in this chapter entitled 'Resign or be fired' and 'Termination by mutual agreeement' because there are other legitimate procedures your employer can use to procure your agreement not take a claim of unfair dismisal to a tribunal.

Q Must I have a minimum of two years service to be able to claim unfair dismissal?

A Yes, normally, but there are exceptions. Where dismissal is on account of sex or race discrimination, pregnancy, trade union membership or activities, health and safety activities, or asserting a statutory right, you can make a claim for unfair dismissal regardless of length of service.

Q I have been promoted to a new job, but am not coping very well with the work, despite training. My boss has indicated that, unless I master the job within the next six months, I could be dismissed. Surely this would be unfair?

A Such a dismissal could be fair, provided your employer had previously given you a reasonable chance to reach the required standard, including sufficient training. This would fall into the category of a dismissal on the grounds of lack of capability.

Q Nine months ago I became ill and have been unable to work ever since. I have supplied regular medical certificates to my employer, and have also been examined by the company doctor. Recently one of the company's senior managers visited me to discuss my position, and indicated that the company was reviewing whether to terminate my employment. Considering my illness is genuine, surely I cannot be dismissed?

A Long-term ill-health is well established as one of the potentially fair reasons for dismissal (in the category of lack of capability), even where the illness is genuine and fully certificated. Your employer must, of course, treat you in a reasonable manner, including proper investigation of the facts and proper consultation with you, otherwise the dismissal would be likely to be unfair.

Q What types of misconduct could I be sacked for?

A There is no law defining the types of misconduct for which you could be dismissed – most companies produce their own list as part of their disciplinary rules / procedure. Typically the type of misconduct you could be dismissed for (called gross misconduct) would include assaulting another employee, defrauding the company, deliberately damaging company property, gross negligence in carrying out your duties, etc. Other less serious misconduct, such as lateness, unauthorised absence from work, etc. would probably lead initially to a warning.

Q If I am dismissed for misconduct, what pay, etc., would I be entitled to receive?

A If you are dismissed after a series of warnings for misconduct, then you would be entitled to receive your pay up to the last day you worked, plus pay in lieu of your notice entitlement (according to your contract). You may also be entitled to pay in lieu of holidays not taken (depending, again, on the terms of your contract of employment).

If, on the other hand, you are dismissed for gross misconduct, you would be entitled to nothing beyond the wages you had already earned. This is known as summary dismissal.

Q I was dismissed recently for something I had done wrong. But I wasn't even given a chance to discuss the matter – just told to leave. I feel I was treated unfairly, and that the problem was not entirely my fault. What can I do about it?

A If you have a minimum of two years service, you can make a claim for unfair dismissal to an industrial tribunal. Even if your employer had a sound reason to dismiss you, the tribunal would examine whether your employer acted reasonably and followed a fair procedure. Giving an employee a proper opportunity to explain his side of the story is a fundamental element of fair procedure. Because this did not happen in your case, it is likely that your dismissal would be ruled unfair.

You would find, however, that the level of compensation a tribunal would award you would be reduced in proportion to the degree of your 'misconduct' prior to your dismissal — i.e whatever you did wrong will be taken into account in assessing the level of compensation.

If you have less than two years service at the date of your dismissal, there is nothing you can do about your dismissal.

Q My employer has dismissed me for drinking on duty, even although I had received no previous warnings. My boss termed what I had done 'gross misconduct'. Is this legal?

A If you are guilty of 'gross misconduct', i.e. misconduct of a serious nature, then your employer can dismiss you immediately, even if you have had no previous warnings. This is quite legal.

Q If I am convicted of a fairly minor criminal offence which took place outside work and in my own time, can I be automatically dismissed from my job?

A You cannot be automatically dismissed from your job — there is always a responsibility on your employer to investigate, consult, and follow certain other principles of procedure (described in this Chapter and in Chapter 10). In the case of criminal offences outside of work, dismissal may be fair if the nature of the offence makes you unsuitable to continue in your job, or if, as a result of your crime, your colleagues find the prospect of working with you genuinely unacceptable.

Q I have heard the term 'constructive dismissal'. What does this mean?

A Constructive dismissal occurs where you resign as a direct result of something your employer has done which is in breach of your contract of employment. Examples include pay cuts, major changes to working hours, transfer to a less senior position or some other major change to the terms of your employment to which you have not agreed. Full details are given in this Chapter and in Chapter 3.

Q The firm I work for has just been bought over by another business. Does the new employer have to keep me on?

A Yes, dismissal of an employee on account of the transfer of a business is automatically unfair — but there is one exception. If the employer has an 'economic, technical or organisational reason entailing changes in the workforce', then he may dismiss you. So, for example, structured redundancies — arising from the need to cut costs or reorganise the company after a company take-over — could be fair.

Q Having been dismissed recently from my employment after a series of warnings, I have just received my final pay cheque. I have not been paid my full notice period (my contract stipulates three months notice and I have only been paid for one month). Because I was employed with the company for less than two years, I assume I have no legal come-back. Am I right?

A No, you do have some rights in a case like this. What you describe is an example of wrongful dismissal – which means dismissal in breach of contract. In your case, failure to pay you for your full contractual notice period amounts to a breach of contract, and you are consequently eligible to make a claim for wrongful dismissal. Such claims, unlike claims for unfair dismissal, do not depend on length of service.

14
Redundancy and Lay-off

Redundancy occurs where an employer needs, due to genuine business reasons, to reduce his workforce. The circumstances in which redundancy may arise are:

● Where your employer has ceased trading;
● Where your employer has closed down a particular business premises (because either he has moved to other premises, or closed down completely);
● Where fewer employees are required (or are expected to be required) to do the kind of work you are employed to do. This can occur, for example, where a company has less work of a particular kind than previously, or following on from the introduction of new technology or methods of work.

Normally your job must have disappeared, or be about to disappear, before you can be made redundant. If your employer engages a direct replacement for someone who has been made redundant, then there is no redundancy in law.

More recently, redundancy has been defined (for the purposes of notification and trade union consultation) as 'any dismissal for a reason not related to the individual concerned'.

Redundancy is one of the potentially fair reasons for dismissal. Redundancy dismissals will normally be fair provided the redundancy is genuine

215

and the employer follows fair and reasonable procedures prior to dismissing the employee(s) concerned. Later sections in this chapter examine the various aspects of fair redundancy procedures.

CASE STUDY

Peter Maverick was the finance manager in a company which manufactured boxes and crates for use mainly in the fishing industry. He had worked for the company for 15 years, having been promoted from the post of accountant three years ago when the previous manager retired.

The managing director was concerned with Peter's performance – during the past 12 months, certain budget and expenditure decisions had been authorised which had had negative consequences for the company. Additionally it had come to light that the company's cash-flow position was not being monitored efficiently, resulting in unacceptably long delays in receiving payment from customers.

The managing director discussed the matter with the personnel manager and took a decision to make Peter redundant. This would provide the opportunity to reorganise the finance department, and examine efficiency improvements.

Peter was made redundant with three months pay in lieu of notice, statutory redundancy pay plus an ex-gratia sum equivalent to another three months' salary. Following the redundancy, the managing director promoted Sandra, the senior accountant, to the (newly-created) post of accounting manager where she was to take responsibility for the accounting, taxation and budgeting aspects of Peter's old job. The other accountant, Tom, took over responsibility for invoicing and credit control. Additionally, a new post of accounts assistant was created.

Peter Maverick subsequently made a claim to an industrial tribunal for unfair dismissal.

Q What were Peter's chances of success in his unfair dismissal claim?

A His chances were good. On examination of the facts, it would become clear to an industrial tribunal that the true reason for Peter Maverick's dismissal was not redundancy. In other words there was no reduction in the work which required to be done, nor in the numbers of people required to do it, but rather the work had been re-arranged and a different job title introduced.

The company might possibly have been able to dismiss Peter on the basis of capability, provided there were sufficient grounds for doing so, and provided a proper procedure was followed prior to dismissal. But because the label of redundancy was attached to a dismissal which appeared to be motivated by factors which had nothing to do with redundancy, the dismissal would probably be unfair. The fact that redundancy pay was awarded would make no difference to the outcome, although it would ultimately affect the level of compensation which Peter could receive.

How do you stand in a situation where your employer moves to new premises? In law this creates a situation where the entire workforce is potentially redundant. This is because employees are deemed to be redundant when their job ceases to exist at a particular place of work, even if a new job is available at a new workplace. If, however, the new workplace is reasonably near to the old, it would be normal for employees to transfer on the basis that working at the new location is a suitable alternative. No redundancy pay is due to you where you move to new premises under these circumstances.

If you have a mobility clause in your contract of employment, and your employer moves to new premises, then you are not technically redundant because your contract allows for you to be moved to another place of work. In this case you would be contractually obliged to move to the new premises.

For more information on what constitutes suitable alternative employment, please refer to the section on this subject later in this chapter.

CASE STUDY

Mrs Barrett worked for a company in Birmingham and was able to walk to work in 10 minutes. The company decided to move from Birmingham to Redditch and, in order to make the move as easy as possible for staff, made arrangements for a coach service and for ex-gratia travel allowances.

For Mrs Barrett, however, the new location meant a journey of 13.5 miles, taking about 40 minutes. She felt that she could not move to Redditch because she suffered from travel sickness. She did undertake a trial period in the new location, but afterwards decided that she could not continue.

The company considered that the offer of work in Redditch was suitable and that because Mrs Barrett had refused it, she had, in effect, resigned. Mrs Barrett, however, made a claim to an industrial tribunal for redundancy.

Q Was the company's offer of alternative employment in Redditch a suitable one, and was Mrs Barrett's refusal under the circumstances reasonable?

A The tribunal decided that a 40-minute journey to work was not unusual or unreasonable and the additional journey did not make the job offer unsuitable.

On the question of travel sickness, whilst the tribunal sympathised with Mrs Barrett, they considered that she could have taken steps to solve the problem by seeking medical advice. Her refusal to accept the alternative employment was consequently unreasonable. She therefore lost her case.

Based on the case *Barrett* v *Boxfoldia Ltd.*

Where the business you work for has been transferred to a new owner (for example in a take-over or merger) then you are not redundant because in law all contracts of employment are transferred automatically. It is automatically unfair to make employees redundant on account of the transfer of a business.

Volunteers for redundancy

If your employer asks for volunteers for redundancy, then this does not necessarily mean that those who do volunteer will be accepted. Most employers retain the right to have the final say as to whether or not a particular employee is to be made redundant.

If, however, you do volunteer for redundancy during a company-wide redundancy programme, then your employer must treat you for all purposes in the same way as those chosen by the company. In other words, as a volunteer you will have the same rights to redundancy pay and other considerations as individuals whom the company has selected.

Your right to be consulted

Under the terms of the EU collective redundancies directive, employers must ensure that workers' representatives are informed or consulted in a collective redundancy situation. Consequently, employers are obliged to consult a recognised trade union (if there is one) or elected representative of employees who will be affected by redundancy. This requirement exists where twenty or more employees are to be made redundant.

Consulting a recognised trade union

Employers who recognise an appropriate trade union have a legal duty to consult that union in advance about the proposed redundancies. The time periods for consultation are laid down in law and are:

- Where twenty or more employees are to be made redundant, the company must allow at least a 30-day consultation period.
- Where 100 or more employees are to be made redundant, the consultation period must be at least 90 days.

These are minimum periods of consultation – the law also states that consultation should take place in good time.

If the company fails to consult, the trade union involved can make a claim for a 'protective award' (this is explained in the next section).

The consultation must be genuine, and must cover the following areas:

- The reasons for the redundancy proposals;
- The numbers and categories of employees who are expected to be affected;
- The proposed criteria to be used for selection (i.e. the methods to be used to choose who will be made redundant);
- The proposed method of carrying out the redundancies;
- Whether anything can be done to reduce the need for redundancies, or reduce the number of employees to be dismissed, or to lessen the consequences of the dismissals;
- The proposed method of calculating the amount of any redundancy payments over and above the statutory minimum payments.

Protective awards

Where an employer has failed to carry out proper consultation in accordance with the stipulated time frames, the trade union concerned may apply to an industrial tribunal for a protective award.

A protective award is in effect compensation paid to employees for a company's failure to consult. The amount of the award will depend on what an industrial tribunal considers reasonable in the circumstances. It will usually be equivalent to pay for the period of time during which the company should have consulted, i.e. up to 30 days or 90 days pay (depending on the number of employees who are being made redundant). The period of the protective award is known as the protected period.

CASE STUDY

The company recognised the GMB union, and when it went into receivership on 12 July, the union continued to be recognised by the receivers. On 19 July, 22 employees were made redundant without any advance notice to the union. On 30 August, because no buyer for the company had been found, the receivers decided to close the factory and made the majority of the remaining employees redundant. This too was done without any advance notice of the redundancies being given to the union. The union applied to an industrial tribunal for a protective award.

Q Was it reasonable, in the circumstances, for the company to fail to comply with the consultation requirements?

A Despite the fact that it is common to reduce numbers of staff prior to the sale of a company in receivership, and despite the fact the company had no work on its order books, the lack of consultation could not be justified in law. A protective award was thus made for a period of 90 days.

Based on the case *GMB* v *Rankin & Harrison*.

Under the Trade Union Reform and Employment Rights Act 1993, the protective award cannot be offset against other sums of money paid to employees, for example pay in lieu of notice.

Consulting employees' elected representatives

If there is no recognised trade union in your company, employers have a duty to consult employees' elected representatives regarding forthcoming redundancies. Failure to consult would be regarded by an industrial tribunal as a breach of fair procedure, liable to render any subsequent redundancy dismissals unfair.

CASE STUDY

Mr Cowley had been employed for many years as a fork-lift truck driver with a small firm. His employer suffered a down-turn in trade and decided to make two of their staff redundant. There was no trade union involvement and no agreed procedure for redundancies. The company's managing director selected Mr Cowley and one other employee for redundancy on the basis of their particular skills, and dismissed them without warning or consultation. Mr Cowley claimed unfair dismissal.

Q Did lack of consultation make this dismissal unfair?

A Yes, the dismissal was found to be unfair despite the fact that there had been a genuine redundancy situation within the company. Mr Cowley's dismissal was procedurally unfair due to lack of warning / consultation. He was awarded only a small sum, however, (the equivalent of two weeks' wages) as the tribunal considered that, even if the workforce had been warned about the redundancies, Mr Cowley would still have been selected for dismissal.

Based on the case *Cowley* v *Manson Timber Ltd*

Another case which demonstrates the importance of consultation in redundancy situations was heard by an industrial tribunal in Scotland in 1992. A branch manager of a national company was taken outside on to the pavement and told, without prior warning, that his job was redundant and 'he'd better just go now'. Not surprisingly, the tribunal found that the manner in which the company dealt with the situation was 'wholly unreasonable in employment terms'. The dismissal was unfair, despite the fact that the company was facing a genuine redundancy situation.

There can, however, be exceptions to the rule requiring employers to consult employees about forthcoming redundancies if there are special circumstances which make it impracticable for the employer to comply, or if consultation would be futile. The following case study is an example:

CASE STUDY

Mr Leese claimed unfair dismissal when he was made redundant without consultation or any offer of alternative employment. His employer, a food company, had, however, been pressed by the Ministry of Agriculture to reorganise its structure within a strict timescale, and instructed to do so secretly.

Q Did lack of consultation make this dismissal unfair?

A No, in this case there were exceptional circumstances which made consultation impossible. The employer acted reasonably under all the circumstances.

Based on the case *Leese* v *Food from Britain*.

Your right not to be unfairly selected for redundancy

Some employers have an established procedure for handling redundancies, which would include details of the methods to be used to select those who are to be made redundant (the criteria). Dismissal on the grounds of redundancy may be unfair if the employer unreasonably fails to follow an agreed procedure for selection, or changes his mind on a whim.

Criteria for selection

The criteria for selection must be seen to be reasonable, objective and fair. Criteria can include, for example:

- Length of service (last in, first out, or LIFO as it is usually known). This method of selection is easy to apply objectively and, until relatively recently, was the most commonly used.
- Capability and skill in performing the job. This method of selection may be used if, for example, the company operates an appraisal scheme on which employees are assessed annually.
- Qualifications.
- Experience.
- Flexibility/adaptability.
- Attendance or disciplinary record.

These days the majority of employers use several criteria, rather than just one, and often aim to achieve a balanced workforce in relation to skills and capability once the redundancies have been carried out. Thus an employer may reasonably decide to use a combination of, for example, job skills, experience, flexibility, special qualifications, general employment record and work performance as the criteria for selection.

Criteria must be clearly defined and not too vague. If, like one company in 1986, your employer states that the criteria for selection will be 'the retention of a balance of skills in each department' then this is likely to be found unreasonable if referred to an industrial tribunal, because it is too vague. Another example in 1990 was a company whose criteria was 'to retain personnel best suited for the needs of the business under the new operating conditions'. A tribunal ruled that dismissals on the basis of this criteria were unfair because the criteria were subjective and no records were referred to in making the selections.

Once the criteria for selection have been agreed, your employer must not deviate from them. If, for example, your employer has established that skills and qualifications are to be used as the criteria for selection, and then subsequently selects an employee for redundancy on the grounds of a poor attendance record, then this would be an unfair dismissal.

What employers may do, however, is establish differing criteria for different groups of employees. So long as the criteria are subsequently applied consistently, then this would be quite in order.

CASE STUDY

An employer nominated 'productivity, absenteeism, attitude to work, and cooperation with requests to work extra hours' as criteria for selection in a redundancy programme. These criteria were applied to employees over the last two years of their employment. Mrs Greene was selected on the basis of the criteria and claimed unfair dismissal. She had been absent from work on maternity leave and therefore had scored badly on the various criteria.

Q Why was this dismissal unfair?

A The dismissal was unfair because, although the criteria themselves were reasonable, the company had not applied them in a fair manner. Mrs Greene's record prior to her maternity leave had been excellent, but in applying the criteria over a period of only two years, she had gained a false score.

Based on the case *Eurocasters Ltd v Greene*.

For a dismissal on the grounds of redundancy to be fair, the criteria must also be applied in a reasonable fashion. Management who are involved in selection must apply the criteria objectively, consistently, fairly and reasonably. This means that managers' personal opinions, likes and dislikes, etc. must not be taken into account.

Criteria which may not be used are those which would obviously be illegal, for example selection on the grounds of sex, race or trade union membership.

'Bumping'

Sometimes an employer may adopt a policy of 'bumping' in a redundancy exercise. Bumping occurs when job A is redundant, but instead of selecting employee A for redundancy, the employer moves employee A into job B with the result that employee B is made redundant. This approach is consistent with the concept of redundancy being due to a job disappearing. It is a sort of transferred redundancy, and is perfectly legal. Nevertheless, in the event of a claim for unfair dismissal following such a redundancy, an industrial tribunal would examine very carefully whether the redundancy had been carried out in a fair and objective manner, and would be careful to ascertain that there was no sinister reason behind the 'bumping'!

Your right to be offered suitable alternative employment

Employers should make a genuine effort to identify suitable alternative employment for employees whose jobs are to be made redundant. This is because employees are not redundant unless there is no work available for them to do under their contracts of employment. If the employer fails to attempt to find alternative work, then this is likely to mean that any subsequent claim for unfair dismissal by a redundant employee will succeed. 'Suitable' in this context means work which the employee can reasonably be expected to do, and which is on terms and conditions not substantially less favourable.

It is a legal requirement that any offer of alternative employment must be made prior to the expiry of the employees' notice period. The new job offer would normally be within the same company,but employers may be expected to look beyond the immediate working environment, for example to associated companies.

In the event of a company moving to new premises, if the new workplace is some distance from the old, for example in a different town, then an offer of alternative employment in the new location may not be suitable and you would be entitled to refuse any offer to move and claim redundancy pay. This, however, would not be the case if you have a mobility clause in your contract of employment. If you have such a mobility clause in your contract, then your job would not be redundant in the event of a move to new premises, as you would be contractually obliged to move.

Where alternative employment is offered, the new job must be available to start within four weeks of the termination of the original job, although in most cases would run consecutively with the old job. In this situation continuity of service is preserved because the employee is, in fact, not being made redundant.

Although the onus is on your employer to look for alternative employment, you have every right to enquire of your employer whether there is any chance of alternative employment within your company or an associated company. There is no harm in making your wishes known to your employer, who may, for example, be unaware that you would be willing to move to an alternative location, or accept work of a different kind.

If you unreasonably refuse suitable alternative employment, you will lose your right to redundancy pay. You will, however, still be regarded as having been dismissed for redundancy, and therefore retain the usual right to claim unfair dismissal.

If an offer of alternative employment made to you is unsuitable, then you are entitled to refuse it and still claim your redundancy pay. In some cases, even if an offer is suitable, provided you have reasonable grounds for refusing it, then you would still be entitled to redundancy pay. An example of this could be where an alternative job with slightly different hours would create family difficulties for you.

Trial period in the new job

Where you accept an offer of alternative employment, your employer must allow you a four week trial period in the new job to establish whether or not it really is suitable for you, and that you are capable of doing it. If re-training is required for employment in the new job, the trial period may be for a longer period than four weeks, in which case there must be a written agreement covering the extended trial period.

You are not limited to just one statutory trial period, but may have any number of trials in different jobs. If they all prove useless and your employment is finally terminated, then you are still deemed to have been dismissed for redundancy on the date your original contract came to an end.

If you reject the new job before the end of the trial period for good reasons, then you will be considered to have been made redundant from the date on which the original job ended, and will be entitled to redundancy pay.

Factors which tribunals have often taken into account when assessing the suitability of an alternative job offer are:

- Place of work;
- Working hours / shift pattern;
- Loss of pay – usually an employee would be justified in refusing an offer of alternative work on lower pay;
- Loss of responsibility or status, or job prospects;
- Working environment – for example an employee with a dust allergy may reasonably refuse to work in an environment where the allergy would be aggravated.

To an extent, the 'suitability' of an alternative position can be viewed subjectively. For example, you may be offered an alternative position in a different location. The suitability of this could well depend on where you live in relation to the new location, your means of transport and family circumstances. The offer may suit one employee perfectly well, but be unsuitable for another person due to personal factors. Each case would have to be considered individually.

The timing of the offer could also be a relevant factor. For example if an alternative job offer is made to you only days before the date your contract is due to terminate, and you have already secured a new job elsewhere, then you may well be acting reasonably in refusing the alternative offer from your employer.

CASE STUDY

Mr MacGregor worked in the civil engineering and construction industry. As a result of redundancy, his employer, William Tawse Ltd, offered him work at a site in the Hebrides from where he would only be able to travel home one weekend in every six. Mr MacGregor refused to move to the new job.

Q Was Mr MacGregor's refusal to move reasonable?

A The tribunal held that Mr MacGregor's refusal to move to the Hebrides was unreasonable, as the work was suitable and a degree of mobility was to be expected in the construction industry.

Based on the case *MacGregor* v *William Tawse Ltd*.

Contrast the outcome of the preceding case with the next case:

CASE STUDY

Mr MacCallum also worked for William Tawse Ltd and was made an identical offer to Mr MacGregor in the case above. In this case, however, Mr MacCallum refused to move because he had a wife and five children, two of whom were in poor health. His wife was not able to look after the family for prolonged periods without help.

Q Was Mr MacCallum's refusal to move to the Hebrides reasonable?

A In this case the tribunal found that, even although the work offered to Mr MacCallum was suitable, his special domestic circumstances made his refusal reasonable.

Based on the case *MacCallum* v *William Tawse Ltd.*

Your right to paid time off work to look for another job

Employees who are under notice of redundancy are entitled to reasonable time off work with pay to look for alternative work, or to make arrangements for training. This provision only applies, however, to employees with two or more years service, although in practice employers may allow all staff such time off work.

The law has not defined how much time off is 'reasonable' in this context, but industrial tribunals have indicated that a maximum of two days per week would not be unreasonable.

Your right to notice

After the period of consultation has elapsed, employees must be given their normal periods of notice, according to their contracts of employment. For full details of your rights to notice, see Chapter 12.

Leaving early

If you wish to leave before the expiry of your notice period, for example if you have found another job, then provided your employer agrees to vary your notice period, you may leave early without losing your right to redundancy pay. If you leave early without your employer's agreement, however, that is a different matter and you may lose your right to redundancy pay.

There is, however, a formal provision where (once your employer has given you notice) you can give 'counter-notice' in writing that you intend to leave on an earlier date. Provided this date falls within the statutory notice period (or your contractual notice period if this is longer), then you could leave early and retain your right to redundancy pay.

The timing of this provision is critical and rather complicated. For example, supposing at the end of June your employer gives you three months notice of redundancy (which would take you to the end of September). Suppose further that under your contract of employment, you are entitled to only two months notice of termination of employment, so in fact your employer has given you an extra month's notice. It is the two months notice period which is critical here. If you serve a counter-notice on your employer to leave earlier than the end of September, your new leaving date must not be before the end of July, which would represent the beginning of your contractual notice period. If you leave before the end of July in this example, you would lose your right to a redundancy payment.

Most employers will comply with a reasonable request to leave early, if the reason is that the employee has found another job. But it is as well to be very careful as to the timing of your early departure!

Your right to redundancy pay

To be entitled to redundancy pay, you must have been continuously employed by your employer for at least two years. The amount of redundancy pay increases according to the number of complete years you have worked for your employer. Entitlement to redundancy pay applies to part-time workers as well as to full-timers.

In calculating your length of service, it is important to remember that any periods during which you have been on strike do not count towards continuous service. You therefore have to subtract the length of any such periods from your total service, to come up with the correct number of complete years. Part years do not count towards calculation of redundancy pay.

You cannot, of course, receive redundancy pay twice for the same period of employment. This means that if you were previously made redundant by your employer (and paid redundancy pay), re-engaged and subsequently made redundant again, the first period of your employment will not be counted in calculating your second redundancy payment.

Employees who volunteer (and are accepted by the company) for redundancy are also entitled to redundancy pay in law, provided they have at least two years service.

If you are made redundant, there is no need for you to put in a claim for redundancy pay as it is your employer's responsibility to calculate it and make payment. If, however, you do not receive the redundancy pay to which you think you are entitled, you should make a written request to your employer, or alternatively you may make a claim to an industrial tribunal.

You must make any such claims within six months of the date of the termination of your employment.

If your employer is insolvent, or is unable to pay your statutory redundancy pay, you can apply to the Department of Employment for a direct payment from the Redundancy Fund. Such an application will only be considered if you have first applied in writing to your employer for payment. Please refer to the section on Insolvency in Chapter 12 for further information.

A redundancy payment will not affect your entitlement to any rights you may have to pay in lieu of notice, nor to unemployment benefit.

Employees excluded from receiving redundancy pay
Certain employees are not eligible for redundancy pay as follows:

- Employees who are over the company's normal retirement age, or if no normal retirement age exists, aged 65 or over;
- Employees working outside Great Britain, including those working in Southern Ireland (unless the employee has been recalled to Britain before the employment contract ends – but even in these circumstances the service abroad may not count for redundancy pay purposes).
- Domestic servants who are members of the employer's immediate family and work in a private household;
- Share fishermen;
- Merchant seamen covered by the National Maritime Board Redundancy Payment Agreement;
- Crown servants and employees in public service (who are covered by other arrangements);
- National Health Service employees (who are covered by other arrangements;
- Employees of the government of an overseas territory;
- Apprentices, whose service ends because the apprenticeship contract has expired.

Calculation of statutory redundancy pay
Statutory redundancy payments are calculated according to a fixed formula and depend on the individual employee's age, length of service and pay.

There is a ceiling put on 'a week's pay' by the government, which is reviewed each year. At the time of writing the ceiling is £205 per week. This means that if you earn more than £205, then your redundancy pay will be calculated as if you earned £205 per week, and if you earn less than

£205, then your redundancy pay will be calculated on the basis of your actual weekly pay.

The calculation is as follows:

Completed Years of Service	Amount of Payment
Number of years service between age 18 – 21 inclusive	0.5 week's pay per year
Number of years service between 22 – 40 inclusive	1 week's pay per year
Number of years service over age 41, up to age 64 inclusive	1.5 week's pay per year

Men and women aged 64 have their statutory entitlement reduced by one twelfth in respect of each month they remain in employment. In other words their payment is tapered as they approach age 65. Statutory redundancy pay may also be reduced if you are in receipt of a pension from your employer, or are entitled to receive a pension within 90 weeks of dismissal.

The maximum length of service which can be taken into account in a redundancy pay claim is 20 years, and the maximum amount of money you can receive is currently £6,150. The formula for arriving at this calculation is 20 (years) × 1.5 (weeks) × £205. Service under the age of 18 does not count for redundancy pay purposes.

There is, of course, nothing to stop an employer from offering additional sums of redundancy pay over and above the statutory amount, and many employers in fact do this. Payments are currently tax free up to £30,000.

Employers are obliged to give redundant employees a written statement indicating how their redundancy payment has been calculated.

Short-time working and lay-off

Short-time occurs where, because of a reduction in work, the employee works less than half a week. Lay-off is where no work at all is available under the contract of employment.

In either case, the employer must continue to pay your full salary, unless there is an express or implied term in your contract of employment allowing payment to be reduced or stopped.

If you are in any doubt, you should check your contract of employment to see whether there are any terms relating to short-time working or lay-off. If such a term is included within the contract, then your employer is entitled to reduce or stop your salary.

In the absence of a term in the contract which allows your employer to lay-off or introduce short-time, you would be entitled to treat any suspension of pay as breach of contract. This means that you would have the right to put in a claim to an industrial tribunal for unlawful deduction of wages, or (provided you have two years service) to resign and claim constructive dismissal. Periods of lay-off or short-time working still count towards your continuous service with the company.

Your right to a redundancy payment during a lay-off or short-time working

Normally you will be entitled to a redundancy payment only if you have been dismissed by your employer on account of redundancy. However the one exception to this situation is during lay-off or short-time working. Employees who have been laid-off or kept on short-time for four or more consecutive weeks, or for a series of six or more weeks within a continuous 13 week period, can choose to treat themselves as redundant if they wish.

Here you must initiate the claim for redundancy pay and your claim must be put in writing. If your employer believes that normal working is likely to be resumed within four weeks, then the claim may be resisted by serving a counter-notice.

Guarantee payments

If you are laid-off (without pay) from your work, you become entitled in law to a guarantee payment for up to five days in any period of three months. Guarantee payments do not apply where you have worked for part of a day.

CASE STUDY

Mr Bloomfield worked in a factory which closed down for five days at Christmas. As he had not been with the company for long, he was not entitled to holiday pay, and was forced to take unpaid leave on the days when the factory was closed. He claimed guarantee pay.

Q Was Mr Bloomfield entitled to guarantee pay in these circumstances?

A The tribunal found that the annual shut-down over Christmas had been agreed between the employer and the union, and had been incorporated into employees' contracts of employment. The days in question were therefore not days when Mr Bloomfield would normally be required to work. Consequently his claim for guarantee pay failed.

Based on the case *Bloomfield v RHM Ingredient Supplies Ltd.*

Guarantee payments are stated as a daily amount, the current level being the vast sum of £14.10. So the maximum you can receive would be five times this amount, i.e. £70.50. These amounts are reviewed each year by the government.

To qualify for a guarantee payment, you must have at least one month's service with the company.

To be eligible for guarantee payments, you must be available to work, be willing to accept suitable alternative work and not be on strike.

Questions and Answers

Q I have decided to stop work and take some time off to take a college course. Can I ask my employer for redundancy?

A Redundancy occurs where a job has disappeared, the amount of work has decreased, or fewer people than before are required to do the same work. In your case, your job and the amount of work have not changed, on the contrary you personally are choosing to leave. This is not redundancy.

Q I was made redundant from my last job, but a few weeks afterwards someone else was recruited into my old job. Is this legal?

A No, it sounds as if the true reason for your dismissal was not redundancy, because the job continues to exist.

If you have two years (or more) service, you could make a claim for unfair dismissal to an industrial tribunal, and you would have a good chance of succeeding. Your claim would have to be made within three months of the date of the termination of your employment.

Q My employer is planning to reduce staff numbers in order to cut costs. A letter was sent to all staff requesting volunteers for redundancy. If I volunteer, would I still be entitled to redundancy pay?

A Yes, provided there is a genuine redundancy situation, volunteers for redundancy are treated in all respects in the same way as employees selected by the company.

Q There are rumours in my department that some of us are to be made redundant, but no-one, including my department manager, seems to know what is happening. Isn't management supposed to consult people about redundancies?

A Yes, they have a duty to consult the employees who are affected by the proposed redundancies, or their representatives. Failure to consult can ultimately lead to subsequent redundancy dismissals being unfair.

Q I have known for several weeks that the company I work for was proposing to make about 40 people redundant. Now the managing director has sent out a letter detailing how people are to be selected for redundancy. This is to be based on 'skills, aptitude and job performance'. I thought that selection for redundancy was usually based on length of service, and since I have been here for nearly 20 years, I am now worried that my job might not be as secure as I thought. Can you clarify this for me?

A Selection for redundancy does not have to be based on length of service. The 'last in, first out' principle is one of many different criteria on which an employer may base selection for redundancy.

Many employers are today using criteria such as job skills, experience, flexibility, special qualifications, general employment record and work performance. So long as your employer applies the criteria consistently, objectively and fairly, then he is acting legally.

Q My job is being made redundant, but I have been offered another job in a different department on the same pay and conditions. The work will be different, however, and I am not sure it would suit me. How do I stand in law?

A You are entitled to a trial period of four weeks to see whether the new job is suitable for you, i.e whether the work is within your capabilities and reasonable in relation to your experience and level of seniority. If the work proves unsuitable, then you may leave and retain your right to redundancy pay.

If, on the other hand, you unreasonably refuse a suitable offer of alternative employment, then you will lose your right to redundancy pay.

Q I am working out my notice since being told my job is redundant. Am I entitled to get time off work to attend job interviews?

A Yes, provided you have at least two years service. If you are entitled to time off, then it must be paid for.

Q My employer has announced redundancies and I have been given three months notice in accordance with my contract. I have been lucky enough to find another job, however, and would like to leave sooner. If I do this, how will it affect my redundancy pay?

A Your best course of action is to seek your employer's agreement to an earlier leaving date. Provided your employer agrees, you may leave early without losing your right to redundancy pay. If you leave early without your employer's agreement, however, that is a different matter and you may lose your right to redundancy pay.

Alternatively, there is a formal provision where you can give 'counter-notice' in writing that you intend to leave on an earlier date. So long as this date falls within your contractual notice period, then you could leave early and retain your right to redundancy pay. Details are given in this chapter.

Q Having worked in the same job for 10 years, I have been informed that my job will be redundant. How much redundancy pay will I get? I am 35 years old.

A Statutory redundancy pay is calculated according to a defined formula, which is explained in this chapter. The formula is based on your age, length of service, and pay. In your case you would receive 10 weeks pay, but your actual statutory redundancy payment could not exceed £2,050, since there is a 'ceiling' on a 'week's pay' of (currently) £205.

Your employer may choose to pay you a higher amount of money to compensate you for redundancy. In other words, an ex-gratia payment can be paid over and above the statutory redundancy pay due to you. Redundancy payments are tax-free up to a total of £30,000.

Q I have been laid off work for four weeks now and there doesn't appear to be any prospect of work picking up again. Can I claim redundancy?

A Yes, if you have been laid off for four or more consecutive weeks, then you have the right to regard yourself as redundant. In this situation it is up to you to claim redundancy pay from your employer, and your claim must be put in writing.

15

Industrial Tribunals

The function of an industrial tribunal

Industrial tribunals were established in the 1960's to allow ordinary people to have access to justice in an informal, inexpensive and speedy fashion. Industrial tribunals are independent from all government bodies. Most of the larger cities and towns in Britain have tribunal offices and hearings take place around the country. The decisions of tribunals are required by law to be kept in a register and this register is available centrally for inspection by members of the public.

Today tribunals deal with about 40 different types of employment-related disputes. Unfair dismissals, including redundancy dismissals, form the bulk of tribunal work, but claims for redundancy payments and claims under the Wages Act are also common. Other issues dealt with include sex and race discrimination claims, maternity rights in employment and trade union membership rights.

Tribunal procedure

Sometimes the parties to a dispute settle 'out of court' in advance of the tribunal hearing. This happens in more than half the claims which are raised.

Where, however, a case does reach a hearing, the procedure is informal, straightforward and flexible. No-one wears gowns or wigs in the hearing room and everybody is seated. Applicants may present their own case if they wish without legal representation, or alternatively they may elect to be represented by another person. Each party may question their own witnesses and those introduced by the other party. Tribunal panel members may also ask questions of both parties and their witnesses, in order to obtain information or clarify a particular issue.

Whilst giving evidence both parties and their witnesses are required to take the oath, but after that they are free to explain their case openly. The approach taken is very much non-confrontational and it would be unusual for an applicant or witness to be intimidated in any way.

Tribunal hearings are normally open to the public, including the press. However, in certain cases a tribunal may agree to a private hearing, for example in a case dealing with alleged sexual harassment.

For cases of unfair dismissal the onus is on the employer to prove the reason, or the principal reason, for the dismissal. The tribunal will then proceed to hear the evidence from both sides and to consider whether, under all the circumstances, the employer acted reasonably in deciding to dismiss the employee, and whether proper and fair procedures were followed.

For sex or race discrimination cases the burden of proof is technically on the applicant to prove that discrimination occurred (you are the applicant if you are making a claim that you have been discriminated against). In practice, however, tribunals may draw an inference that discrimination has occurred without actual proof being shown by the applicant. This happens particularly in cases where the employer is unable to provide a material defence against the claim.

Over time tribunals have developed 'tests of fairness' that are used in reaching decisions on various cases. In other words, tribunal decisions depend largely on precedent. Therefore where a particular decision has been taken by one of the higher courts (for example the Court of Appeal) in the past, a tribunal is obliged to make a similar decision if the present case is similar. Thus consistency is assured.

Witnesses/documents

It is customary for both parties to bring witnesses to the tribunal hearing who can present personal knowledge of the matters in dispute and help establish the facts. If you are bringing a case to a tribunal it is likely to be in your own interests to arrange for any relevant witnesses to attend the hearing.

Similarly it is normally in an applicant's interests to bring along to the hearing any documentary evidence which might help their case. If you have difficulty in persuading someone to give evidence on your behalf, the tribunal may grant an order requiring the witness to attend.

Similarly if there are documents which you wish to cite as evidence, and you are unable to obtain them from the other party, then the tribunal may order the disclosure of such documents if, in their opinion, there is good reason to do so.

Appeals

After the tribunal hearing and decision, there is a procedure for appeal (to the Employment Appeal Tribunal, or EAT as it is known). However, appeals can only be brought on a point of law, and not because you do not like the decision! What this means is that if the tribunal has made a mistake regarding the legal principles relevant to your case, or where there is no evidence to support its decision, then an appeal can be lodged.

When you receive your copy of the tribunal's decision, you will be informed as to the procedure for making an appeal. The appeal must be made in writing within 42 days of the date on which the decision was sent to you.

What are your chances of success?

The number of cases dealt with by industrial tribunals continues to rise each year. At the time of writing, the most recent statistics available are those pertaining to the year 1993–1994. During this period a total of 69,612 cases were registered with industrial tribunals across the UK, of which the majority (42,757) were for unfair dismissal. This represents a rise of 30% over the year before. Of the total number of applications, 18,565 were settled via ACAS (Advisory, Conciliation and Arbitration Service), 23,997 were withdrawn, 11,687 were successful at tribunal hearing, and the remainder unsuccessful at tribunal hearing.

Out of the unfair dismissal claims, 15,249 were settled through ACAS, 12,680 withdrawn and 5,952 were successful at tribunal hearing.

The success rate at tribunal hearing varies considerably according to the type of claim involved. Of the unfair dismissal claims which reached hearing, 44 per cent succeeded and 56 per cent were rejected. Claims for redundancy pay on the other hand were successful at tribunal in 71 per cent of cases, whereas only 29 per cent failed. For Wages Act claims the figures were 64 per cent succeeding and 36 per cent failing.

For sex discrimination claims, only 38 per cent were won at tribunal and for race discrimination the figure was even lower at 29 per cent. It must be remembered of course that these figures represent only those cases which actually got as far as the tribunal hearing. The majority of cases were settled out of court – resolved through ACAS, settled privately or otherwise withdrawn. Many of these no doubt had satisfactory outcomes for the applicant.

Very few unfair dismissal claims result in an award for reinstatement or re-engagement. Only 1.2 per cent of all successful unfair dismissal claims resulted in such an order during 1993–1994. This is partly due to the fact that the majority of applicants do not want re-employment, but seek compensation instead.

The average compensation award for unfair dismissal during 1993–1994 was £2,773, which was an increase of 6 per cent over the previous year. For sex discrimination the average award was £2,999, although this statistic is likely to be blown out the window in the future now that the upper limit on sex discrimination awards has been abolished. For race discrimination, almost half the awards were in the range of £1,000–£1,500.

The total number of cases appealed to the Employment Appeal Tribunal was only 951 (representing 4.2 per cent of cases heard at tribunal). Of the 951, 44 per cent were withdrawn, 32 per cent dismissed at hearing and 24 per cent allowed or remitted to another tribunal for re-hearing. It is much more likely for cases of alleged discrimination to result in an appeal – 12 per cent of sex and race discrimination cases which when to tribunal resulted in an appeal (as opposed to the overall figure of only 4.2 per cent).

Eligibility for claims to an industrial tribunal

All individuals have the right to pursue a claim through an industrial tribunal, subject to length of service (see next section). If your employer attempts to persuade you to sign an agreement to settle a claim for unfair dismissal, on the basis that you will agree not to bring proceedings before an industrial tribunal, this will be unenforceable in law. Even if you actually sign an agreement and accept a payment of money, this will not prevent you from pursuing your claim through the tribunal.

There are two exceptions to this, the first being where an agreement and settlement are reached under the guidance of a conciliation officer from ACAS, using a prescribed form known as a COT3 form. The second method is through obtaining legal advice and entering into a written agreement via an independent qualified lawyer, i.e. a lawyer who is not acting for the employer or an associated employer.

Qualifying periods for applying to an industrial tribunal

The qualifying period for making a claim to an industrial tribunal varies depending on the type of claim you are making. For some claims, including most unfair dismissal claims, the qualifying period is two years continuous service. For other types of claim, e.g. sex/race discrimination there is no service qualification at all. Please refer to the section dealing with your type of complaint for information on qualifying periods.

Time limits for applying to an industrial tribunal

You must submit your tribunal application within the prescribed time limit. For most claims, the time limit is three months after the relevant event. For unfair dismissal claims this means that your application must be received at the tribunal office within three months of the date of the termination of your contract of employment, and for claims of discrimination within three months of the discriminatory act in question. To give a precise example, if your contract of employment terminated on 15 March, then your application would have to be with the tribunal by 14 June at the latest.

CASE STUDY

Ms Corrigan was dismissed on 5 February 1992. She consulted her solicitors on 19. March and instructed them to commence unfair dismissal proceedings. The tribunal application and a covering letter, dated 25 March, were prepared and posted to the Central Office of Industrial Tribunals.

By July, having heard nothing, Ms Corrigan asked her solicitors what was happening with her application. It was then discovered that no acknowledgement of the application had been received from the Tribunal Office. A fresh application was submitted on 4 August, some three months out of time.

Q Would the tribunal accept the case in these circumstances?

A An appeal tribunal decided that the applicant or her advisers had failed to take all steps reasonably necessary to ensure that the application was presented in time. The solicitors should have checked to see that the application had been received and registered. It was not enough to assume that, because the application was posted, it would be delivered. Unfortunately for Ms Corrigan, therefore, she lost the opportunity to have her claim of unfair dismissal heard.

Based on the case *Capital Foods Retail Ltd* v *Corrigan.*

Tribunals do have limited discretion to accept complaints made after the time limit has elapsed, if they consider that it was not reasonably practicable for the person to make the complaint earlier. It is much safer, however, to ensure your application is lodged in time so that you do not risk losing the right to have your case heard.

Situations where it is 'not reasonably practicable' to present an application in time might include abnormal postal delays (although this may not always be accepted as a valid reason), faulty advice from a member of tribunal staff (but not faulty advice from a solicitor or trade union representative), or, in some cases, genuine ignorance of unfair dismissal rights or of the time limit for applying. Now that you have read this far, the latter should not be a problem!

CASE STUDY

Ms Taylor was compulsorily retired (under protest) on medical grounds and told that she was entitled to a pension. More than three months after her retirement, she discovered that she was not, after all, entitled to a pension from her ex-employer. She only then became aware that her dismissal could have been unfair.

Q Would a tribunal make an exception to the three-month time limit under these circumstances?

A Yes, there was sufficient evidence to show that Ms Taylor had accepted the termination of her employment only because she genuinely believed that she was entitled to a pension. The tribunal concluded that it had not been reasonably practicable for Ms Taylor to have presented her claim in time. When she did find out about the pension, she lodged her claim for unfair dismissal immediately. Thus her case was accepted for hearing.

Based on the case *Grampian Health Board* v *Taylor*.

How to apply to an industrial tribunal

To make an application to an industrial tribunal, you should obtain an application form, known as an IT1, from any local tribunal office, employment department office, job centre or citizens' advice bureau. The form is fairly straightforward and includes an open section for you to state the grounds on which you are making your complaint.

The application should be sent directly to your local tribunal office, the address of which should be stated on the form.

If you need help in filling in your tribunal application, your trade union or a citizens' advice bureau may be able to give you help, and advise you as to how you should proceed.

Normally your application will be acknowledged within a few days and a copy sent to your employer or ex-employer (the respondent). The respondent is asked to complete a form known as the 'notice of appearance' on which he must state whether he intends to contest the application and, if so, his grounds for contesting it. You will subsequently receive a copy of the notice of appearance. Finally a date for the hearing will be arranged to suit both parties.

If you change your mind and decide to withdraw your application before it reaches hearing, then you must write to the tribunal office and inform them of your withdrawal.

In most cases, copies of all the relevant documents are sent to an ACAS conciliation officer who will try to assist you to reach a mutual settlement, thus avoiding the need to proceed to the hearing.

The waiting list for tribunal hearings varies from area to area – some areas of England have in the past had quite a long waiting period (more than a year), although they have reduced recently as a result of new simplified procedures for handling certain cases. Scotland has generally fared better with a 16-week average waiting period.

Preliminary hearings

A preliminary hearing may be ordered prior to your case being heard by the tribunal. Preliminary hearings deal with one specific point of jurisdiction. For example, if the employer believes that your application for unfair dismissal is out-of-time (more than three months have passed since the date of termination) or that you do not have the required two years service, then he may apply for a preliminary hearing to determine this particular point.

Preliminary hearings are therefore designed to determine whether the case can legitimately proceed to a full hearing.

Pre-hearing reviews

At any time before the tribunal hearing, either you or your ex-employer may request a pre-hearing review. The tribunal itself may also instigate a pre-hearing review.

The purpose of a pre-hearing review is for the tribunal to determine whether the case has a realistic chance of succeeding. The tribunal will hear both sides' evidence and / or review written representations, and subsequently give its opinion in writing.

If, at the hearing, the industrial tribunal considers that either the claim or the defence is unlikely to succeed at a full hearing, they will say so, and warn the party concerned that if he pursues the claim regardless, and loses, an award of costs may be made against him. So, if after a pre-hearing review, you are informed that, in the tribunal's view, your claim is unlikely to succeed, but you continue with your claim regardless, you may end up having to pay for the costs of the other party. Note that the tribunal cannot actually stop you from pursuing your claim, rather they will issue a written statement informing you of their views.

The chairman of a pre-hearing review has the power to require either of the parties to pay a deposit of up to £150 if they wish to proceed with the case.

The make-up of a tribunal

The government is keen to reduce the time it takes for cases to reach a hearing and thus introduced new rules in 1993 to allow certain cases to be heard by a tribunal chairman sitting alone, rather than by the usual complement of three tribunal panel members.

Normally, however, a tribunal is composed of three persons:

- A legally qualified chairman;
- An employer representative – i.e. a lay-person from industry, typically a personnel manager;
- An employee representative – e.g. a trade union official.

The objective is to ensure that the panel members have, between them, sound knowledge and experience of both legal matters and current employment practices.

Representation at tribunal

It has always been the purpose of tribunal hearings to enable individuals to have access to legal remedies without undue expense or formality.

You have the right, therefore, if you wish, to represent yourself at a tribunal hearing. Alternatively, you may prefer to be represented by a friend or trade union official. There is no need to have a solicitor present, although nowadays many people do elect to employ a solicitor.

If you wish someone else to represent you, then you must state your representative's name and address on your application form IT1.

If you decide to present your own case, and you find that the other party is represented by a solicitor, there is no need to feel intimidated. One of the functions of the chairman of the tribunal panel is to ensure a fair hearing. If, therefore, only one of the parties is represented, thus creating a possible 'advantage', then the chairman will work to redress the balance. Thus the chairman may offer you guidance as the hearing progresses, and will certainly ask questions to ensure that all the relevant facts are allowed to come out into the open.

How much will it cost?

Normally you will be responsible for all your own costs connected with bringing a case to industrial tribunal. However, since there is no requirement for you to be represented by a solicitor, the costs need not be substantial. You do not have to pay the tribunal members, as their fees come out of public funds. Often there will be more of your time involved, than money!

Expenses

Certain allowances may be paid to you by the Employment Department, including travelling costs for yourself and your witnesses. There is also a subsistence allowance payable for periods of absence from home, including overnight if this is necessary. Loss of earnings can also be claimed for at a fixed daily rate.

To claim expenses, you should apply to the clerk of the tribunal for a form of application. Expenses can only be claimed, however, after the tribunal hearing has taken place.

Award of costs to the other party

It is not regular practice for tribunals to 'award costs', i.e. order the party who loses to pay the costs of the party who wins the case. This is different from the general rule in civil litigation that the winner's costs are paid by the loser.

A tribunal does, however, have the power to award costs and expenses in the event that one of the parties has, in its opinion, acted frivolously, vexatiously or otherwise unreasonably' (a lovely phrase!). This could occur if you pursue your case in circumstances where it is obvious that you have no chance of winning, perhaps because (for example) you wish to seek revenge on your ex-employer for dismissing you. More recently it has also been established that a person who acts 'abusively or disruptively' may have costs awarded against them. This could, for example, cover a person who acts disruptively during the tribunal hearing by interrupting constantly or hurling insults at the other party.

A tribunal may also order you to make a payment to the other party if you postpone the hearing for no good reason or at the last minute. This could occur, for example, if you come to the hearing unprepared to deal with issues which may be expected to arise, and as a result there has to be a postponement to allow you to check your facts, investigate records or call appropriate witnesses.

If you wish to apply for your costs to be awarded to the other party, then you should make your request to the tribunal chairman at the hearing. Do bear in mind, however, that in normal circumstances you will be unlikely to succeed in your request.

What remedies are available in cases of unfair dismissal?

There are three possible remedies for unfair dismissal, two of which involve you being re-employed by your employer. The third, and most common, remedy is financial compensation.

It is up to you to inform the tribunal as to whether or not you wish to be re-employed if you win your case. No tribunal will order re-employment if the applicant does not wish it.

If you do seek re-employment, the tribunal will take into account whether it is practicable for the employer to take you back. There may be circumstances which make it impracticable for the employer to re-employ you, for example if your job has in the meantime been made redundant, or if working relationships have been seriously damaged. In this case, even if you have asked for re-employment, the tribunal may not order it.

One other factor which a tribunal will take into account in considering whether to order re-employment is whether you were wholly or partly to blame for the dismissal. Again, if this was the case, the tribunal may decide against an order for re-employment.

Reinstatement and re-engagement

Re-employment may involve either reinstatement or re-engagement. The two are quite similar:

- *Reinstatement* is re-employment in your old job on exactly the same terms and conditions. You are treated in all respects as if the dismissal had never happened.
- *Re-engagement* is re-employment under a new contract of employment, either in the same job or a different job. Terms and conditions may not necessarily be exactly the same as before, but the job and terms must be comparable to your old employment.

If you succeed in your case, and an order for re-employment is made, then your employer must also pay you all your back-pay from the date of your dismissal to the date of re-employment. Financial compensation must also be paid to cover loss of employment 'perks' (for example employer's pension contributions) during the same period. The amount paid to you must take into account any pay increase which you would have received if you had not been dismissed. Once re-employed, your length of service is regarded as continuous from your original start date, and includes the period of absence between dismissal and re-employment. Thus you do not lose out if, for example, you are later made redundant and your length of service is being calculated for the purposes of redundancy pay.

Certain deductions may also be made, however. These would include amounts equivalent to any ex-gratia payments which your employer made to you when you were dismissed, and any money you have earned in the meantime through working with another employer. In other words, the award will be based on what you would actually have earned, had you not been dismissed. There is no upper limit on the amount of back-pay you may receive.

Unfortunately a tribunal cannot actually enforce a re-employment order. If your employer refuses to take you back despite an order being made, you need to re-apply to the tribunal for additional compensation. There is an element of compensation specifically set up to provide for this, known as the 'additional award', and an enhanced compensatory award may also be made. Information on how unfair dismissal compensation is worked out is given in the next section.

In practice less than one and a half per cent of unfair dismissal cases involve re-employment, and the more common remedy is to award a sum of money as compensation.

Compensation

Compensation in most cases consists of a basic award, which is calculated according to a fixed formula, and a compensatory award which is an amount which the tribunal will decide based on a number of different factors. The next section gives more details.

Usually part of the industrial tribunal's compensatory award will involve an amount to compensate you for loss of earnings for the period since the dismissal up to the tribunal hearing.

If you have already received unemployment benefit or income support during this period, the money you have received will be deducted from your compensation before it is paid to you.

The good news is that income tax and national insurance contributions are not deducted from tribunal awards of compensation (where the employment relationship has ended). If, however you are to be re-employed, then tax and national insurance contributions will be deducted from the award of back-pay, because this award is equivalent to your normal wage or salary which would have been taxed.

How compensation for unfair dismissal is worked out

Compensation for unfair dismissal consists of two primary elements, a basic award and a compensatory award, and two special additional elements. Each of these is considered below.

Basic award

The basic award is calculated in a similar way to redundancy pay, according to a fixed formula which depends on the person's age, length of service and pay. The current official maximum level of a 'week's pay' is £205 and the overall maximum basic award is £6,150.

The calculation is as follows:

Completed Years of Service	Amount of Payment
Number of years service up to and including age 21	0.5 week's pay per year
Number of years service between age 22 – 40 inclusive	1 week's pay per year
Number of years service over age 41, up to age 64 inclusive	1.5 weeks' pay per year

The only difference between the calculation of the basic award and the calculation of redundancy pay is that service under the age of 18 counts when calculating the basic award (whereas it does not count for calculating redundancy pay).

The basic award can be reduced if:

- You refuse a reasonable offer of re-employment;
- Your conduct before dismissal was such as to contribute towards, or cause, the dismissal (for example if you were dismissed for gross misconduct) and the dismissal was found unfair purely on procedural grounds;
- You have already received an ex-gratia sum from your ex-employer which is in excess of the amount of the basic award;
- You have received statutory redundancy pay;
- You were within a year of age 65 at the time of your dismissal.

Depending on the above factors, the amount of the basic award could be nil (for example where you have received full redundancy pay).

Note that where the dismissal is as a result of trade union membership/non-membership/trade union activities or health and safety reasons, there is a minimum basic award, currently £2,700.

Compensatory award

The amount of the compensatory award, which is paid over and above the basic award, is as much as the tribunal considers just and equitable in all the circumstances, taking into account your financial losses arising from the dismissal. It is not calculated to a formula and does not depend primarily on the concept of a 'week's pay' used to calculate the basic award.

Factors which the tribunal will take into account when assessing the amount of a compensatory award are:

- Net loss of wages and benefits up to the date of the hearing;

- Loss of future income (estimated);
- Loss of statutory employment protection rights (because in your next job you will be starting out with no continuous service);
- Loss of future company pension contributions;
- Loss of any other employment benefits (e.g. a company car);
- Expenses incurred in seeking new employment.

The present maximum compensatory award is £11,000. This amount is reviewed annually by the government.

The compensatory award can be reduced where:

- You have earned money from a new job, or were paid money by your ex-employer as an ex-gratia payment;
- Your actions caused or contributed to your dismissal;
- You failed to mitigate your loss, e.g. refused other available employment or failed to make reasonable efforts to obtain another job;
- (If the dismissal is unfair purely on procedural grounds) where there is a high likelihood (in the tribunal's view) that you would have been dismissed anyway, even if a fair procedure had been followed.

CASE STUDY

Mr Gilroy was employed as a supervisor, but sometimes helped out with driving duties. He was a keen soccer fan and in 1990 took his two weeks holiday to go to Sardinia for one of the World Cup games. When, shortly afterwards, England got into the semi-finals, Mr Gilroy requested immediate time off to go to Italy.

His employer, however, needed him to drive to Edinburgh that day and told him that if he went to Italy he would not have a job to come back to. Despite this, Mr Gilroy decided to go to Italy, and he was subsequently sent his P45, from which he deduced that he had been dismissed. He claimed unfair dismissal.

Q What level of compensation would Mr Gilroy be likely to win if the dismissal was found to be unfair?

A Firstly, the dismissal was found to be unfair on procedural grounds, because the manner in which Mr Gilroy's employment was terminated was unsatisfactory.

The tribunal concluded, however, that because Mr Gilroy had committed misconduct serious enough to justify dismissal, he did not deserve any compensation. He had contributed to his own dismissal by 100 per cent and therefore it would not be just to make either a basic award or a compensatory award. He received nothing.

Based on the case *Gilroy* v *Ken Bell (International) Ltd.*

There is one circumstance in which the maximum amount of £11,000 does not apply. The limit may be lifted in cases where your employer has refused to take you back after an order for re-employment has been made by the tribunal. In this situation, if you had been re-employed, you would have received arrears of pay from the date of your dismissal up to the date of your re-employment.

Hence the amount of the compensatory award in this situation will be calculated to reflect the amount specified as arrears of pay and benefits in the original reinstatement or re-engagement order. Thus your compensatory award will be at least equal to the amount of net pay lost between your date of dismissal and what should have been the date of your re-employment. This compensatory award is paid in addition to the basic award and, in these circumstances, the additional award (see next section).

Note that the compensatory award does not include an amount to cover injury to feelings or loss of job satisfaction, although in cases of discrimination, compensation may be awarded for injury to feelings. Equally there is no financial element to reflect the idea of punishment of the employer who dismissed you

Other factors which a tribunal will take into account in assessing the amount of the compensatory award are your age, skills, qualifications, and from these factors, your likelihood of success in finding future employment if you have not already done so.

Whilst an industrial tribunal is likely to be sympathetic towards you if you have lost your job through unfair dismissal, you are still expected to have minimised your losses by making a reasonable effort to find another job. If it comes to light that you have failed to do this, the tribunal's sympathy (and the compensatory award) may well be considerably reduced!

Additional award

The additional award is intended to compensate you for the additional loss you inevitably suffer if your ex-employer unreasonably refuses to re-employ you after an order for re-employment has been made by the tribunal. The additional award is based on a 'week's pay' (currently £205 per week):

The normal additional award is between 13 – 26 weeks' pay:	Maximum 26 × £205 = £5,330
If the reason for the dismissal was related to sex or race discrimination, or if it was for an inadmissible reason:	
The additional award is between 26 – 52 weeks' pay:	Maximum 52 × £205 = £10,660

Remember that in this situation, you may also be entitled to an enhanced compensatory award (see previous section).

Special award

A special award is payable in very limited circumstances where your dismissal was because of reasons related to trade union membership, non-membership or activities, and you asked for re-employment, and either the tribunal did not order it, or your ex-employer failed to comply with it. The amounts are calculated using the 'week's pay' concept, as follows:

Where the tribunal did not order re-employment, the special award is based on 104 weeks' pay.	Minimum £13,400 Maximum £26,800.
Where the tribunal did order re-employment but the company did not comply and could not satisfy the tribunal that it was not practicable to comply the special award is based on 156 weeks' pay.	Minimum £20,100 No maximum

The tribunal may reduce the amount of the special award if, in its opinion, your conduct before dismissal justifies a reduction, or if you have unreasonably refused an offer of re-employment from the employer.

The special award is made in addition to the basic award and the compensatory award. You would not, however, be entitled to receive both the special award and the additional award – these latter two are mutually exclusive.

As from April 1990, awards made by industrial tribunals are subject to the addition of simple interest, if they are not paid in full within 42 days of the tribunal decision being notified to the parties.

Compensation for sex / race discrimination

The maximum amount of compensation available from an industrial tribunal on account of sex or race discrimination used to be £11,000, an amount which was subject to annual review. Following on from a European Court declaration in 1993 that this upper limit was illegal, the Government passed legislation which removed the upper limit completely. Today, individuals who win claims of sex or race discrimination must be compensated in full for the damage and loss they have suffered as a result of their employer's discrimination. There is no limit on the amount of money which may be awarded in cases of sex or race discrimination. The industrial tribunal will examine the facts of each case in order to award an amount of money which is just and equitable. Compensation may include an amount for injury to feelings, according to the discretion of the tribunal.

Questions and Answers

Q What kind of cases do industrial tribunals deal with most often?

A Industrial tribunals deal with about 40 different types of employment-related complaints. The most common is unfair dismissal, representing approximately 60 per cent of all claims. Other frequent cases are redundancy pay claims, complaints of illegal deductions from wages, sex or race discrimination, maternity rights and trade union membership rights.

Q I have been advised that I have a solid case against my ex-employer for unfair dismissal, but I am concerned about going to an industrial tribunal. Is it very formal, or complicated?

A Industrial tribunals were set up to be informal, straightforward and inexpensive, so that ordinary people could have access to justice in employment matters. You do not need any special skills to apply to an industrial tribunal, or to present your case — tribunal staff are normally willing to provide plenty of help and guidance.

Q What happens at a tribunal hearing?

A Tribunal procedures and the order of events vary according to the type of complaint being dealt with. Essentially you will be given the opportunity to explain your complaint fully, and you will have the chance to question any witnesses from your side and also those introduced by the other party. Equally the other party may ask you questions. Tribunal panel members may also ask questions of both parties and their witnesses, in order to draw out information or clarify a particular issue.

Whilst giving evidence you will be required to take the oath, but after that you are free to explain your case openly. The approach taken is very much non-confrontational and it would be unusual for an applicant or witness to be intimidated in any way. The aim is to establish whether your employer (or ex-employer) acted reasonably, and not to put you 'on trial'.

Q What are the time limits for making a claim to an industrial tribunal?

A Normally there is a three-month time limit for the majority of complaints. For claims of redundancy pay, and dismissal on account of strike action, the limit is six months (from the date your employment ended).

Q How do I go about making a claim to an industrial tribunal?

A You need to complete a form known as an IT1, which you can obtain from your local tribunal office, employment department office, job centre or citizens' advice bureau. The form is straightforward and not too long. When complete, the application should be sent directly to your local tribunal office, the address of which should be stated on the form.

Q Who sits on an industrial tribunal panel?

A An industrial tribunal panel consists of three people. The chairperson is always a qualified lawyer, whilst the other two members are usually people with a background in industry. Typically, one would have a personnel management background and the other trade union experience or involvement.

The objective is to ensure that the panel members have, between them, sound knowledge and experience of both legal matters and current employment practices.

Q Do I have to hire a solicitor in order to make a claim to an industrial tribunal?

A No, you can either present your own case, hire a solicitor to represent you, or ask someone else, for example a friend or trade union official, to represent you. The choice is yours.

Q How much does it cost to bring a case to an industrial tribunal?

A The answer to this depends on whether or not you choose to hire a solicitor to represent you. If so, you would have to pay the solicitor's fees yourself, as legal aid is not available for industrial tribunal cases.

If, on the other hand, you present your own case, costs should be minimal. You do not have to pay the tribunal panel members.

Q If I win my claim for unfair dismissal at industrial tribunal, will I be given my old job back?

A You will be asked whether or not you wish (in the event of your claim succeeding) to be re-employed in your old job. If you do not wish re-employment, then the tribunal will not order it.

If you do request re-employment, the tribunal will decide whether it is appropriate to make an order of re-instatement or re-engagement, and will do so according to whether the circumstances of the dismissal make it practicable. Otherwise you will receive financial compensation.

Q What level of compensation can I expect to get if I am successful in my claim for unfair dismissal?

A This depends on the circumstances of your case. There is, firstly, a basic award calculated according to the same fixed formula as redundancy pay (based on your age, length of service and pay). The current maximum is £6,150.

Secondly there is a compensatory award which is an amount (up to a maximum of £11,000) which the tribunal considers just and equitable to compensate you for your financial losses. Both basic and compensatory awards are payable.

In certain cases, there are additional amounts payable over and above the basic and compensatory awards.

A typical award for unfair dismissal would be in the region of £3,000, and payments are tax-free. Full details are given in this chapter.

Conclusion

Industrial tribunals are becoming busier. As mentioned earlier, during the year 1993–1994 the total number of cases registered with industrial tribunals was 69,612 which represented a 30 per cent increase on the previous year. More and more people are becoming aware of their employment rights and asserting them through the industrial tribunal system.

Good luck if you should decide to go this route in the future!

Index